D0488109

THE AFRICA THAT NEVER WAS

Four Centuries of British
Writing About Africa

The AFRICA *That Never Was*

FOUR CENTURIES OF BRITISH WRITING ABOUT AFRICA

by

Dorothy Hammond and Alta Jablow

TWAYNE PUBLISHERS, INC.
NEW YORK

301.296

Copyright © 1970 by Twayne Publishers, Inc.
All Rights Reserved

Library of Congress Catalog Card Number 78-77035

MANUFACTURED IN THE UNITED STATES OF AMERICA

To LORD GREYSTOKE

Foreword

The Africa that Never Was is a brilliant essay in the sociology of knowledge. With painstaking scholarship and keen insight, Dorothy Hammond and Alta Jablow have demonstrated the relationship between the perceptions of Africa and Africans by British writers, on the one hand, and the latters' political and economic interests, on the other. They have also shown that these writers have revealed more about themselves and British society than they have told us about Africa.

Five interrelated themes impressed me in reading this work:

(1) An early and persistent dichotomy divides sub-Saharan Africans into *noble savages* and *bestial savages*. The former are found in earlier writings almost exclusively among indigenous rulers, although some whole peoples are seen as noble. The latter category seems to include some rulers and all of the ordinary Africans, with the exception of some loyal servants of Europeans and occasional soldiers during the period of empire. Closely related to this characterological bifurcation of the African population is the tendency of many writers to ignore indigenous African people altogether. Often the literary stereotype of the Continent consists of breathtaking landscapes, noble beasts, magnificent flora, but no people!

(2) British writers reflect the rise and establishment of a racist ideology as a principal handmaiden to the slave trade, slavery, and empire.

(3) Assessments of the human qualities of black Africans have varied with the manner in which they fit into the plans of white settlers, missionaries, or proconsuls. Changes in descriptions of the Zulus of Southern Africa reflect this tendency. At one period, their adaptability to Western life styles and beliefs was perceived

as reflecting an openness to Christianity and "civilization." At a later period when they had begun to make demands, some of which were based upon their adopted ideology, their behavior was seen as evidence of deracination and degeneration. The essential behavior had not changed, but it changed from honorific to pejorative in the eyes of the beholder.*

(4) A strongly androcentric, if not misogynist, mystique permeates British writings on Africa, particularly during the nineteenth century. Muslim tribes are admired, for example, for keeping women in a frankly inferior position and for "knowing how to deal with them." With few exceptions, women authors stress their own manly virtues.

(5) Whether they have been bearers of the white man's burden or idealizers of the "unspoiled Masai," British writers see Africa as the obverse of England. A "fixed gulf" separates the black African from the European, a gulf that is seen in genetic, rather than cultural terms. The European—the Englishman in particular—is seen as rational, mature, and exceedingly well disciplined, while the black African is perceived as non-rational (if not irrational), childlike (if not childish), and quite undisciplined.

It is a truism of intergroup relations that subordinated groups tend to see themselves as they are seen by those who dominate them. Most women probably accept the misogynous attitudes of an androcentric society. Many Jews are anti-Jewish, a phenomenon called "self-hatred" by the late Kurt Lewin. Fanon observed that the victims of colonialism tend to value themselves in terms laid down by the imperialists; and the fact that Negro Americans have generally accepted and internalized the esthetic standards, as well as the moral and characterological stereotypes of the dominant Caucasian population has been well documented by social scientists and pundits alike. The tendency of the weak to emulate the strong, of the powerless to identify with the powerful, and of the oppressed to see themselves through the eyes of their oppressors is an understandable response to subordination, de-

* CF. B. Schreike-*Alien Americans* (Viking Press, N.Y., 1936) for a study of similar changes in stereotypes about Chinese and Japanese immigrants in the 19th century.

plorable as it may be in consequences for personal self-esteem and group enhancement.

Recent years have seen an apparent and happy reversal of the self-hatred syndrome among Negro Americans. *Black* was formerly a term of derogation within the group. It is now perceived—or at least proclaimed—as *beautiful*. The sub-Saharan African heritage, formerly ignored or even despised, is now a source of pride. The strengths, beauty, and survival values of the plantation past and the ghetto present are being increasingly recognized. Our sorrow songs and blues are being transformed into instruments of overt protest and bitter triumph. The Black Experience is celebrated as a source of personal enhancement and group salvation; and being "blacker than thou" has become a form of subcultural gamesmanship.

Much health is resident in the newfound blackness of Negro Americans. Even the overtones of protesting too much are quite in harmony with the traditional patterns of developing ethnicity in America. Professors Jablow and Hammond note that, for most British writers, Africa is the obverse of England. Much of today's black rhetoric is a mirror image of the imperialists' view of indigenous Africans, of the white supremacists' view of black Americans. Earlier generations of Negro leaders sought to deny racist imputations of non-rationality, differential sex morals, and lack of personal discipline or to explain them in terms of environment or opportunities denied. Many of today's most articulate blacks "repudiate" Western rationality, lay claim to greater sexuality, and profess to reject "whitey's" putative moral standards. *Soul* and *Negritude*—and various vulgarizations thereof—come very close to restoring the fixed gulf, for much of the defense of these concepts is based upon frankly racialist, if not racist, assumptions. *The Africa that Never Was* should help to place some of these very relevant current issues in context.

This volume has been more than a decade in the making. The time was well spent.

Charles R. Lawrence
Professor and Chairman, Department of Sociology
Brooklyn College, The City University of New York

Preface

While it may seem a departure from the usual anthropological objectives, interest in and concern with a people's views of other and alien ways of life has had a long and honorable tenure in anthropology. In a sense, any anthropological research into early writings has been of this nature, since the culturally determined biases of the writer are so much a part of how he sees and what he reports. The modern researcher must learn to distinguish relevant data from biased observations. Such research eventually led us to a concern with the nature, not so much of the data, but of the modifying biases themselves.

We began our work on the Western fantasy of Africa in 1960 with two articles published in the periodical, *Africa Today*. These articles indicated the existence of a governing literary tradition in the European and American popular writing on Africa. Each of us had also written a doctoral thesis on separate aspects of this broad problem. The articles and dissertations proved to be the seedbed for this book. While our basic idea of a Western fantasy based on ethnocentrism still prevails, much new data has been added, and with the passage of time and further study, our views of the problems have changed their shape. Our original concepts have been rethought, redefined, and greatly modified.

Our approaches and points of view have been, throughout, so totally compatible, and our collaboration of such a nature, that it is impossible for us to now distinguish any individual contribution or idea. Thus, we must both share an equal responsibility for the entire work.

There was no need to treat fiction and nonfiction separately since both are governed by the same tradition. The fiction, however, does give more forceful phrasing to the images because of the concentration of each novel upon a single complex of images. Marguerite Steen, for example, focuses on the image of Africa as dark, alien, and evil. With this imagery she elaborates upon the conventions of the brooding and implacable jungle and the uncanny powers of African witchcraft. Richard Llewellyn's *A Man in a Mirror* stresses the image of Africa as an open sunlit land inhabited by "noble savages." Nonfiction is more apt to include diverse images, none as fully developed as in the more integrated works of fiction.

Fictional and nonfictional treatments of African material differ only in respect to greater or lesser consistency and integration. The fiction is by no means more fanciful than the nonfiction. Of the following passages the second and the fourth are from novels, the first and third from nonfiction:

> The stagnation of Africa is chiefly due to that jealous tribal law which forbade any man to be wiser or cleverer or richer than his neighbors. For thousands of years, Africa, like a modern dictator, has oppressed the natural freedom of the mind, and thrown away all its increase.[1]

> Ibu . . . was an intelligent child. This quality had probably been her ruin. All intelligent, good-looking persons are exposed to jealousy, and jealousy is the subconscious source of the hatred which produces injurious fear; and from fear, an accusation of witchcraft. In this way Africa has destroyed every year for some millions of years, a large proportion of its more intelligent and handsome children.[2]

> Africans have remained for thousands of years at virtually the same level of culture. They seem almost alone among the major races of the world to have halted in the stone age, too comfortable to go any further.[3]

> People who have lived precisely the same way for hundreds of years, because they have discovered a corporate existence, which wholly satisfies them.[4]

Analysis of the images pointed up still another regularity. It became obvious that there existed a dependent correlation between the image of the Africans and that of the British. One is in reciprocal contrast to the other. Where the British are brave, the Africans are cowardly; where the Africans are carefree, the British are beset by many anxieties; where the British are gracious in granting favors, the Africans accept them without gratitude. The literature on Africa does present a very clear self-view of the British in Africa. To test the validity of this self-image we turned to commentaries and observations on British character and society. They conformed to the British self-view in the African literature. Our last chapter treats in detail the British self-view. Some readers may prefer to read this chapter first.

There are those who share none of the responsibility for the finished product, but who nevertheless contributed to its completion. We must first express our deepest gratitude to Professor Joseph Jablow for the initial impetus he provided, and for many years of patient support, advice, and encouragement. We are grateful to Professor Alexander Lesser for his sound advice and needed exhortations. We should also like to take this opportunity to express our belated thanks to our dissertation advisers, Professors Conrad Arensberg, Morton Fried, and Charles Wagley. Finally, we owe a tremendous debt of gratitude to Carl Withers for his painstaking reading of the manuscript and his many valuable suggestions.

Contents

Introduction

Since classical times Africa has exerted a powerful hold on the European imagination. The ancient world knew little of Africa other than Egypt and the Mediterranean littoral. Imagination transformed the rest of the continent to a strange and wonderful land where were to be found tailed men, men with heads beneath their breasts, and men who did not dream. To this classical heritage were added in time tales of other prodigies and of great riches. It was interest in the fabulous as much as interest in geography that spurred Prince Henry of Portugal to send his ships in exploration of the lands lying southward. In the sixteenth century the British followed the lead of the Portuguese and voyaged to Africa to fill their pockets and the coffers of Elizabeth's treasury. European exploration and expansion brought sober fact to dispel the old legends, but new legends took their place. Africa remained a field for the free play of European fantasy.

Western literature provides the record of the fantasy, and because it is a lurid fantasy, it has resulted in a sensational literature. It has always had wide popular appeal, especially for young readers. This literature was, in fact, the path which led us ultimately to our interest in African anthropology. Sir Henry M. Stanley along with Tarzan and Allan Quatermain were our most unlikely guides to the scientific study of African cultures. But anthropology is intolerant of fantasy, and we found ourselves looking at the literature that had given us so much pleasure with coldly professional eyes.

There are two Africas, different and incompatible: the Africa of anthropology and that of popular "literary" conception. Anthropology discerns an Africa infinitely varied, complex, and changing, inhabited by people neither more nor less human than anyone else. The anthropological view of Africa has always been subject to revision as knowledge increased. In popular writing Africa is strangely homogeneous and static; differences between past and present and between one place and another are obliterated. Africans, limited to a few stock figures, are never completely human, and Africa exhibits few changes over time. It became and remains the Africa of H. Rider Haggard and Joseph Conrad. In short, the literary image of Africa is a fantasy of a continent and a people that never were and could never be.

Films also have familiarized Westerners with an Africa composed of the old notions of the Dark Continent inhabited by archetypal figures: howling savages, faithful servants, sinister half-breeds, white hunters, and gallant colonial officials. In the face of their appeal, durability, and pervasiveness, reality has little chance of acceptance.

With few exceptions, no matter how different in style, form, or content, the books—and naturally the films based upon them—present the same fantasy of Africa. With remarkable consistency the fantasy is expressed through the same idioms and figures of speech. These rhetorical devices may seem merely a manner or style of writing about Africa. Yet by persistent reiteration, a manner of speaking can become the substance of what is said. In book after book about Africa identical images appear expressing similar attitudes and concepts, often similarly phrased. Literary license allows each author to depict Africa in much the same way as every other author. Such conformity cannot be the result of chance. It clearly indicates a governing literary tradition, quite different from the tradition guiding the scientific writing.

Distinction between the two traditions is possible only for recent times. Trained anthropological observation in the field began only in the early part of the twentieth century. Before then, armchair theorists relied on the literature of voyage and exploration to supply their raw data, which was too often inadequate as well as biased. The study of man has moved steadily toward emancipation from the inevitable errors stemming from reliance on amateur and secondary sources. However, what has been discarded as unreliable by anthropology has been retained in the popular literature. The errors and biases so perpetuated have by now acquired an inviolable tenure.

Africa of the popular literature is a myth, but myths have a place and function in the societies which create them. They support cultural values and mediate points of stress. Within this context of social reality myth is subject to anthropological study. This book is an attempt to analyze the British myth of Africa, to trace its historical development, to establish its modern usages, and to indicate its relationship to other aspects of British life.

Although the British were not alone in creating a myth of Africa, we chose, for a number of reasons, to concentrate on the British writing on Africa. The British were the predominant European colonial power in Africa. In sheer volume their popular literature far exceeded that of any other nation, and much of what they wrote was accessible to us. An obvious advantage in dealing with the English material was that problems of translation were eliminated. Moreover, the investigation of the historical development of the tradition has been possible because four centuries of British contact with Africa has produced not only an enormous literature but one of unbroken continuity.

The literature of this popular tradition yields relatively little empirical knowledge about either Africa or the history of the British in Africa. Reality is nearly irrelevant to the tradition. What is relevant, and indeed, integral to it, is ethnocentrism. This means that all perception is made through the lenses of one's own system of values and beliefs. An ethnocentric point of view admits only one valid way of life. Cultures which differ from one's own are perceived as negations of that single set of values, rather than as expressions of other and different systems. Those who do not worship the God of the Christians are not necessarily worshiping the Devil of the Christians; they may be adherents of a religion to which the tenets of Christianity are totally irrelevant. Ethnocentrism, however, does not permit the possibility of alternative and perhaps equally valid ways of life. A literature dominated by ethnocentrism is bound to be unrealistic in its omissions and misinterpretations.

It is not going too far to say that ethnocentrism is a nearly universal human attitude. All people are so thoroughly conditioned to their own culture that their habits and learned modes of behavior seem the inevitable expression of basic human nature.

Other people with different habits acquired from their cultures seem to behave unnaturally or perversely. This is the basis of all preconception about alien cultures and the seedbed of the stereotypes by which they are described. Differences are almost always exaggerated. Even in the absence of difference, strange and unnatural behavior is projected onto the alien group simply because they *are* alien. These are not random projections, but reflect important and dearly held values of the perceiver. Alien behavior is made to serve as an object lesson—the contrast that highlights and affirms the worth of one's own patterns of behavior. Thus, ethnocentrism produces myths of aliens that often seem to be antagonistic, even if hostility was not intended.

Katherine George describes the European view of Africa in the literature prior to the nineteenth century as an "antagonistic fantasy."[1] She refers primarily to Dutch, Italian, and Portuguese materials, and only minimally to English accounts. Her work indicates that all the Europeans were equally biased about Africa, and their literatures reflect those biases. This remains equally characteristic of the literatures of the nineteenth and twentieth centuries.

The British view of Africa appears to be, at best, quite absurd, and at worst, the results of malice and cynicism. Yet the British have been neither malicious nor cynical; they have merely been ethnocentric. The absurdity lies in the nature of ethnocentrism itself.

With no hope of being exhaustive we have read and analyzed some five hundred volumes of fiction and nonfiction covering the period from earliest British contact with Africa in the mid-sixteenth century to the present. Our focus is on the image of Negro Africa. We have, therefore, excluded works dealing with the Sahara and North Africa since they are better understood within the context of the Moslem world. We have intentionally omitted the early works of British explorers of Ethiopia; they are sufficiently distinctive to constitute a subtradition. The modern protest literature on race relations, mainly in South Africa, has also been omitted as not directly germane to our purpose.

Writers were not and could not be selected for literary merit. There are, therefore, many more "bad" writers than "good" ones in the sample. The better writers handle the conventions with greater skill and subtlety, but all conform to the literary traditions.

The continuing dominance of the tradition can be partly accounted for by its acceptance as the only appropriate way to write about Africa. Authenticity seems assured when a writer gives his narrative "verisimilitude" by using the expected conventional images. In addition, it cannot be denied that the conventions impart a color and vitality which can rescue otherwise dull narratives. Thus, it is no wonder that so many writers continue to incorporate this useful tradition into so variegated a literature.

The British have written about Africa in many literary forms. In the earliest contact period and for a long time after, the predominant type of literature was the narrative of trade and exploration. As the British became increasingly committed to Africa there appeared many new kinds of writing: polemic tracts and romances dealing with the issues of slavery and colonialism, memoirs and reminiscences, accounts of travel on the Dark Continent, and an ever-increasing number of novels. Fiction (aside from the anti-slavery romances of the eighteenth and nineteenth centuries) did not really hit its stride until the end of the nineteenth century; by the middle of the twentieth century it was the outstanding type of popular writing about Africa.

The wide range of styles and genres presented the problem of dealing with a very heterogeneous body of material. It was, nevertheless, possible to abstract striking regularities from these works. The fundamental and unifying theme is the confrontation between Great Britain and Africa. The continent, the Africans, and the British themselves are depicted by sets of interlocking images that are consistently employed throughout the literature. These images are built up out of a stock of stereotypes formulated in highly conventional idioms and metaphors. The typical form is the narrative of travel which appeared from the beginning of British contact and has continued to the most recent present. Travel ranges from the standard trek on foot to travel in every possible conveyance: hammock, bathchair, sedan, jeep, motor bicycle, and even a balloon. It is quite rare to encounter a book in which the protagonists stay in one place. So entrenched is this convention that even books dealing with quite other matters incorporate a journey. A love story or an account of medical practice must be so written as to describe some travel. This form is appropriate to the focus of interest upon the British protagonist, whether in fact or fiction, for a journey provides a variety of African stimuli. Obviously, the more exciting and varied the stimuli, the more excited are the responses, and the livelier the book.

We have allowed direct quotations from many sources to illustrate the nature of the conventions. Generally, one or two citations must stand for an almost limitless supply, and our selection of the most suitable quotation from among such riches was often an agonizing decision. Though we might have illustrated each convention by citations from any number of writers, not every writer uses all the conventions—only those appropriate to his book. The preponderance of material from a limited group of writers should not be taken to indicate that they alone made such comments, but that we preferred their particular phrasing.

Our study of over four centuries of British writing about Africa has disclosed elements of both continuity and change. For each period certain historical factors determined the precise content of the images. These factors include the nature of British-African contact and of the personnel and the particular ideology of a given period. Yet the continuities are far more striking than the changes, since they are the result of the unifying and constant force of ethnocentrism. Ethnocentrism created and preserved until today a persistent fantasy: the civilized Briton in confrontation with savage Africans in an Africa that never was.

CHAPTER I

First Light on the Dark Continent

Commerce in Commodities and Human Beings: 1530–1800

BRITISH contact with Africa began in the mid-sixteenth century as part of the developing commerce between the European maritime nations and the coastal states of West Africa. From the first recorded British voyage of William Hawkins in 1530 to the early nineteenth-century voyages of exploration, British relations with Africa were dominated by the concerns of trade. Initially small in scope and sporadic in nature, the trade was in the West African commercial staples of ivory, pepper, and gold. These early ventures were profitable; John Lok's voyage of 1554 returned ten times the capital invested,[1] and William Towerson exchanged a "copper Bason" for gold equivalent to thirty pounds sterling.[2]

The earliest literature clearly reflects the overwhelming preoccupation with trade. It is a sparse literature and consists of brief accounts of trading voyages in Richard Hakluyt and Samuel Purchas,[3] and a few separate accounts such as the one by Richard Jobson.[4] The narratives emphasize the details and mechanics of trade: compass and sailing directions, lists of place names, and items bought and sold. The new land and its people were only incidentally described, and then within the limited geographical range of a few coastal areas. British writing of this early period nowhere indicates an interest in the life of the Africans equal to that of the Dutch and Portuguese writers of the same period.

British accounts briefly described the location, topography, and climate of the coastal areas, casually noted the novel flora and fauna, and briefly commented on the people. Occasionally the writers larded their own sketchy observations with borrowings from classical writers. For example, Eden's account of the voyage captained by Lok in 1561 mingles observed details with fantasy from the classical tradition.

. . . Negroes, a people of beastly living, without a God, lawe, religion, or common wealth. . . . There also other people . . . whose women are common: for they contract no matrimonie, neither have respect to chastitie . . . the region called Troglodytica, whose inhabitants dwel in caves and dennes: for these are their houses, and the flesh of serpents their meat, as writeth Plinie, and Diodorus Siculus. They have no speach, but rather a grinning and chattering. There are also people without heads . . . having their eyes and mouths in their breast. . . . Among other things therefore, touching the maners and nature of the people, this may seeme strange, that their princes and noble men use to punce and rase their skinnes with pretie knots in divers formes. . . . And albeit they goe in maner all naked, there are many of them, and especially their women, in maner laden with collars, bracelets, hoopes, and chaines either of gold, copper or ivory. I my selfe have one of their braslets of Ivory. . . .[5]

In general, the early British traders seem to have found the Africans strange and perhaps not entirely to their liking, but they were viewed as real or potential partners in a commercial arrangement in which the British recognized their own dependence upon them. The writers did not engage in polemics or invidious comparisons; even when they indicated distaste at what they saw, it was not made an occasion for moral judgment. Certainly the Africans were savages, but one could trade as profitably with savages as with anyone else; and these particular savages were just as eager as the British to engage in commerce. As trade partners they were respected; for, savage or not, they were shrewd traders and skillful bargainers. Eden, in recounting Lok's voyage, found them to be

. . . very wary people in their bargaining, [who] will not lose one sparke of golde of any value. They use weights and measures, and are very circumspect in occupying the same. They that shall have to doe with them must use them gently; for they will not trafique or bring in any wares, if they be evill used.[6]

Towerson's comment indicates how tightly organized the African traders were in this period.

> The 16. day in the morning we went into the river with our Skiffe, and tooke some of every sort of our merchandize with us, and shewed it to the Negroes, but they esteemed it not . . . so that this day we tooke not by estimation above one hundredth poundweight of Graines, by meanes of their Captaine, who would suffer no man to sell any-thing but through his hands, and at his price: he was so subtile, that for a bason he would not give 15. pound weight of Graines . . . and when he saw that wee would not take them in contentment, the Captaine departed and caused all the rest of the boates to depart. . . .[7]

Aside from a few displays of reading in the classics, this is a matter-of-fact literature, and in a matter-of-fact way it adumbrates the image of the continent as the White Man's Grave. The most portentous statistics deal not with profits but with disease and death. In this early period, the history of the British on the West Coast often reads like a series of death notices: "And of seven score men came home to Plimmouth scarcely forty. . . ." [8] Towerson, writing of his third voyage, states that "The crews began to fall sick even before the Mina coast was reached"; on the way home by way of the Cape Verde Islands, the crews of three ships were reduced to only "30 sound men." [9]

The gains from commodities paled into insignificance beside the enormous profits made from the buying and selling of slaves. The British slave trade began on a very small scale in the 1560's with several voyages of John Hawkins to the "coast of Guinea . . . where he got into his possession, partly by the sword and partly by other meanes, to the number of three hundred Negroes. . . ." [10] From then on the continuity and growth of the slave trade were ensured; its enormous rewards far outweighed the high risks. By the beginning of the eighteenth century British trade with Africa had become almost exclusively a trade in slaves.

The British merchants bought their slaves from African traders, who in turn obtained them in the interior, a time-honored practice which established the middle-man position of the African coastal chiefs. This procedure effectively limited the British to the littoral and restricted their contacts mainly to their African suppliers.

The chiefs were anxious to prevent Europeans from penetrating the hinterland, afraid that they might gain influence and eventual control of the mainland trade. Up to the nineteenth century, in fact, the African chiefs and traders had the upper hand; their power was sufficiently strong to check the growth of British power and to limit the British area of operations.

The dangers of travel in the interior also prevented inland expansion. The dense rain forest and the untraversable swamps were formidable obstacles, and the ever-present fever was, perhaps, an even greater deterrent. Besides, the British merchants were interested above all in their profits. As long as these were forthcoming, there was no compelling motive to brave the hazards of the interior. Small wonder, then, that as late as the beginning of the nineteenth century, the sum of British holdings in West Africa consisted of the tiny colonies at Freetown and Gambia, maintained precariously by traders with government aid, and a string of forts and factories along the coast, held largely on leasehold and at the sufferance of local chiefs.

By mid-eighteenth century certain aspects of the British situation in West Africa had changed. The hitherto powerful competition of the Dutch and Portuguese had finally been eliminated by the Treaty of Utrecht. The trade was no longer hit-and-run, for the British were ensconced in relatively permanent trading posts along the coast from the Senegal River to the Oil Rivers. They could support an established and settled trade, although their operations were still clearly dependent upon the good will of the Africans.

Accounts of British activity in Africa during the eighteenth century are contained in J. Churchill's compendium[11] and in several individual works: Robert Norris and Archibald Dalzel both recorded their observations of the Kingdom of Dahomey, and William Smith and William Snelgrave recounted their voyages to Guinea.[12] Continuity with the earlier writing was maintained; the emphasis was still on trade and its circumstances. But there was a marked change in the tenor of the literature. Its content shifted from almost indifferent and matter-of-fact reports of what the voyagers had seen to judgmental evaluation of the Africans. John Phillips, a trader of this period, referred to the "swinish manner" of the Negroes and their "murderous treachery."[13] Dalzel described the king of Dahomey as a cruel and bloody tyrant,[14] and Norris concurred.

> . . . and he sports with [his subjects], with the most savage and wanton cruelty. Piles of their heads are placed as ornaments before his palace . . . and the floors leading to his apartments are strewed with their bodies. . . .[15]

Eighteenth-century comments placed inordinate emphasis upon the sanguinary aspects of West African cultures. African behavior, institutions, and character were not merely disparaged but presented as the negation of all human decencies. African religions were vile superstition; governments but cruel despotism; polygyny was not marriage, but the expression of innate lusts. The shift to such pejorative comment was due in large measure to the effects of the slave trade. A vested interest in the slave trade produced a literature of devaluation, and since the slave trade was under attack, the most derogatory writing about Africans came from its literary defenders. Dalzel, for instance, prefaced his work with an apologia for slavery: "Whatever evils the slave trade may be attended with . . . it is mercy . . . to poor wretches, who . . . would otherwise suffer from the butcher's knife."[16] Numerous proslavery tracts appeared, all intent upon showing the immorality and degradation of Africans. Basil Davidson cites an anonymous pamphlet from eighteenth-century Liverpool to this effect.

> Africans being the most lascivious of all human beings, may it not be imagined that the cries they let forth at being torn from their wives, proceed from the dread that they will never have the opportunity of indulging their passions in the country to which they are embarking?[17]

Enslavement of such a degraded people was thus not only justifiable but even desirable. The character of Africans could change only for the better through contact with their European masters. Slavery, in effect, became the means of the Africans' salvation, for it introduced them to Christianity and civilization.

The slave trade was the subject of bitter controversy. People of diverse beliefs and backgrounds united in opposition to slavery, and their protest eventually achieved its abolition in the early nineteenth century. The leading spokesmen for the antislavery movement included such forceful personalities as William Wilberforce, James Fox, John Wesley, Harriet Martineau, Hannah More, and Sir Charles and Lady Middleton. Theirs was a direct approach, concerned with the philosophical and moral issues in slavery. They wrote tracts, made speeches, and engaged in political action. In short, they produced a literature of abolition, but it did not contribute to the image of Africa.

There were, however, among the publicists of the antislavery movement—along with less well-known writers—a group of the most distinguished literary figures of England, such men as Daniel Defoe, Joseph Addison, Thomas Day, Thomas Chatterton, William Cowper, and Samuel Johnson. As the antislavery campaign entered the nineteenth century, its adherents included almost every distinguished novelist and poet of the times. These professional literati embellished their antislavery writing with literary inventions and created a new Africa inhabited by a new breed of Africans.

For the White Man's Grave inhabited by beastly savages, the antislavery writers substituted an Arcadian landscape where dwelt people of the greatest nobility, beauty, and refinement. In the light of modern knowledge the available accounts of Africa may not seem the height of factual realism, but in the eighteenth century such accounts provided all the "facts" there were. It was a remarkable literary feat to have put aside all data and to have completely transcended the "facts." The following description by Michel Adanson, an eighteenth-century voyager, is a model of the antislavery idylls of African life:

> Which way soever I turned my eyes, I behold a perfect image of pure nature: an agreeable solitude bounded on every side by a charming landscape; the rural situation of cottages in the midst of trees; the ease and quietness of the negroes . . . temperate, moral religiously inclined folk, intelligent and industrious. . . .[18]

Robert Burns, safe in Scotland, succumbed to the geographical vagaries about Africa in his compassionate "Slave's Lament."

It was in sweet Senegal that my foes did me enthrall
For the lands of Virginia, O;
Torn from that lovely shore, and must never see it more,
And also I am weary, weary, O!

All on that charming coast is not bitter snow or frost,
Like the lands of Virginia, O;
There streams forever flow, and there flowers forever blow,
And also I am weary, weary, O! [19]

The motives of these writers were clear enough. One of the proslavery arguments was that the coast was so pestilential that it could only benefit the Africans to remove them to more wholesome lands. This argument was countered by a bold denial from the antislavery writers. Their Africa was thoroughly salubrious; it thus could not constitute a kindness to take people away from rural delights. In the employ of polemics, the literary imagination created a pseudo-Africa.

The antislavery writers created a pseudo-African to dwell in pseudo-Africa. Counter to the "beastly savage" of the slavers was the "noble savage" of the antislavery romancers. The noble savage is a well-established literary figure, a device often used in criticism of the writer's society. The convention proposes that man in nature is free, innocent, and virtuous. Uncorrupted by civilization he is naturally noble in character. This very old literary contrast between natural virtue and civilized vice received new formulation as a by-product of the Age of Discovery. The explorers Sir Francis Drake, Sir Walter Raleigh, and Philip Amadas seemingly with an eye toward promoting colonization, praised the virtues of savage men in savage lands. Elizabethan drama and poetry began to laud exotic heroes. William Shakespeare's Othello and Christopher Marlowe's Tamburlaine were more than life-sized exemplars of the devotion and valor of barbaric noblemen.

The noble-savage convention came late to Africa with Mrs. Aphra Behn's novelette, *Oroonoko.* Othello may have been the model for Oroonoko, but Oroonoko himself was the undisputed antecedent for innumerable African romances of the noble-savage genre. The hero, an African prince of royal blood and bearing, and his equally royal love, Imoinda, are captured and enslaved.

Their tribulations at the hands of brutal white men and their heroic deaths constitute the plot of the tale. It was dramatized by Thomas Southerne in 1696 and appeared in many other adaptations through the eighteenth century. From 1696 to 1801 some version of the play was performed in England every year. Apart from actual adaptations of the Oroonoko tale there were even more imitations of it, all immensely popular and confirming the presence of noble savages in Africa.

Oroonoko and his like were taken up with enthusiasm by the abolitionists as suitable vehicles for antislavery propaganda. Antislavery sentiment provided a new function for the noble-savage romance. Its role shifted from a critique of civilization to an attack upon slavery. What justice or humanity could there be in the cruel enslavement of such a noble figure as Oroonoko?

> The most illustrious courts could not have produced a braver man, both for Greatness of Courage and Mind, a Judgement more solid, a Wit more quick, and a Conversation more sweet and diverting. . . . He had an extreme good and graceful Mien, and all the Civility of a well-bred Great Man.[20]

European attitudes toward nobility were pivotal in selecting those virtues granted the noble savage. He was depicted as the counterpart of the contemporary English aristocrat. The "noble savage" and the "beastly savage" were conventions equally lacking in realism; both represented opposite poles on the single scale of English values. As the noble savage epitomized the ideal of British character, so the beastly savage was its antithesis. The symbolism also pertained to physical appearance. The beastly savage was disgustingly ugly. The noble savage was, on the other hand, the beau ideal of manly beauty, wanting only a light skin to be entirely perfect. We again return to that paragon, Oroonoko, for illustration.

> He was . . . of a Shape the most exact that can be fancy-d: The most famous Statuary could not form the Figure of a Man more admirably turn-d from head to foot. His face was not that brown rusty Black which most of that Nation are, but a perfect Ebony, polished Jett. . . . His nose was rising and Roman, instead of African and flat.

His Mouth the finest shaped that could be seen; far from those great turn-d lips which are so natural to the rest of the Negroes.[21]

The convention of the noble savage was never extended to the entire African population. All the African noble-savage heroes and heroines are princes and princesses whose nobility of character matched the aristocracy of their lineage. The fundamental impropriety and shame of slavery was the degradation of an aristocrat to servile status. Not only had the function of the noble-savage convention undergone a sea change, its basic meaning had altered. The noble savage no longer referred to natural man; "noble" described his social status quite as much as it did his character.

In the more operatic protests against slavery the common Africans barely exist. At best, the commonality is pitiable in its enslavement and suffering. Quite often, however, the lower classes appear venal and ignoble. The Reverend William Dodd wrote many poems in the noble-Negro tradition which were reprinted in numerous anthologies. His regal Africans disdain the "rabble of ordinary slaves of manners brutish who mock'd my sufferings and my pangs renew'd, and lament the humiliations of enslaved *royalty*" (italics ours).[22] Thus, at least in part, the noble-Negro romance incorporates the more pervasive major convention of the beastly savage.

Aside from the fantasy of the classical tradition, there were no set conventions from which the early British writers on Africa could draw. They did utilize the pattern of ethnocentric description which characterized the literature on other "savage" peoples, such as the American Indian.[23] The usual ethnocentrism in writing about non-Europeans and the special context of the slave trade gave rise to the dual conventions which form the basic themes of the tradition to be echoed and elaborated through the years.

The Early Nineteenth Century: West Africa

The extremely lucrative traffic in slaves was legally terminated early in the nineteenth century. The slave trade went on *sub rosa* for a number of years, but it had a limited future. Thus, the English traders looked for alternative commodities on the West Coast and for this reason even penetrated the forbidding hinterland.

The quest for new commodities was a compelling purpose and converged with another major current of contemporary interest: scientific geography and exploration. For the first time not all voyages to Africa were undertaken as purely mercantile ventures. The newly formed African Association's chief concern was to map the West African hinterland and to determine the exact course of the Niger River.[1] Profit and science could be served simultaneously. As new areas were explored and new people were contacted, their trade potential could be assayed and tapped.

Geographical exploration was stimulated by the Enlightenment and its scientific and humanitarian concerns. Commercial motives took on fresh value as profit-seeking was also phrased in humanitarian terms. The slave trade could be brought to an end only by the substitution of profitable trade in other commodities. It was clear that the issue of slavery and the slave trade had not disappeared with the abolition of slavery. It was, and continued to be for a long time, the major ideological theme in the literature on Africa, as part of the general motive of philanthropy. The combined motives of philanthropy, advancement of science, and development of commerce are explicitly stated by the explorer Hugh Clapperton in the beginning of his *Journal of a Second Expedition into the Interior of Africa.*

> Such exploration should provide a favourable opportunity of establishing an intercourse with the interior of Africa, and probably of putting an effectual check . . . to a large portion of the infamous traffic carried on in the Bight of Benin, and also for extending the legitimate commerce of Great Britain with this part of Africa and at the same time adding to our knowledge of the country. . . .[2]

These newer motives, though more altruistic, contained the germs of condescension. The British were beginning to regard themselves as the bearers of enlightenment to the Dark Continent. This attitude was not yet fully developed, however, and is in this period almost tentatively expressed in the literature. Captain Allen of the 1841 Niger Expedition addressed the Africans with whom he was to make a trade agreement as follows:

Englishmen will bring everything to trade but rum or spirits, which are injurious. If you induce your subjects to cultivate the ground, you will all become rich, but if you sell slaves the land will not be cultivated, and you will become poorer by the traffic.[3]

British missionaries, the most obvious vanguard of enlightenment and philanthropy, were on the littoral of West Africa early in the nineteenth century. The Church Missionary Society and the Church of England were in Sierra Leone as early as 1806; Fourah Bay, a college to train African clergy, was founded in 1827. In Nigeria missionary work began only in 1844, when the Church Missionary Society founded its mission in Abeokuta. On the Gold Coast, the Wesleyans established the first mission in 1835, though in 1752 Thomas Thompson at his own request was sent by the Church of England to convert the Africans. No real headway in missionary activity in the interior was made until mid-century.

The West Coast pioneers of Christianity were few,[4] and theirs is a record of personal hardship, isolation, and death, rather than of the joys of enlightenment bestowed. Yet even these accounts contributed to the developing British attitude of condescension toward Africans. The missionaries inevitably saw the Africans as subjects for change and amelioration—the "benighted savage."

Though it was part of the great philanthropic and humanitarian work to be undertaken in West Africa, missionary enterprise could not be divorced from its total context of combined motives. Commerce and missionary efforts are mingled in the lyrical plea of the Reverend Montgomery.

And now where savage waters wind their lonely course—unwhitened by a single sail—there may commerce lift her thousand signals, streaming in the gale; instead of the forest depths where the tiger preys and the lion howls—there may the thronged city, the busy wharf, the crowded street be hereafter seen, with all the glow of commercial life and the grace of social advancement; and instead of the war-whoops of contending tribes, the tyrant's lash, the clank of chains and thralldom's bitter sigh—there may be heard the voice of prayer, the sound of praise and the sweet music of the "church going" bell.[5]

The outstanding literary figures of mid-century are neither traders nor missionaries, but the noted explorers of the West African hinterland. They came to West Africa with immediate purposes: to seek out prospects for trade and to fill in the map. Their time was always limited. The imminent onset of the rainy season, their progressive physical debilitation, and the shortage of supplies kept them continuously on the move. The rains flooded rivers and land making passage impossible; heat and damp brought fever. They were doubly constrained by the problems of supplies; on the one hand there was a need for haste lest their supplies be exhausted; on the other hand, they were constantly delayed by the difficulties of transport. It was not possible to live off the land. Here was nothing like the abundant game of South Africa, nor was camping out feasible. The explorers and their retinues were dependent upon African hospitality, and their precious goods went quickly for payment. They were obliged to pay for porters, guides, for *laissez-passers,* and to oil the machinery of trade. Such were the hazards and circumstances of West African travel: they were certainly not conditions which made for dallying or leisurely contemplation.

The explorers' journals are permeated with a sense of urgency. This very urgency had a way of creating even greater difficulties for the already beset traveler. Alexander Laing expressed his frustration at the constant need for haste.

> Although I was now obliged to abandon the hope of actually reaching the source of the Niger . . . the endeavour to accelerate an undertaking in Africa is almost certain to occasion its failure; and although well aware of this fact, yet my time was so limited, that I was compelled to act contrary to my judgement.[6]

There was neither time nor inclination to study or to indulge in speculation. The explorers saw a great deal and they saw it well; there is much detailed description, but all of it is literal, treating only of surface aspects. The bulk of description is that of the physical appearance of people and places. Crafts are often carefully described, but in technological rather than social or esthetic terms. Political observations were limited to commentary about rulers and their entourage. If any behavior or culture trait could be subsumed under a known European rubric, there was no more to say: trade was trade, farming was farming, and a ruler was a ruler. If, on the other hand, behavior or culture was alien to the European, it was "savage."

Most of these early nineteenth-century West African explorers were men of action. They were young, mostly from an impecunious middle class, and ambitious to make their way in the world. There was little room at home for upward-striving youth. The post-Napoleonic period was a time of economic distress, to say nothing of lack of opportunity. Most of the explorers were determined young Scotchmen who looked to Africa for adventure and careers, just as many others of their countrymen looked outward from Britain to other faraway and exotic lands. The historian Wallace Notestein comments on this point.

> . . . the chief reason why the Scot went so far away from home was because his own country had so few resources and he had imagination enough to guess that he might better his chances by seeking out richer countries. . . . They were to become explorers, even more than the English, explorers who discovered and opened up new parts of Canada, Australia, New Zealand and Africa to the white man[7]

Despite the poverty and lack of opportunity that prevailed throughout Great Britain, the parish and burgh schools of Scotland and the grammar schools of England did a creditable job of educating the young men, and many went to universities and on to careers in civil and military professions. Their journals of exploration are literate and in some cases even elegantly written; the observations of natural phenomena indicate a trained regard for meticulous recording of detail.[8]

Such personal backgrounds and ambitions, linked to the commercialism of British motives in Africa, did not make for a literature of philosophical speculation, nor for flights of poetical fancy. The explorers are as prosaic and practical as if the hazardous journey up the unknown Niger were an outing on the Clyde. They recorded what was to be seen, kept marvellously accurate book of goods given and goods received in the same manner that they entered the record of death, illness, and disaster—the most methodical of madmen!

Every one of the explorers was strongly individualistic. However, the prevailing tone of the journals is quite remarkable for its homogeneity. The journals were primarily narratives of personal adventure of men who shared a similar background of culture, interest, and aspiration. Their ethnocentrism was tempered by the egocentrism typical of them all. In their compulsion to get on with the journey, they were apt to judge the Africans encountered—if they noticed them at all—in terms of whether they were a help or a hindrance. All Africans were savages, but the African who aided the explorer was more pertinently a "good" man. Park described a helpful king as the kindest of men—no savage he.

> I thanked the king for his affectionate solicitude, but told him that I had considered the matter and was determined, notwithstanding all dangers to proceed. The king shook his head, but desisted from further persuasion; and told me the guide should be ready in the afternoon. About two o'clock the guide appearing, I went and took my last farewell of the good old king.[9]

In their preoccupation with self and immediate purpose, the explorers demanded help and were indignant when it was not forthcoming. They could not perceive the anomaly of their position from the African's point of view; to him British motives were inexplicable and British manners lacked courtesy. African suspicions were often aroused by the fact that the explorers marched directly from one group to its enemies without regard to traditional rivalries or feuds. The explorers' haste often made them rude, and their demands for hospitality and aid were sometimes excessive as well as inconsiderate.

The conditions of travel, quite apart from the exigencies of haste, determined in a large measure the nature of the observations made by the explorers. Their contacts with the Africans were largely limited to the political and social elite. According to African custom, they were passed on from chief to chief and were formally received by the chief or his representatives. From the moment of entrance to a town, the explorer and his party were under the protection of the chief, and it was to his hospitality that they owed their well-being, if not their lives. Most often such hospitality varied in proportion to the generosity of the traveler. If he was well supplied and gave many gifts to the chiefs and retainers, he could expect hospitable treatment. This was, in fact, a sore subject of grievance. Few of the explorers were aware that it was not purely gift-giving, but the proper form with which to *repay* the chief and his town for hospitality and protection, and an accepted mechanism of economic distribution. Consequently the European found himself haggling exasperatedly over gifts which he felt he should be free to give or not. The journals repeatedly refer to the greedy and exploitive Africans who constantly demanded "presents." The following are such complaints from the journals of Richard and John Lander and Mungo Park:

> This old rascal had muttered and grumbled at everything which was offered him; *this* was of no use, and *that* of no value, and he would desire all that we had, such was his covetousness.[10]

> I assured him that Europeans would much rather run risque of being plundered in a hostile manner, than have their goods . . . extorted from them by such exorbitant demands.[11]

Park's first journey in West Africa was exceptional because he was then in closer contact with the African people. He was alone and without goods for either trade or "presents" and hence was left to make his way unassisted. He recorded that several times he would have perished if not for the charity shown him by the women of the poorer class.[12]

Usually the explorers dealt almost exclusively with the men in power. When making treaties or trade agreements or when trying to gain favor they had to know something about the individual chiefs. In fact, the only character portrayal of Africans in this literature is of chiefs or kings.[13] For the rest, description was limited to the details of bearing, clothing, and ornaments. The interest in clothing was an exaggerated one, reflecting the attitude, perhaps, that "clothing maketh the man." The fashion reports are most elaborate in the numerous accounts detailing the panoply of African courts and the regalia of the monarchs. Those who visited the great kingdoms of Ashanti and Dahomey were awed by the "barbaric splendours." Bowdich says of Ashanti:

. . . they had not prepared us for the extent and display of the scene which here burst upon us; an area of nearly a mile in circumference was crowded with magnificence and novelty. The King, his tributaries, and captains were resplendent in the distance, surrounded by attendants of every description, fronted by a mass of warriors which seemed to make our approach impervious. The sun was reflected with a glare scarcely more supportable than the heat, from the massive gold ornaments which glistened in every direction. More than a hundred bands burst at once on our arrival with the peculiar airs of their several chiefs . . . the general blaze of splendour and ostentation. . . . Gold and silver pipes and canes dazzled the eye . . . the warriors sat on the ground . . . and so thickly as not to admit of our passing without treading on their feet. . . . We agreed in estimating the number of warriors at 30,000. . . .[14]

Not all the sights were so splendid and shining in these kingdoms. The observers witnessed with horror gory war trophies: skulls, human bones, and scalps.[15] They saw executions, human sacrifices, and mutilations. These instances of "bloody brutality" contributed to the high drama of the barbaric pageantry, adding just the proper note of *frisson* to the usual review of troops and fashions. Additionally, such terrible scenes reinforced the generalized stereotype of the savage African.

As to the analysis of the political systems themselves, the explorers were, as in other cultural matters, limited to surface aspects and to ethnocentric comparisons with European systems. However involved they were with the ruling groups and alert to palace intrigues and tribal rivalries, they were still imperceptive of the actual functioning of the state, unaware of the complex of reciprocities and forces within the polity. They saw the kingdoms as purely personal despotisms and the kings as absolute monarchs. Thomas Bowdich described the Ashanti state as a "military despotism" and the monarch as having life-and-death power over all his subjects.[16] The depth of Bowdich's misconception can best be seen if his view is contrasted with the view of modern anthropology on the Ashanti state, stated first by R. S. Rattray in *Ashanti Law and Constitution* (London, 1929) and still held by contemporary anthropologists. Here is Robert Lystad's statement:

Ashanti is . . . a government of imperial cast and of remarkable complexity for the nonliterate world, being bureaucratic and heirarchic in its structure but using a principle of decentralization of authority which permitted the member states to manage all affairs which did not affect the Confederacy.

At the summit of the Confederacy stood the King. . . . At his side stood the Asanteman Council, composed of the paramount chiefs of the member states . . . near equals to the King in the direction of Ashanti affairs . . . they governed with district chiefs, town chiefs, village heads and heads of families . . . picked by choice requiring the approval of the constituent commoner groups, and a poor selection could be deposed by popular demand.[17]

In these "First Light" descriptions of African rulers, they are represented as an inversion of the British ideal of kingship. Benevolent and enlightened rule could not apply to the African monarch. He was a savage for whom rule could only mean self-aggrandizement and the unequivocal and brutal exercise of unlimited personal power.

In general, the commonality were viewed with disapproval, if not outright contempt, the observations limited only to traits of appearance that seemed bizarre, such as hair styles and facial markings. The travelers found the manners of the people offensive: they were too noisy, and their dancing was indecorous. The rigidly conservative John Duncan and the more easygoing, gentle Alexander Laing express the same shocked dismay at the dancing.

Their dances, however, are anything but what an Englishman would consider dancing. . . . Another motion used by them, which is considered the most amusing in the dance is a rotatory movement of hips, changing to a backward and forward motion of a most disgusting description.[18]

. . . when commenced a most grotesque kind of dance in which was more action than elegance and more labour than grace. The dancers scarcely moved their feet, but made up for their deficiency in that respect by twisting their bodies into attitudes completely serpentine . . . displaying their activity in a manner which was rather distressing than agreeable to witness. . . .[19]

Religion, even as superstition, received literary short shrift. Far more space was devoted to almost any detail of costume than to description of West African religions. Bowdich, rather more interested in "native customs" than most of the explorers, devoted an entire chapter of a scant dozen pages to the "superstitions" of the Ashanti, of which fully five pages are given over to a description of aggry beads and conjecture as to their origin.[20] Avowing distaste for "native superstitions," the explorers most often remained uninterested and uninvolved. Duncan, however, to show the extent of his distaste, forced his way into a sacred enclosure, manhandling the attendant priestess. He recorded this as a heroic episode to elicit admiration for his crusading Christian spirit, and the reader is indeed struck with wonder that he lived to record it at all.[21]

Samuel Crowther, who later became the first Anglican Bishop in West Africa, was himself a European-educated Yoruba. He was a missionary accompanying the 1854 Niger Expedition. It is not possible to judge whether his social position as an African and a missionary on an exploratory expedition was a source of difficulty, since in this regard he was a model of literary discretion, but it is possible that his position might have been a source of constraint in his extra-expedition relations. One might legitimately expect greater attention to native religion from a missionary, if only in terms of that which must be combated. Yet Crowther barely mentioned religion in his entire journal of the expedition, and when he did it shared equal honors with clothing and cannibalism, in what seems an unparalleled example of the *non sequitur.*

I asked whether the inhabitants of Gomkoi were Pagans or Mohammedans; and was informed that they were all Pagans; that the males wore some sort of cloth around their loins, but the females only a few green leaves. On asking whether they were cannibals; I was answered in the negative.[22]

These apparently disparate traits—pagan, naked, and cannibal—form a syndrome. The basic attitudes which arbitrarily relate these essentially unrelated qualities are those which assign all cultural differences to the single category of savagery; any one trait as it distinguishes a savage from a European becomes an index to the existence of the other traits which are part of the syndrome. Thus, nakedness may well imply that there is also cannibalism and that the people are "fetish-worshippers." A clothed cannibal is somehow a contradiction in terms. Such a typology also provides an ethnocentric scale of judgment: where differences are less marked, the people are less savage. This may well account for the remarkable concentration of the explorers upon the clothing of the Africans. It served as an obvious and facile measure of the state of civilization or savagery.

The First Light explorers did not label the Negro per se as inferior or ugly. The Africans were inferior because they were savages; whether they were deemed ugly or not depended upon the extent of the writer's cultural chauvinism. There was a general tendency to regard the less Negroid physical type as better looking, but this was probably more the result of xenophobic predilections than of explicit racism. The writers were more apt to notice and comment on the fine features and bearing of members of the African aristocracy, so that if overt racism did not color their judgments, class-consciousness certainly did. Richard Lander describes the King and Queen of Boussa as follows.

> The features of the royal couple bore a closer resemblance to the European than the Negro cast, and might be styled handsome, even in England.[23]

And Laird and R. A. K. Oldfield describe Osiman, King of Nupe.

> His manners were dignified and imposing, his conversation free and easy, and his remarks shrewd and sensible. . . . He was rather good-looking around the eyes which were dark and piercing. . . .[24]

The consistent and determinant attitude was a matter-of-fact acceptance that the Africans were savage and hence inferior to civilized Europeans, and what constituted either savagery or civilization was evident in items of dress, material culture, and overt behavior.

In the light of the established tradition, these writings of the early nineteenth century seem to be more antagonistic toward Africans than they actually were. Critical comments of this period were later repeated as the component idioms of the tradition, and the later tendentiousness overlooks the many comments which describe Africans as intelligent, kindly, and decent, and exaggerates the pejorative nature of the descriptions, if only by such omission.

Descriptions of the land in this period were literal, without romantic embellishments. Yet it was during this time that the term "White Man's Grave" became common, and the image of Africa as hostile and repelling was firmly implanted. The phrase itself was the title of a work by F. Harrison Rankin[25] about Sierra Leone in which he describes an attractive land and bids for European colonization. It may have been Rankin's phrase, but not the work itself which established the image. Undoubtedly the term attained such wide usage because of the popular impression that had been gained from high disease and mortality rates and the heat and extremes of weather, which made exploration and philanthropic endeavors so hazardous, all of which were publicized by the secular press and by such widely read works as Charles Dickens' *Bleak House*.

The reader must create his own synthesis to construct a coherent image of Africa from the material provided by the First Light writers. Later writers created just such a synthesis and developed the conventions which are in the first half of the nineteenth century only dimly outlined.

The Golden Land: South Africa, 1800–1850

The contrast between "White Man's Grave" and the Cape of Good Hope quite fortuitously gives the key to the difference in the British response to the West Coast and to South Africa. South Africa was an inviting territory; combining a fertile and beautiful land, a temperate climate, and open, easily traversed terrain. Colonization rather than trade was the compelling motive. The foundations for settlement were already laid; the farms and towns of the Dutch and Huguenot immigrants had demonstrated its feasibility. The Cape of Good Hope became a British colony early in the nineteenth century, long before areas in West Africa that had had contact with the British since the sixteenth century.

Unlike the rather intimidating West Coast Africans, the natives of South Africa seemed picturesque or pathetic. The Bushmen and Hottentots close to the Cape had already been subjugated by the early settlers, and the survivors were slaves and servants of the Dutch Boers. The great mass of the Bantu, although in the path of future expansion, were in the early nineteenth century still to the north and east of the European settlements. The Europeans in the south were not dependent on the good will of powerful chiefs and generally had a freer hand.

The British never engaged in slave trading in the south, and slavery itself took on a different significance than it had in West Africa. It was the Boers who had virtually enslaved the Hottentots. The British protested against Boer inhumanity and pitied the victims whose wretched condition inspired the philanthropic endeavors of British mission societies. Their energetic activities and outlook dominated the literature on South Africa.

The generally felicitous conditions were reflected in a body of literature characterized by more thoughtful observation and discussion, less urgency, and on the whole, a more optimistic attitude than that of the west. During the first fifty years of British possession a steady stream of travelers published their observations and impressions to make the British at home aware of the worth of their new colony.

The British in South Africa in this period were a mixed bag, comprising missionaries, settlers, officials, and gentlemen of leisure who had come to regain their health, to enjoy the unparalleled opportunities for hunting, or to study natural history.

In 1795 John Barrow described a journey he made through the colony at the request of the British government to investigate conditions. His attitudes toward both Boers and Africans reflected his role as an agent of the government. Boer intransigence seemed to him the most serious obstacle to successful British colonization. He believed that the Boers were a stubborn and brutal lot, and commented:

> By habitual indolence, excess of food, and fondness for indulging in sleep, they become no less gross in their persons than they are vulgar in their manners.[1]

Barrow's hostility to the Boers accompanied a corresponding sympathy for the Africans. In reference to the Hottentot he wrote:

These weak people, the most helpless, and in their present condition perhaps the most wretched of the human race, duped out of their possessions, their country, and their liberty, have entailed upon their miserable offspring a state of existence to which that of slavery might bear the comparison of happiness . . . their extreme poverty, scantiness of food, and continual dejection of mind, arising from an inhuman and unfeeling peasantry [the Boers] who having discovered themselves to be removed to too great a distance from the seat of government to be awed by its authority, have hitherto exercised, in the most wanton and barbarous manner, an absolute power over these poor wretches whom they had reduced to the necessity of depending upon them for a morsel of bread.[2]

To Barrow the Hottentots were evidence of Boer cruelty and the "Kaffirs" were a glowing contrast to Boer baseness. His portrayal of "Kaffirs," especially that of Gaika, the Xhosa chief, comes perilously close to the noble savage. The theme of the noble savage, always a polemic device, was this time the weapon with which to belabor the Boers. The "Kaffirs" were "modest, kind and brave," even quite splendid. Shades of Oroonoko!

Though black, or very nearly so, they have no one line of the African negro in the shape and turn of their person . . . and a line from the forehead to the chin drawn over the nose is as a Roman or a Grecian countenance. In short, had not Nature bestowed upon him the dark-colouring principle . . . he might have ranked among the first of Europeans.[3]

Some years later, when the "Kaffirs" stood in the way of British expansion, the writers were not as disposed to extol "Kaffir" nobility and beauty. Correspondingly, the Boers were favored. Steedman, writing approximately thirty-five years after Barrow, cited a settler, Mr. Shaw, as saying

. . . it has been the practice of various writers to give such glowing descriptions of the noble and generous-minded Caffers, that many

> persons . . . find it difficult to believe that a Caffer chief would degrade himself by sanctioning robbery and murder. Nothing can be more misleading than statements which produce this impression. . . . The frequent robberies committed by them . . . may fairly be ascribed . . . to their own imperfect moral perceptions, deeply rooted habits, and defective mode of government.[4]

Steedman agreed with this estimate of "Kaffir" character and consequently found the Boers to be admirable people. He commended their "plain and frugal manner" of living and their patriarchal character.[5]

Throughout the literature on South Africa, anti-Boer sentiment has its echo in pro-native sentiment, and vice versa. The British either had to placate the Boers at the expense of native Africans or to engender Boer antagonism by protecting the Africans. Whichever line a writer followed, he was bound to be critical of one of the two as he reflected the ups and downs of historical circumstance and British policy.

The dominant context of the literature was not political, but religious. The Boers had been reluctant to establish missions, and before the arrival of the British the only successful mission on the Cape was the German Moravian mission at Genadendal. The British were more zealous. In England, the Age of Enlightenment was ending; Deism and religious indifference were being replaced by the religious revival of the nineteenth century. This was a time of rapid growth of sectarian movements as well as of reform and expansion within the Anglican Church. There was new impetus and eager support for Christian missions abroad.

South Africa proved congenial to British missionary efforts to bring salvation and enlightenment to a population "sunk into the lowest depths of ignorance, superstition, disorganization and debasement"[6] and "enveloped in ignorance and vice."[7] The work of the missions entailed far more than conversion alone. Christianity and civilization were to be promoted together.[8] The image of the missionary, and one that is long-lived in the tradition, was here laid down. He was the self-sacrificing bringer of light for whom no task was too menial or arduous. He did whatever had to be done to meet all the needs of his people. The image, in short, is that of the wise, benevolent father and heroic martyr. David Livingston thus described the strenuous life of an African missionary.

> After family worship and breakfast . . . we went to keep school for all who would attend. . . . While the missionary's wife was occupied in domestic matters, the missionary himself had some manual labour as a smith, carpenter, or gardener, according to whatever was needed for ourselves or for the people. . . . After . . . the wife attended her infant school; or she varied that with a sewing school. . . . During the day every operation must be superintended, and both husband and wife must labour till the sun declines. After sunset the husband went into town to converse . . . sometimes on religion. On three nights of the week . . . we had a public religious service, and one of instruction in secular subjects aided by pictures and specimens. These services were diversified by attending upon the sick and prescribing for them, giving food and otherwise assisting the poor and wretched.[9]

In reports of missionary activities, the literature for the first time indicates a more-than-superficial knowledge of the Africans. The missionaries lived and worked intimately with particular groups and reported something of their cultures. Such works[10] are the chief sources of early data, invaluable to modern ethnographic research. The data, however, often have to be sifted out of their missionary matrix. Missionaries' accounts of African religion are particularly difficult for modern ethnographers to use. In their discussions, fact and judgment are almost inextricably combined, for the purpose of the missionaries was to root out the native religions —to convert the heathen.

The early work of Livingstone belongs to this period. Like other missionaries, his writings reveal no doubts about the absolute truth of Christianity and the superiority of British culture. However, his work was as much a reflection of scientific interests and training as of missionary zeal, a fact that modified its entire nature. Much of his discussion about Africans, even of African religions, sounds a modern note of cultural relativism.

> As for the rain-makers, they carried the sympathies of the people along with them, and not without reason . . . in order to understand their force, we must place ourselves in their position, and believe as they do.[11]

Livingstone's evaluations of the intelligence and morality of the Africans had a like objectivity, which set him apart from most other writers of the period.

> . . . but in questions affecting their worldly affairs, they were keenly alive to their own interests; they might be called stupid in matters which had not come within the sphere of their observations, but in other things they showed more intelligence than is to be met with in our own uneducated peasantry.[12]

> . . . I have found it difficult to come to a conclusion on their character. They sometimes perform actions remarkably good, and sometimes as strangely the opposite. . . . After long observation, I came to the conclusion that they are just a strange mixture of good and evil as men are everywhere else.[13]

The course of Livingstone's career as a missionary was altered by a virulent case of the geographer's itch. He sought always to go deeper into the interior, ostensibly to search out new areas for Christian endeavor. In time, however, geography and exploration took precedence, at least in his writing, over more orthodox missionary labors. His *Last Journals*,[14] which cover the years from 1865 to his death in 1873, demonstrate his personal evolution from exploring missionary to Christian explorer. In both time and emphasis, these journals represent a distinct shift from the South African missionary tradition, and they properly belong with the works of the next period on East Africa. They indicate Livingstone's involvement with the mid-nineteenth-century explorations in search of the sources of the Nile. Douglas Woodruff writes of this change in Livingstone.

> Without abandoning his calling, he shifted his emphasis, and in the end he stood first and foremost for the discovery of unknown land and the intrepid conquest of natural obstacles and it was only secondarily that he was thought of as a missionary. The consular cap which he always wore after he left the London Missionary Society in 1856 and became the leader of expeditions was a far-reaching symbol.[15]

In the early nineteenth century, conversion of the heathen concerned the settlers as greatly as it did the missionaries. To the settlers, a Christian population meant a population which would neither harass nor threaten the European community. In fact, it was thought a settlement of Christian natives could be an admirable buffer against unruly heathens. It would also provide a supply of clean, willing, and honest servants, for when Africans were converted to Christianity they were also expected to accept the values of cleanliness, work, and respect for private property. British settlers rejected the Boer ideal of the isolated, independent frontier farmer; they envisioned the establishment of an orderly, close-knit community, which required a "civilized" native population.

The British plainly felt that the Boers had been derelict in their Christian duties, but even more, they identified true Christianity with the British brand. Such ethnocentrism involved more than religion, which was the banner for the onward march of civilization, subsuming manners as well as morals and literacy as well as salvation. British zeal was boundless, their vision huge, and the groundwork was thus laid for empire. Pringle in the 1820's was already envisioning empire.

> Let us enter upon a new and nobler career of conquest. Let us subdue Savage Africa by justice, by kindness, by the talisman of Christian truth. Let us thus go forth, in the name and under the blessing of God, gradually to extend the moral influence . . . the territorial boundary also of our colony, until it shall become an Empire—embracing Southern Africa from the Keisi and Gareep to Mozambique and Cape Negro —and to which, per adventure, in after days, even the equator shall prove no ultimate limit.[16]

Though Christian optimism was the prevailing tone, some believed that the Africans were incorrigible and unredeemable. Since South Africa was so pleasing to Europeans, the presence there of such a "greedy, heartless, silly set of savages," [17] as Francis Galton termed them, was a serious inconvenience. Since they were not educable, other means of dealing with them had to be found. Alfred W. Cole suggested that conversion to the less refined faith of Islam might prove possible and would improve the Africans by its much-needed discipline. He thought it more likely, however, that contact with civilization would bring about an inevitable and total extinction of the native population and thus effectively remove the inconvenience of their presence.[18] Sir William Harris, on the other hand, placed no such trust in inevitability.

It does indeed furnish matter of amazement to every thinking person . . . how those who have legislated for the affairs of the colony should not long ago have seen the imperious necessity, dictated alike by reason, justice, and humanity, of exterminating from off the face of the earth, a race of monsters. . . .[19]

Whether they were sanguine or choleric, the observers categorized the Africans as heathen savages. All were uniformly heathen, but a certain elasticity was given to the term "savage." The various African groups were ranked according to degrees of savagery; on this scale the Bushmen were invariably at the bottom as the most savage and closest to the beasts. Robert Moffat, for example, considered them to be "the link between rational and irrational creation." [20] They were often pitied, for the writers ascribed their miserable existence to the persecutions they had suffered. The Hottentots were a rung higher than the Bushmen because they were pastoralists, not wandering hunters. Hugh Murray felt their low condition "to have been in a great measure produced by their degrading subjection to the Dutch Boors [*sic*]." [21] The Gricquas and Bastaards were granted superior intellect and ability; their partial European ancestry accounted for the higher estimation in which they were held.

The Bantu-speaking people, the "Kaffirs," were ranked by some at the top of this scale. Though not Europeanized, neither were they degraded victims. None of the early writers professed any need to pity them; they were disliked or respected, depending upon the bias of the observer. General opinion held that the southern Bantu were savages who merited some respect because they were manly and warlike. Henry Methuen, for example, thought that they shared the "nobility" of the American Indians in the novels of James Fenimore Cooper.

They reminded me very much of the North American Indians, as described by Cooper; their warriors are, in general, models of symmetry, tall, of graceful carriage, elastic step, and independent air, so that no one can help admiring them. . . .[22]

South African travelers surpassed West African explorers in their interest in natural history. The primary purpose of some was the collection of scientific data. W. J. Burchell meticulously described and sketched the plants and animals of the Cape, and discovered several new species of both which are named for him. All the writers, even those lacking a special scientific interest, describe the landscape, flora, and fauna *ad infinitum*.

Many books are little more than lovingly detailed chronicles of the outdoor life, of camping and hunting. These initiated a most persistent theme in the literary tradition, that Africa was a Hunter's Paradise. Like many others, Harris had come to Africa for the hunting, and it fully lived up to his expectations.

. . . the landscape literally presented the appearance of a moving mass of game. Their incredible numbers so impeded their progress that I had no difficulty in closing with them, dismounting as opportunity offered, firing both barrels of my rifle into the retreating phalanx, and leaving the ground strewed with the slain. Still unsatisfied, I could not resist the temptation of mixing with the fugitives, loading and firing, until my jaded horse suddenly exhibited symptoms of distress, and shortly afterwards was unable to move.[23]

Hunting was much more than the mere killing of animals; an entire ethos was built around it. For the English related it to two major sets of values, that of personal character and of social status. Hunting not only demonstrated character, it also helped to inculcate the virtues of courage and action. Livingstone was sufficiently a man of his times to agree with the notion.

I sometimes felt annoyed at the low estimation in which some of my hunting friends were held; for, believing that the chase is eminently conducive to the formation of a brave and noble character, and that the contest with wild beasts is well adapted for fostering that coolness in emergencies, and active presence of mind, which we all admire, I was naturally anxious that a higher estimate of my countrymen should be formed in the native mind.[24]

The sport had long been the prerogative and avocation of the British upper classes. A display of the proper enthusiasm for hunting and proper conduct in it carried the cachet of "gentleman." To the Africans, hunting was a matter of subsistence, not sport. The British considered this view of game to be gluttonous and vulgar, rather like the poaching of the lower classes at home. Livingstone's observations upon the contrast between British and African attitudes toward hunting are perceptive and pertinent. He reports his conversation with an African, which indicates the difference in values.

Have these hunters, who come so far and work so hard, no meat at home? —Why, these men are rich, and could slaughter oxen every day of their lives. —And yet they come here, and endure so much thirst for the sake of this dry meat, none of which is equal to beef? —Yes, it is for the sake of play besides. (the idea of sport not being in the language). This produces a laugh, as much as to say, "Ah! You know better"; or, "your friends are fools." When they can get a man to kill large quantities of game for them, whatever *he* may think of himself or of his achievements, *they* pride themselves in having adroitly turned to good account the folly of an itinerant butcher.[25]

The first, and for a long time the only, British novel about South Africa was Captain Frederick Marryat's *The Mission,* a tale primarily of big-game hunting on the South African veldt. Once having disposed of a slender plot of shipwreck and the search for survivors, the writer was free to devote himself and the reader's attention to the excitements of the chase.

. . . now he was most anxious to go to Africa on his own account. The narratives of combat with wild animals, the quantity and variety of game to be found, and the continual excitement which would be kept up, inflamed his imagination and his love of field sports. . . .[26]

Marryat was a professional novelist who exploited not his own adventures, but material already available in print. The initial plot of shipwreck he based on newspaper reports of the wreck of the H.M.S. *Grosvenor* off Delagoa Bay, and the rest of his tale came from various accounts of African adventure and sport.

Thomas Pringle, in particular, was a rich source of material for Marryat. A secondary plot, which deals with the English hero's adoption of a clever Bushman boy, is directly out of Pringle. With Marryat's novel, there is clear evidence of the literary cribbing which is one of the processes by which the tradition has become established and maintained.

Two basic themes were characteristic of this early South African literature. The first derived from the environment itself: in happy contrast to the White Man's Grave, South Africa was a White Man's Paradise. The image of a beautiful, sunlit, golden land became a permanent component in the literature on Africa.

The second distinguishing theme derived from the emphasis on the missionary effort and the Christian ethos. It permeated the literature with a philanthropic flavor. Ethnocentric comments were pitying or patronizing rather than hostile. Christian philanthropy added a new dimension to both the image of the African and of the British: the British were the bringers of enlightenment; the Africans, still savages, became the heathens as well. The African was savage because he was not Christian, and Christianity was equated with civilization.

The identification of the savage with the heathen did not prove as persistent in the tradition as either the "beastly" or the "noble" savage. As Christian optimism waned and the new problems of empire arose, the theme of the heathen became attenuated, occasionally cropping up again in missionary writing, but never again as an important convention in the total tradition.

CHAPTER II

The Dawn of Empire: Mid-Century

The Saga of Exploration

THE history of British involvement in Africa throughout the nineteenth century was one of progressive complexity, accelerating tempo, and expanding territorial interests. By the middle of the century East Central Africa, hitherto considered Portuguese or Arab preserve, became the new and predominant locus of British activity. Britain's colonies in Asia, primarily India, were her major concern. The original purpose even in the British annexation of the Cape Colony in 1806 had been "to secure the master link in connection between the western and eastern worlds." [1] The Suez Canal—the new, short route to India completed in 1869—placed East Africa in a position of strategic importance. Increasing pressures of international rivalry, especially with France and Germany, made it imperative for Great Britain to maintain dominance in East Africa to further safeguard the "jewel in the Imperial crown."

From its inception, the Cape Colony had been a base for expansion to the north and east. The Boer treks and the growing British population made such expansion almost inevitable, despite government reluctance to extend territorial responsibilities in Africa. The authors of *Africa and the Victorians* point out the effects which expansion from the south had on the British government.

> . . . they [the settlers] were lengthening and disturbing frontiers which placed an increasing strain upon the imperial Exchequer, the War Office, and the tempers of Cabinet and Parliament.[2]

The missionaries had moved out from Cape Colony well ahead of the colonists. David Livingstone established a base for the

London Missionary Society in Kuruman, Bechuanaland. Making his way north, he reached the Zambesi in 1850. The Reverends Robert Moffat and John Mackenzie (in 1854 and 1863) were among the first Europeans in Matabeleland. They were the vanguard, but other missionaries soon arrived from Great Britain via Zanzibar to establish stations in Nyasa and Uganda.[3]

The missionaries, especially Livingstone, brought the East African slave trade to public attention. This publicity served to heighten interest in the area as well as arousing philanthropic groups in Britain. Sentiment against the trade gained wholehearted support, as every writer on Africa during this and later periods inveighed against Arab slave raiding. Suppression of the trade provided the moral purpose for the penetration and subsequent annexation of East and Central Africa.

Another factor in the awakened interest in East Africa was the still new and flourishing interest in scientific geography, which turned its attention to the ancient mystery of the source of the Nile. The great figures of this period are, in fact, the explorers, and in the course of their explorations, the mystery of the source of the Nile was solved.

Britain's increasing concern with overseas expansion gave new purpose to exploration. The explorers were committed to the idea of British dominion in Africa and saw themselves as the vanguard of an advancing empire. The explorers of the Niger in the earlier nineteenth century had been intent upon discovering new trade commodities and new geographical knowledge; the explorers of mid-century were the true conquerors of Africa, the heroes of nascent empire.

In West Africa, too, the British were sounding the fanfare that preceded empire. From 1850 on they were energetically spreading the gospel of Christianity and of civilization. Mid-century West African accounts add new knowledge, but do not inaugurate any new theme in the literary tradition. The writers on both West and East Africa repeat the same ideology and reiterate the same stereotypes of Africans and of their own role. There is even overlapping in personnel. The explorer, Richard Burton, was at least as active in West Africa as in the east, though his fame rests mainly on his work in East Africa. V. L. Cameron, Henry M. Stanley, and

Joseph Thomson also figure in the annals of both East and West Africa.

The records of East African exploration are the apogee of African travel literature. They provided the spectacle of the full-scale expedition: intrepid British leaders, gunbearers and servants, and the long line of porters. These expeditions were carried out on a much grander scale than ever before. Some of the explorers now even traveled in high style. Stanley transported his elaborate solid silver tea service complete with table linens from Zanzibar to Ujiji on the shores of Lake Tanganyika. Samuel Baker had with him at all times the delightful Mrs. Baker, and a portable bath which could be converted into a dinghy or a wine tub. Burton's list of equipment was prodigious; it included everything necessary for a long, eventful journey, from five dozen bottles of brandy to three hundred and eighty pounds of lead bullets and fifty pounds of nails in addition to the enormous load of cloth, beads, brass, and wire for gifts and trade.[4] Even foresighted provisioning did not always achieve its purpose. The British suffered in East Africa as they had in the West from losses due to robbery and desertion. Illness was here a serious hazard, too, but there were fewer deaths because of the increasing use of quinine as a specific against malaria and the easier conditions of East African travel.

East African exploration constituted a great, continuous, cliff-hanging saga. The narratives still make exciting reading about explorers lost, and search parties sent to find them, of the race to discover the sources of the Nile and the struggles to put down Arab slave raiding. The same names, African and British, appear over and over again in the various journals. Tippu Tib, Kumrasi, Livingstone, Mr. and Mrs. Baker and the others must have been familiar figures to the English reading public. The accounts were further enlivened with thrilling encounters with wild game, savages, and even cannibals. Alan Moorehead's history of the explorations of the Nile comments on how such narratives delighted an eager audience at home.

> In the Victorian age, explorers' books exerted an extraordinary power over peoples' minds. . . . In the sixties the great outpouring of these African publications began. . . . One would have thought that

NATIONAL CITY PUBLIC LIBRARY

there was enough here to inform, confuse, and finally satiate the most besotted student of African travels, but still the public could not have enough.[5]

The explorers were well aware of the public interest, and they were not averse to its exploitation. In a letter, John Hanning Speke urged John Petherick to take full advantage of the popularity of African material in what seems a somewhat too-calculating manner for the dedicated man of science and exploration.

It has just struck me that you could not do better than write a short description of your travels in Africa, well loaded with amusing anecdotes and fights with the natives: the thing would tell admirably just at present, and for the future would keep the world looking anxiously for your peregrination.[6]

The literature provided the Victorian reader with more than mere entertainment. It was primarily dedicated to the advancement of knowledge and moral purpose, and the Victorian sought, even in his entertainment, instruction and elevation. With these qualities the African literature was generously endowed. Its enormous popularity was not fortuitous.

The accounts reiterated and stressed the basic values of the Victorian ethos, and the explorers appeared as paragons of Victorian manhood. Dedicated men with the highest morals, devoted to the advancement of Progress, Christianity, and Civilization, the explorers were held up as models for the instruction of the young and the inspiration of all. The example they set of courage and commitment seemed of utmost importance to a "period in which the alarming increase of both the commercial spirit and religious doubt made moral inspiration a primary need." [7]

The British were committed to industrial and commercial growth, but they also felt a lingering regret over the progressive loss of a landed aristocracy who need take no thought of trade and money. The explorers, too, seemed to have an aristocratic disregard for such concerns. Stanley stated that he "would not have even the appearance of personal profit out of Africa." [8] Speke was insistent that he be regarded as a gentleman and not a trader.[9] Burton certainly considered himself a good cut above "a warm man of business with a good ledger."[10] Whether the explorers were rich or poor, whether their travels were financed by missionary society, geographical society, government, or themselves, they were uniformly dedicated to a far grander goal than making money. They were all knights in shining solar topees! One of the most truly splendid examples of such gallantry was the young Joseph Thomson, who wrote:

We may be a nation of shopkeepers but we have a warm heart to everything which keeps burning brightly the sacred lamp of that chivalry, in which there is as much daring, more self-denial, and a more tender regard for the weak and the oppressed than was ever practiced by the flower of ancient knighthood.[11]

In an age of doubt and controversy about religion and the entire purpose of human existence, the explorers were heartening. They were supremely confident of the righteousness of their purposes, which they identified with those of civilization itself. Because they *were* civilized men, they determined to accomplish these ends: to determine finally the source of the Nile, to map unknown territory, to introduce the blessings of Christianity and the benefits of just government to Africa. The most explicit purpose, upon which all their hearts were set, was the civilized and civilizing mission to end the slave trade. The following statements from Sir Samuel Baker and Verney Cameron expressive of this attitude can be found in almost any work of this period.

If Africa is to be civilized, it must be effected by commerce, which, once established, will open the way for missionary labour; but all ideas of commerce, improvement, and the advancement of the African race that philanthropy could suggest must be discarded until the traffic in slaves shall have ceased to exist.[12]

Africa is bleeding out her life-blood at every pore . . . its population . . . daily depleted by the slave trade. Should the present state of affairs be allowed to continue the country will gradually relapse into jungles, and wilds, and will become more and more impenetrable to the merchant and traveler. That this should be a possibility is a blot on the boasted civilization of the nineteenth century. Let us hope that the Anglo-Saxon race will allow no other nation to outstrip it in the efforts to rescue thousands of fellow-creatures from the misery and degradation which must otherwise infallibly fall to their lot.[13]

Suppression of the slave trade was but the first step toward the greater imperative of civilizing the Africans. No responsible Briton could, even after putting down the slave trade, leave the Africans to their own devices. Speke wrote that only British rule could prevent the extinction of the Africans.

How the negro has lived so many ages without advancing, seems marvelous, when all the countries surrounding Africa are so forward in comparison; and judging from the progressive state of the world, one is led to suppose that the African must soon either step out from his darkness, or be superseded by a being superior to himself. Could a government be formed for them like ours in India, they would be saved; but without it I fear there is very little chance; for at present the African can not help himself. . . .[14]

By mid-century the conviction of British superiority entailed commitment to action; the superior *should* take on the responsibility for the inferior. Here were the essential ingredients for the ideology of imperialism. It is a matter of interest that two men so far apart in character as Livingstone and Baker should be as one in their clear statements of British responsibility in Africa.

It is on the Anglo-American race that the hope of the world for liberty and progress rest. . . . But in Africa the land is cheap, the soil good, and free labour is to be found on the spot . . . the inborn energy of English colonists would develop . . . resources. . . . By linking the Africans to ourselves . . . it is hoped that their elevation will eventually be the result.[15]

England . . . possesses a power that enforces a grave responsibility. She has the force to civilize. She is the natural colonizer of the world . . . to wrest from utter savagedom those mighty tracts of the earth's surface from the creation of the world,—a darkness to be enlightened by English colonization.[16]

Perhaps nowhere could this new commitment be so clearly exemplified as in a typical safari. An East African expedition was a large enterprise, employing as many as several hundred Africans, over whom the explorer had complete authority. It was an imperium in miniature. Stanley, ever the extremist, hanged men for theft or desertion;[17] others flogged their men for various infractions of the rules. Even Livingstone, the most humane of men, once resorted to force, and then abjured its use by himself at least, saying, "I felt I was degrading myself, and resolved not to do punishment myself again." [18]

We are told by Thomson's brother and biographer that throughout his career as an explorer "he had the high and glorious distinction of never having caused the death of a native." [19] When Thomson made his first journey as the geologist and naturalist in the expedition of the Royal Geographical Society, he was barely twenty-one. The leader of the expedition died, and young Thomson took charge. It is clear from his own writings that the older, experienced Africans in his party were touched by his youth and charm; they looked after him and were amused by attempts he made to enforce discipline. When most enraged, Thomson would throw a boot in the general direction of the offender, and usually missed him. His account of this expedition is almost unfailingly good-humored.[20] The later exploration through Masailand was quite different. Then older, more experienced, and less affable, he led a more typical safari. Describing his porters as "the refuse of Zanzibar rascaldom," [21] he kept them under strict discipline, beating them when he felt it necessary. And on his return to Zanzibar he felt that the Africans had been "morally and physically regenerated." [22]

Livingstone, and Thomson as a young man, were unusual, for most of the explorers were not reluctant to use force. On the contrary, its exercise was thought to be a clear demonstration of the authority of the British leader, besides being the only effective way to deal with Africans who were by nature uncontrollable. Furthermore, stringent discipline was justified by its ultimately good effects. Most explorers would have agreed readily with the mature Thomson that rigorous discipline was salutary.

If the expedition leaders did not spare their men, neither did they spare themselves. They were undaunted by hardship, danger, or disease. One can only marvel at their reservoirs of energy and courage which even triumphed over illness. The standard prescription for everything, from a touch of the sun to a bad case of malaria, was to dig down into one's British character and come up with hard exercise.

Face the sun and fatigue, get hard exercise, fight against the anaemic state that threatens you, the disinclination to work, and the extreme lassitude and craving for sleep; above all do not lose your temper, but always manage to have some occupation, and no healthy Englishman need be afraid of a sojourn on the East Coast.[23]

James Elton, explorer and administrator, was not voicing untried notions in the statement above; such drastic measures were common. Activity was considered prime therapy, and yielding to illness an immoral and suicidal indulgence. Most explorers kept going no matter how ill they were. We quote from Thomson:

The day after my arrival I was thoroughly prostrated by the fever, and I approached unpleasantly close to the stage of delirium. Notwithstanding that, and remembering the efficacy of exertion in such cases, I set off on the second day, and braced myself up by a six-hours march.[24]

Implicit in the prodigious activity of the British was their self-image as superior beings. That superiority had to be upheld at all costs. To give way to illness before the Africans would be an admission of unwonted weakness before which prestige and unquestioned authority might waver. Stanley believed ". . . my reputation as a white man would have been ruined had I stayed behind or postponed the march, in consequence of feebleness."[25]

The authors were the heroes of their own narratives in which every incident appeared as a life-or-death event and genuine courage and fortitude took on an operatic bravura. Unlike the mundane recounting of the earlier West African explorers, these journals are suffused with self-dramatization. In his account, Sir Samuel Baker responded as a hero of matchless chivalry to the demand of Kumrasi, King of the Bunyoro, that he be given the golden-haired Lady Baker.

If this were to be the end of the expedition I resolved it should also be the end of Kumrasi, and, drawing my revolver quietly, I held it within two feet of his chest, and looking at him with undisguised contempt, I told him that if I touched the trigger, not all his men could save him: and that if he dared to repeat the insult, I would shoot him on the spot. At the same time I explained to him that in my country such insolence would entail bloodshed, and that I looked upon him as an ignorant ox who knew no better and that this excuse alone could save him.[26]

If at this moment Sir Samuel stood for every gallant British gentleman ready to give his life to defend the honor of his lady, then Kumrasi was certainly miscast as the villain of the piece. For his response deflated high drama to comic opera.

Don't be angry! I had no intention of offending you by asking for your wife; I will give you a wife, if you want one, and I thought you might have no objection to give me yours; it is my custom to give my visitors pretty wives, and I thought you might exchange. Don't make a fuss about it: if you don't like it, there's an end to it: I will never mention it again.[27]

If Baker saw any humor in this episode, it was probably in the preposterous notion that an African should ask for his wife, and in the contrast between the behavior of a Christian gentleman and a crude savage.

There was, usually, no better situation for the display of manly heroics than in the hunting of big game. As in South Africa, certain portions of East and Central Africa were literally happy hunting grounds. Stanley waxed lyrical in his depiction of opportunities for hunting on the East African savannah.

Here at last was the hunter's Paradise! . . . Where is the nobleman's park that can match this scene? Here is a soft, velvety expanse of young grass, grateful shade under those spreading clumps; herds of large and varied game browsing within easy rifle range. Surely I must feel amply compensated now for the long southern detour I have made, when such a prospect as this opens to the view! No thorny jungles and rank smelling swamps are here to daunt the hunter and to sicken his aspirations after true sport! No hunter could aspire after a nobler field to display his prowess.[28]

The journals abound in stirring episodes of hunting. It was a pleasure as well as a necessity for the explorers, and no matter how exotic the animals or the circumstances were, all hunting had to be carried out according to the rules of sportsmanship. Speke expressed his disgust at having to shoot at sitting birds by order of his host, Mtesa, King of the Baganda. This was a situation with which any gentleman could sympathize.

When I arrived, hat in hand, he [Mtesa] smiled, examined my fire-arms, and then proceeded for sport, leading the way to a high tree, on which some adjutant birds were nesting. This was sport; Bana must shoot a Nundo for the King's gratification. I begged him to take a shot himself, as I really could not demean myself by firing at birds sitting in a tree; but it was all of no use—No one could shoot as I could, and they must be shot. I proposed frightening them out with stones, but no stone could reach so high; so to cut the matter short I killed an adjutant on the nest.[29]

Like Baker, Speke was appalled at the conduct of the African monarchs. If kings were so lacking in a sense of propriety, then how base must be the rest of the people? In the literature of this period, there are no noble savages, and this seems to be an index of increasing British arrogance. British assumption of superiority could not admit any Africans as equals, and it angered the explorers that the Africans did not accord them automatic deference. Anger and arrogance are clear in these statements by Speke and Burton.

By the chief officers in waiting, however, who thought fit to treat us like Arab merchants, I was requested to sit on the ground outside in the sun with my servants. Now, I had made up my mind never to sit upon the ground as the natives and Arabs are obliged to do . . . I felt that if I did not stand up for my social position at once, I should be treated with contempt during the remainder of my visit, and thus lose the vantage-ground I had assumed of appearing rather as a prince than a trader. . . . I allowed five minutes to the court to give me a proper reception, saying if it were not conceded I would then walk away. . . .[30]

With the characteristic negro impudence which ever pierces through Dahoman politeness we were directed to remove from under our favorite tree; and naturally we did not.[31]

The British believed that the advanced state of British culture presented most obvious signs of their superiority. Its material progress had an inevitable accompaniment of the moral values of efficiency, commitment to work, and ambition. Conversely, the Africans were inferior because they did not show tangible evidence of progress. There were in Africa no railroads, no steamships, no factories, nor any other sign of industrialism. It followed that the Africans must also lack the moral concomitants. Progress—the dynamic factor for civilization—could be achieved only by hard work. The African must be taught the value of work, chiefly by being compelled to work. African societies, said the writers, did not provide the necessary motivation or compulsion and therefore it was up to the British to provide a government for the Africans that would. Baker wrote "The African . . . instincts being a love of idleness and savagedom, he will assuredly relapse into an idle and savage state, unless specially governed and forced to industry." [32]

The emphasis on teaching Africans the value of labor presaged the day of empire when the Africans would be valued chiefly as a source of labor. Similarly foreshadowing British imperial domination in Africa, the explorers and missionaries at mid-century consistently pointed to the untapped wealth of the continent which could be profitably developed. Some of them, such as Burton, Speke, and Baker, were frankly exploitive; they thought that the wealth of Africa should be outrightly a European property. More often discussions were couched in philanthropic terms: Great Britain should exploit the resources of Africa, but for the ultimate benefit of the Africans. In general, though it is still too soon to find an explicit formulation of the British role as master in Africa, the literature does reflect two features characteristic of it. One is the latent imperialist attitudes of mid-century. The second, specifically and clearly articulated, is the British self-image as that most superior of beings, an English gentleman.

The Setting of the Saga

The Continent. At mid-century the image of West Africa as the White Man's Grave was already entrenched, but there was no similar convention for East Africa. The images of the explorers of the east were still only individual expressions. They are, however, consistent with each other and with the later full-blown tradition. Both Burton and Stanley, for example, described the difficulties and discomforts of Europeans in Africa as if the land itself were willfully rejecting them.

> . . . the European traveller realizes every preconceived idea of Africa's aspect, at once hideous and grotesque. The general appearance is a mingling of bush and forest, which, contracting the horizon to a few yards, is equally monotonous to the eye and palling to the imagination . .. in some parts the traveller might fancy a corpse to be hidden behind every bush . . . apathy and indolence, the physical debility and the mental prostration that are the gifts of climate . . . moist heat and damp cold . . . attest the hostility of Nature to mankind.[1]

> . . . but the great forest which lay vast as a continent before them, and drowsy like a great beast, with monstrous fur thinly veiled by vaporous exhalations, answered not a word, but rested in its infinite sullenness, remorseless and implacable. . . .[2]

The hostility of these personifications can be partly explained as the projections of the individual writers. Burton disliked Africa. He was an ardent Orientalist and Arabophile, and in his descriptions Africa and the Africans suffer from invidious comparison with the Islamic world. Stanley fastened the label of the "Dark Continent" upon Africa, though this may have been merely a journalist's proclivity for sensationalism. He regarded Africa as a personal adversary to be conquered, and his explorations *were* conducted like military operations: Stanley's description of the "great beast" may be viewed as a projection of his own predatory and ruthless passage through the continent. Thomson, on the other hand, was a gentler man, who found much to please him. He presented a less hostile metaphor in which the hazards of African travel appear to guard a precious secret. This eventually became one of the most persistent images in the tradition.

> We might imagine . . . that some all-powerful evil genius held sway over the land and kept some lovely damsel or great treasure deep hidden in the interior, surrounded by a land teeming with horrors and guarded by the foul monsters of disease, of darkness and savagery. That land is the pestilential coast region where so many adventurous modern knight-errants [*sic*] have been doomed to die in their attempts to reveal to the world the fair spirit of Africa.[3]

The continent plays a large part in the drama of exploration. As the setting for high adventure and heroic exploit, it could not be just another ordinary land. What the explorers found in Africa was anything but commonplace; it was all novel and exciting, enough to stir the dullest imagination. The accounts are almost overburdened by descriptions of the varied and awe-inspiring landscapes, the incredible rivers, the rich vegetation, and the many strange animals. Though florid in style, the descriptions are matter-of-fact and more analytical than romantic.

The People. From 1530 on racial differences had been remarked and often described pejoratively, but race had not been in itself an explanation of "savagery." In the First Light period in the south, the chief determinant had been religion; in the west it had been class privilege and power. The literature of East Africa at mid-century was marked by a new and intense consciousness of race differences. Most of the writers ascribed the inferiority of the Africans, as well as British superiority, to racial origins.

Earlier British travelers in West Africa had been keenly aware of African social hierarchies and had accepted the superior status of African rulers. All kings were to be respected, and African kings only slightly less than European. The explorers of mid-century also encountered powerful rulers, yet they submitted to royal power angrily or with mockery, for it seemed to them anomalous, if not ludicrous, that a Negro could be a king. Most of the explorers of this period evinced contempt for African kings, but Baker was probably the least guarded in his sneering reference to Kumrasi.

> We received a message today that we were not to expect Kumrasi as great men were never in a hurry to pay visits. . . . It is very trying to the patience to wait here until it pleases these almighty niggers to permit us to cross the river.[4]

A few African monarchs were portrayed individually; there are excellent descriptions of Kumrasi, of Mtesa of Baganda, and Gelele, King of the West African kingdom of Dahomey. The only other individual portraiture in this literature is of the personal servants or guards of the expedition leaders. Chuma and Susi, Livingstone's servants, Speke's man, Bombay, and a few others reappear as familiar figures in various accounts.

With the increased emphasis placed upon race, however, there was a correspondingly greater tendency to categorize by stereotype, rather than to describe individuals. Social and individual distinctions were blurred; the individual was lost within the tribe, and the tribe within the race. Africans and Negroes were equivalents, all alike, and all equally inferior.

Certain tribes were exempted from the general ascription of total inferiority. They elicited approbation because they were "fighting tribes," who prized the role of the warrior and held the values of personal courage and martial spirit. These attitudes struck a responsive chord in the British. John Petherick held that ". . . the Nuer are the most warlike, noble and courageous negro race that I know of." [5] And Sir Samuel Baker felt that "The Latookas are a fine, frank and warlike race . . . always ready for either a laugh or a fight." [6] Such laudatory descriptions of warrior tribes are as close as we get to the earlier convention of the noble savage, now temporarily in abeyance.

The mid-century stress on race produced protracted discussion of African physical characteristics. Physical appearance was rated on a scale which placed the Caucasoid features high and the Negroid low. Beauty could only be found in the Caucasian type: ". . . this mean and hideous concave nose is the African substitute for the beautiful, the sympathetic and the noble convexity of the Caucasian."[7] If this comment by Burton were not so completely congruent with the rest of the contemporary descriptions, one might almost suspect him of humor. But his statement can be matched, if not outdone, by other writers. Evaluations of physical appearance were accompanied by emotional reactions of marked distaste for the "lower" types and approval for the "higher." Thus, Thomson admired the European features of the Masai whom he contrasted with the Negroid Kavirondo.

These pure-blooded Masai have the finest physical development, are undoubtedly superior to the others in shape of the head, the less depressed nose, and thinner lips. Indeed,—but for a prominence of the cheekbones, a tendency to a Mongolian shape and upward slant of the eyes, the chocolate coloured skin, and the hair with a tendency to become frizzy—they might pass muster as very respectable . . . Europeans.[8]

The Wa-kavirondo are by no means attractive in their appearance, and contrast unfavourably with the Masai. Their heads are of a distinctly lower type, eyes dull and muddy, jaws somewhat prognathous, mouth unpleasantly large, and lips thick, projecting and everted—they are in fact true negroes.[9]

The racial difference between European and African was so exaggerated that they were conceived to be completely discrete categories of humanity. Burton was most explicit and elaborate in his discussion on this point. His letter in response to James Hunt's paper on the "Negro's Place in Nature," given before the Anthropological Society of London, is included in *A Mission to Gelele*. Its racial determinism is typical of the times.

Like other students of anthropology, I am truly grateful to you for having so graphically shown the great gulf, moral and physical, separating the black from the white races of man, and for having placed in so striking a light the physical development of the negro . . . that in the occipetal or lower breeds of mankind, the sutures of the cranium close at an earlier age than amongst the frontal races . . . it assigns a physical cause for the inferiority of the negro, whose psychical and mental powers become stationary at an age when, in nobler races, the perceptive and reflective principles begin to claim ascendancy.[10]

Negro physical characteristics were the criteria by which the British assigned the Africans to a lower level of humanity. There was a fundamental confusion in the failure to separate out just which were physical, moral, or mental differences. A disapproved physical trait, such as concave nose structure, implied a less noble character;[11] black skin was evidence of degradation.[12] The repeated assertion that the Africans have "hard skulls" carried the meanings of either boneheaded stupidity or brutishness.[13]

The mental and moral characteristics ascribed to the Africans were all negations of qualities which the British valued most highly: courage, honesty, responsibility, gratitude, and generosity. Baker's description of African character is not much more than a detailing of the absence of such virtues.

> The obtuseness of the savages was such, that I never could make them understand the existence of the good principle:—their one idea was "power,"—force that could obtain all . . . human nature viewed in its crude state as pictured among African savages is quite on the level with that of the brute, and not to be compared with the noble character of the dog. There is neither gratitude, pity, love, nor self-denial; no idea of duty; no religion: but covetousness, ingratitude, selfishness, and cruelty. All are thieves, idle, envious and ready to plunder and enslave their weaker neighbours.[14]

Stanley presented a similar though more positively phrased picture of the Africans as not quite human, or if human, then only children.

> The dark brother, wild as a colt, chafing, restless, ferociously impulsive, superstitiously timid, liable to furious demonstrations, suspicious and unreasonable. . . . A barbarous man is a pure materialist. He is full of cravings for possessing something that he cannot describe. He is like a child which has not yet acquired the faculty of articulation.[15]

The flat statement, made frequently, that the African was a child, was implemented by a series of attributions which were defined as childlike by Victorian standards. The nineteenth-century adult saw himself as vastly superior to the child in his self-control, virtuous character, and rational mind. Both child and African were ignorant, impulsive, irresponsible, and without powers of reason —"wild as a colt"—and according to Burton, both were guilty of the same heedless cruelty.

> The cruelty of the negro is, like that of a schoolboy, the blind impulse of rage combined with want of sympathy. Thus he thoughtlessly tortures and slays his prisoners, as the youth of England torment and kill cats . . . he mentally remains a child, and is never capable of a generalization.[16]

The image of the African as a childlike being is a significant addition to the earlier conventions, which had portrayed the Africans as savages or heathens, but never as children. The mid-century designation underlined the distinction between Negro and white and rationalized emergent European dominance in Africa.

The other contemporary stereotype was no innovation, but a continuation of the beastly savage of earlier writings. The conventions were retained of the "unthinking savage" who delighted in violence, unable and unwilling to curb his savage ferocity, "men whose hands are at all times ready to be imbrued in blood . . . wild and bloody men. . . ."[17] Travelers in the West African kingdoms had earlier been horrified by human sacrifices and public executions. They had, however inadequately, conveyed their understanding that these were an aspect of the political and religious systems of the society. Mid-century accounts of the East African kingdoms described killings and mutilations purely as a savage addiction to gore, carried out at the whim of a wanton ruler. Buganda, under Mtesa, was undoubtedly the scene of such blood-letting; the accounts of Robert Ashe, A. M. Mackay, and Speke all attest to this.[18] Yet none of these observers suggested any institutional or ideological reason for the slaughter. Nor did they suggest the possibility that Mtesa might have been quite mad. They simply took for granted that such brutal behavior was only to be expected from an African king.

Mid-century explorers perceived all African social institutions in the same way as had the writers earlier in the century. Instead of government, there was only anarchy or bloody despotism; polygyny was a sorry substitute for marriage; music and dance were rude and indecent. The Africans were without any religion worthy of the name, and it followed that they were also without any moral sentiment, sense of duty, conscience, or finer perceptions.

The statements from this period suggest a half-understood and half-accepted concept of sequential development. The writers would have it that the Africans had remained at the lowest level of man's development in a condition of permanent stasis. This is not yet full-blown evolutionism, but bears it a family resemblance, and one congenial to the temper of the time when progress and civilization were inextricably linked.

Mid-Century Fiction and the Work of Winwood Reade

Accounts of exploration continued to be the predominant form of literature on Africa throughout the nineteenth century, but by mid-century sufficient materials had accumulated to provide a basis for the writing of fiction. African exploration was a subject tailor-made for fictional treatment, and the ready reception of the explorers' journals indicated a wide market.[1]

Previous fiction about Africa consisted of the antislavery romances of the late eighteenth century, and a very few other works such as the South African narrative poetry of Pringle in the 1820's and Marryat's novel, *The Mission.* In the 1860's and 1870's more novels and short stories set in Africa appeared. These tales were based more or less upon the "real" Africa of the explorers, rather than on the pseudo-Africa of the romancers;[2] some of the explorers themselves wrote fiction, capitalizing on their firsthand knowledge.

No bibliography exists which lists the African fiction of this period. No student of literature has as yet found it of sufficient literary merit, nor in sufficient quantity to merit scholarly investigation. Libraries have discarded most of the novels; they can be obtained only by diligent search in secondhand bookstores or through sheer serendipitous accident. Though we knew of Joseph Thomson's novel, *Ulu,* from his biographer, it could not be found. Altogether we found four novels, information about several others, and the short stories of Winwood Reade.[3]

Although generalizations drawn from so small a sample of mid-century fiction would be of highly dubious validity, these books have much in common, and their content significantly echoes the nonfiction. The novels reflect the contemporary extension of interest to all of sub-Saharan Africa. The African episode in *A Simpleton* occurs in the south, Stanley's fiction is set in East Africa, Marryat and Skertchly wrote of West Africa. Like the journals, the novels are heavily larded with hunting and adventure episodes and with manifold details of scenery and natural history. They repeat those elements of the literature of exploration which had the greatest popular appeal. The pivotal themes of these novels, however, are reflections of earlier interests: the days of European slave trade, the early Arab trade in East Africa, West African tribal conflicts, and the quest for fortune and the restoration of health in South Africa.

The African characters of this nineteenth-century fiction were indistinguishable from those in the romances of the eighteenth century. Stanley's protagonist, Kalulu, Skertchly's heroic Melinda, and Marryat's Whyna were noble savages par excellence, adhering faithfully to the old conventions: they were all African royalty, as splendid in their virtues as they were in appearance. Here is Marryat's description of Princess Whyna:

> . . . she was uniformly kind and gentle . . . young and generous in disposition. She was a negress as to colour, but not a real negress; for her hair, although short and very wavy, was not woolly, and her nose was straight. Her mouth was small and her teeth beautiful. Her figure was perfect, her limbs being very elegantly formed.[4]

As the Reverend J. B. Thomson described Ulu, the heroine of Thomson's tale, she too apparently conformed to the same convention, since "The character of the lovable, but untutored little maid was intended to illustrate some of the best traits of an utterly uncivilized nature. . . ."[5]

As in the eighteenth-century romances, the masses of Africans were depicted as beastly savages, but in the fuller terms available to the nineteenth-century writers. All the concomitant stereotypes were brought into play. Skertchly described non-royal Africans as "noisy," "ferocious," "lazy niggers," with "hard heads" and a "peculiar foetor." Marryat referred to their "boundless cruelty," "diabolical ferocity," and "lack of all human feeling." Stanley wrote of their "indolence," "drunkenness," and their "callous souls." The much-vaunted nobility of the African protagonists of the novels was clearly anomalous, for the general population was entirely brutish.

The settings, however, unlike the earlier fiction, were not fantasy. The explorers' descriptions were too well known to be dismissed or disregarded even for the sake of artistic effect. Charles Reade's picture of South Africa is based squarely upon published accounts. Skertchly's West Africa is perhaps more a sportsman's paradise than it was in reality, but the major thread of the narrative is a hunting trip undertaken by two English gentlemen, and the descriptions of beasts and terrain were founded upon the author's own considerable observation and experience in West Africa. The locales in *My Kalulu* could easily have been modeled on Stanley's descriptions of East Africa.

The novels' plots are negligible; they were simply the framework for a series of adventurous encounters with wild animals and wilder savages in the African locale. The British protagonists were always portrayed as ideal gentlemen and brave sportsmen, superbly assured of their superiority.

There is not even an incipient imperialism in any of the novels. The factual accounts of the period are far more concerned with the role of the British in Africa and the possibility of domination than is the fiction. The difference was that the novelists were taken up with plots referring to past situations and were either relying upon older accounts or their own memories. The nonfiction not only dealt with the immediate present, but dealt with the future in terms of prediction and of programs of action.

The work of W. Winwood Reade is a link between fiction and the explorers' journals, as well as a most striking example of continuity in the literary tradition. He repeats all the conventions of the past, of his contemporaries—and what is more remarkable —his innovations are prophetic of the future development of the tradition. His *African Sketchbooks* and *Savage Africa* were popular accounts of his West African travels. The *Sketchbooks* included, as well, novelettes and short stories set in Africa. Most of his tales are substantially similar to the other fiction of his period:

they tell of noble savages, the outdoor life, and of British gentlemen engaged in sport. But in some of his stories, Reade wrote of European administrators and traders in West Africa, and these tales introduced new themes reflecting the then current situation in Africa.

Reade said of his fiction that it contained as much truth as did his non-fiction and the "learned dissertations of others." [6] Thus, quite unintentionally, Reade correctly assessed the validity of his work, for his fiction and non-fiction are equally unrealistic. Both drew heavily on the conventions and stereotypes of places and people. In fact, Reade was probably the most complete exemplar of the tradition in his time. It is possible to discover in his work every one of the conventions of his own and of earlier times, from the classical myth of "fabulous tailed men" [7] to the contemporary conventions of the childlike, brutish savage.

> . . . they are only grown-up children after all. Like other children they dance and play, and tell one another stories . . . and sing the same song over and over again, like children they are greedy, cunning, sensitive, loveable and fondling, easily excited to laughter or to tears; like children also their anger is a madness: like children also they are cruel; like children they pilfer on the sly, and beg, beg, beg, without any feeling of shame.[8]

> . . . one might infer that the barbarity of the negro is mere ignorance and thoughtlessness. . . . But negro barbarity is not ignorance alone. . . . It cannot be denied that the Africans are connoisseurs in cruelty, that murder is one of their fine arts.[9]

Reade was just as all-inclusive in his theoretical and ideological positions. He was eclectic, uninhibited by any need for consistency in approach, and expressed himself in terms of almost every accepted theory at one time or another. He was thus both pro- and antislavery;[10] he was both for and against the missionaries and hence committed to the improvability of the Africans and the futility of attempting to improve them;[11] he was both a biological and an environmental determinist.[12] In short, he was the very model of inconsistency, and hence a model for any and all of the conventional ideologies.

The stable and unifying core in all his writings, dominating the mass of stereotype, curiosa, and discrepant argument, was that which was common to the literary tradition as a whole. Whatever traits were ascribed to the Africans were the negations of the virtues ascribed to the British. Moreover, in Reade's conventional derogation of the Africans, one senses the inflation of his own self-image. He described, uniquely and entirely out of the contemporary tradition, African men as effeminate or eunuchoid,[13] by way of contrast to his own virility. The detailing of his amorous encounters with African women was a most radical anticipation of a much later theme.

Reade was clearly an innovator and forerunner of the modern literary tradition in such contravention of Victorian propriety. Though there was in his time a large and receptive audience for pornographic writing, none of the African material had been anything but serious, educational, and morally elevating. Reade attempted to make the best of both worlds and, under the banner of ethnography and exploration, he was exploiting in a minor, muted fashion the taste for the salacious. Even his discussions of evolution emphasized a unique brand of sexual selection.

> Tribes of a higher standard domesticate their prisoners of war. . . . The Women are now emancipated, are married for their beauty, and are allowed to pass their time in sedentary occupations. Long hair being universally admired, long-haired wives are selected by the chiefs, and thus, in the course of countless generations, a new species of woman is produced, and the delicate beauty of the sex thus indirectly proceeds from slavery.[14]

> Mr. Darwin has found the clue . . . in the law of Sexual Selection. Animals not only struggle for existence, but also for the propagation of the species. Partly owing to the custom of polygamy and partly to other causes, matrimonial competition is severe. In most cases the question is decided by duel; the rivals fight and the best man wins: in this manner not only physical strength, but also courage and amorous ardour are gradually developed and improved.[15]

No previous writers had singled out African women for particular notice or extended discussions. There were Mungo Park's comments on the kindness and maternal devotion of the women of West Africa, and Burton does mention the women of various East African tribes—most often with distaste, saying that they generally constituted a "spectacle to make an anchorite of a man." [16] Reade's eye and imagination were obviously caught by the women in West Africa, and he devotes much attention to them in passages that were notable for their length and even more for their suggestion of prurience.

It is true that there are girls here who have such sweet smiles, such dark, voluptuous eyes, and such fond, caressing ways, that one cannot help loving them, but only as one loves a child, a dog, or a singing-bird. They can gratify the desires of a libertine, but they can not inspire a passion of the soul. . . . The negress has beauty—beauty in spite of her black skin. . . . And she is gentle and faithful and loving in her own poor way. . . . Where is the intellect, which is the light in the crystal lamp, the genius within the clay? No, no, the negress is not a woman; she is a parody of a woman; she is a pretty toy, an affectionate brute—that is all.[17]

Reade was, as well, the first to write an elaborate personification of the continent as a woman. Thomson's fantasy quoted earlier in this chapter was actually written twenty years later than Reade's and was a pale effort by comparison. Again Reade proved to be prophetic in his delineation. Reade depicts Africa as a mother, but what an unmaternal image results!

There is a woman whose features, in expression, are sad and noble, but which have been degraded, distorted, and rendered repulsive by disease; whose breath is perfumed by rich spices and by fragrant gums, yet through all steals the stench of the black mud of the mangroves and the miasma of the swamps; whose lap is filled with gold, but beneath lies a black snake, watchful and concealed; from whose breasts stream milk and honey, mingled with poison and with blood; whose head lies dead and cold, and yet is alive; in her horrible womb heave strange and monstrous embryos. Swarming round her are thousands of her children, whose hideousness inspires disgust, their misery compassion. She kisses them upon the lips, and with her own breath she strikes them corpses by her side. She feeds them at her breasts, and from her own breasts they are poisoned and they die. She offers them the treasures of her lap, and as each hand is put forth the black snake bites it with his fatal fangs. . . . Look at the map of Africa. Does it not resemble a woman with a huge burden on the back . . . ?[18]

The Sketchbooks and *Savage Africa* are works that indicate much literary creativity and reveal Reade's undoubted imaginative gifts. This was not sufficient for Reade himself. He longed to be ranked among the scientific explorers, and in particular to be thought of as Alexander Laing's successor. It is nowhere clear why he fastened upon Laing as a model, but it was a strange choice for the flamboyant Reade. Nothing reads less like the modest, dedicated Laing than Reade's defense of his role in Africa.

I make, of course, no pretensions to the title of Explorer. If I have any merit, it is that of having been the first young man about town to make a *bona fide* tour in western Africa; to travel . . . with no special object and at his own expense; to *flaner* in the virgin forests; to flirt with pretty savages, and to smoke his cigar among cannibals.[19]

This statement is in sharp contrast to the serious self-image of the Victorians in general and the explorers in particular. It is frivolous—at variance with the earnest and highly moral purposiveness of Reade's own times. His levity strikes its most discordant note in prophecies about the future of Africa. There was as yet no clearly defined British policy for African development, but the British were very seriously concerned about it. Almost every one of the explorers devoted attention to the pressing problems of abolishing the slave trade, civilizing the Africans, and developing the resources of the continent. Reade's facetious or ironic prediction is entirely out of key.

This vast continent will finally be divided almost equally between France and England. . . . Africa shall be redeemed . . . in this amiable task they [the Africans] may possibly become exterminated. We must learn to look upon this result with composure. It illustrates beneficent law of Nature, that the weak must be devoured by the strong. . . . When the cockneys of Timbuctoo have their tea-gardens in the Oases of the Sahara; when hotels and guide-books are established at the Sources of the Nile; when it becomes fashionable to go yachting on the lakes of the Great Plateau; when noblemen building seats in Central Africa, will have their elephant parks and their hippopotami waters, young ladies on camp-stools, under palm trees will read with tears *The Last of the Negroes*. . . .[20]

CHAPTER III

The Height of Empire

The Bearers of the Burden

BRITISH activity in Africa reached a climax toward the end of the nineteenth century, for by then the British were consolidating their scattered African interests into an African empire. Most British historians emphasize the reluctance with which the government undertook any colonial commitment in Africa.[1] Yet the British were as actively participant as other European powers in the scramble for colonies, and they emerged from the Berlin Conference in 1885 with vast territories.

It is difficult to pinpoint the precise causes for this seemingly paradoxical development. Many factors were at work: the enterprise of dynamic men like Cecil Rhodes and Sir George Goldie, the pressures of international rivalries and influential philanthropic interests at home, the need to protect the existing empire in the Far East and in Australia, the need for markets, and, perhaps, the momentum of more than three centuries of exploration and trade. Despite these factors, the process of the actual acquisition of empire appeared so fortuitous that the historian J. R. Seeley could make the engaging comment that it was "an empire acquired in a fit of absence of mind." [2]

Whether Seeley's comment was justifiable or not, British official reluctance was evidenced by the indirect means by which colonies were finally acquired. The "flag followed commerce" as various commercial chartered companies laid the groundwork for later imperial dominion. Granted a charter in 1884, Goldie's Royal Niger Company was the sovereign power in the Nigerian hinterland until 1899, when Nigeria finally was taken over by the British government. The company's ostensible purpose was trade, yet during its tenure it maintained and used an army, made treaties with local chiefs, and in general behaved as representative and surrogate of the British government, while the government incurred neither expense nor responsibility. Similar roles were played elsewhere in Africa by the Imperial British East Africa Company and Rhodes's South Africa Company. The initial tasks of pacification and organization already accomplished by the companies, it remained only for government to step in and take over.

On the surface the change from company to government seemed inconsequential; the conduct of affairs was essentially unaltered, and there was even continuity in the personnel. Lord Lugard, whose name is inextricably linked with the rise of British Empire in Africa, began his career as an employee of the Imperial British East Africa Company. He went next to West Africa in the service of the Royal Niger Company, moved to the British West Charterland Company, and finally entered government service. When the Royal Niger Company surrendered its charter to the government, Lugard was appointed High Commissioner of the new colony of Northern Nigeria.

The undignified "scramble for Africa" in no way dimmed the fine luster of idealism. The Europeans sharing the spoils were well aware of the political and economic advantages that possession of colonies entailed, but the stated motives were ideologically lofty —the suppression of the slave trade and the mission to civilize. The literature clearly indicates that by this time the British regarded their position in Africa as ordained—the natural consequence of their Anglo-Saxon heritage. On them had fallen the mantle of the Romans as builders of empire and emissaries of civilization.

It had been thought formerly that the lot of the Africans could be improved by means of trade, education, and Christianity. But by the end of the century it was held that such means, though still essential, required a sound government through which the British might ensure the protection and progress of their subjects as well as the prosperity of the empire. The first step toward achieving the necessary stability and order was the establishment of peace by the Pax Britannica, which Lugard insisted would end the illegal raiding and intertribal conflict and "will be the greatest blessing that Africa has known through the ages since the Flood." [3] All of this was, in effect, the substance of the Dual Mandate, the plan for the governing and developing the colonies, propounded by Lord Lugard and incorporated into British policy.

From the 1880's through the first decade of the twentieth century more Britons than ever before came to Africa. There was no longer the stress on exploration; for the empire-builders, mapping territory was only an ancillary activity. There were missionaries, traders, and settlers as before, but their numbers increased and the significance of their work broadened. In addition, soldiers, administrators, engineers, and other technical experts added their contributions to the growing empire. Interest in the new possessions stimulated the first wave of African tourism, and many came just to observe and report on their observations.

The floodgates were raised for a tidal wave of literary production. It is very clear that anyone who was in Africa for any purpose at all was ready to comment on African affairs and the progress of empire. Among the missionaries and officials there were some who became sufficiently interested in native life to produce works that properly belong to an anthropological rather than a popular tradition. But everybody wrote: the "men on the spot," their wives, the tourists, the self-appointed experts, biographers, and novelists.

Even so demanding a task as building the empire did not absorb all the energies of these energetic Victorians. Sir Harry Johnston's literary production alone (there are forty-four works, many in several volumes) staggers the imagination. Where he found time to administer colonies, paint, and do anthropology is a consuming mystery. While no literary match for Sir Harry, Lord Lugard produced two substantial works, each in two volumes, articles, and letters, and he achieved the distinction of being both a pioneer of empire and a model administrator.

It is a matter of both relief and frustration that some of the key figures of imperial history (Cecil Rhodes, George Goldie, and Theophilus Shepstone) made no contribution to the literary flood. In a brief introduction to a book by Ewart Grogan and Arthur Sharp, Rhodes stated that he was unaccustomed to even such minor forays into literature; his method of communication was more commonly the cablegram.[4] Goldie's daughter reported her father as saying, "All that I wish to be recorded of myself can be read under the articles headed 'Nigeria' and 'Goldie' in the Encyclopaedia Britannica." [5] Shepstone, for over thirty years director of native policy in Natal, wrote nothing but official reports. Literary reticence was, however, the exception.

The imperial situation did not alter the traditional form of African accounts; the narrative was still one of personal adventure and accomplishment in the Dark Continent. The authors did not abandon the theme of the journey into Africa, and if it did not constitute the total substance of their tale, it was at least an integral part of it. As before, the narrative was one of action, recorded by the European as protagonist with a heavy stress on the "I." There was not as much self-dramatization as in the previous generation, but this may have been due to the need to share the limelight with the British Empire itself.

The British in Africa were still very much aware of the exotic environment and wrote voluminous descriptions of flora, fauna, and scenic wonders. They continued their interest in the hunt and sport; shooting for the pot, lamenting lost opportunities for hunting and near misses, and exulting in a good bag. It was a standard expectation that Africa would provide the game and that every Briton in Africa would want to hunt. Himself no great huntsman, Winston Churchill describes his East African hosts' overwhelming preoccupation with hunting.

> Nothing causes the east African colonist more genuine concern than that his guest should not have been provided with a lion. . . . He feels some deep reproach is laid upon his own hospitality and the reputation of his adopted country. How to find, and having found, to kill, a lion is the unvarying theme of conversation; and every place and every journey is judged by a simple standard—"lions or no lions." [6]

There was still, and would continue to be, an endless litany of the minutiae of travel in the interior. And the desire for accustomed comforts and the proper way to do things—in short, the British sense of fitness—generally prevailed in preparations for a trip. Stanley's silver tea service and Baker's portable bath–wine tub–dinghy were manifestations of this attitude earlier in the century. Presently Grogan's loss of his two table servants while on safari "rather annoyed" him;[7] and Johnston's penchant for elegant living even in the bush, provoked Joseph Thomson, in expectation of his visit, to ironic comment.

However, I hope to come up smiling by taking care to supply myself with marmalades, jams and other luxuries of that nature to which I have been accustomed. I would like to have adopted a higher level, but alas! Grant has stupidly brought up with him only 2 tins of paté de fois and one tin of caviare. However, we shall keep these, in case of H. J.'s supposing that such is our daily fare, and that we don't belong to the marmalade class. Sheets for our bed are beyond us, and I don't know about table napkins. . . .[8]

Though greatly improved, African travel was still arduous enough to be a test of the mettle of a man, which the British accepted eagerly. Life in Africa held out the possibility of freedom of movement and a general independence from the constraints of life in Great Britain. Lugard spoke for many in his expression of delight with such an opportunity to show one's true measure.

There is a charm in the feeling of independence which a farewell to civilization brings with it, and in the knowledge that henceforward one has to rely solely on one's own resources, and that success or failure depend on one's self.[9]

Although Africa represented a "farewell to civilization," home and its way of life were internalized; the break was never complete. Always, and perhaps "greatly to his credit, he remained an Englishman," and Englishness was intensified by the un-English surroundings of Africa. In his travels through South Africa, James Bryce noted with some pride that not even the tropical heat could dissuade the British from an energetic game of cricket.

The first sign that we were close upon Gwelo came from the sight of a number of white men in shirtsleeves running across a meadow —an unusual sight in South Africa, which presently explained itself as the English inhabitants engaged in a cricket match. Nearly the whole town either played or looked on. It was a hot afternoon, but our energetic countrymen were not to be scared by the sun from the pursuit of the national game. They are as much Englishmen in Africa as in England, and, happily for them and for their country, there is no part of the national character that is more useful when transplanted than the fondness for active exercise.[10]

The tenacity with which the Briton clung to his British identity was central to the maintenance of his self-image in an alien land. Hence, his behavior would maintain the prestige of England and reflect his pride in background and character. This was the same self-image which had remained fairly stable over many decades, but during this period the dynamic factor of empire added to it a new dimension. Imperial responsibility demanded attitudes and behavior appropriate to the new roles of guardians and rulers.

The new roles demanded the same kind of energetic activity that the British in Africa had displayed and valued from the beginning, but now it had new direction and an expanded range. The literature often defines the roles in terms of the particular job to be done. The work of opening up new areas, of organization, and of administration required men of skill, experience, and proven responsibility. But empire in Africa grew faster than administrative personnel available to serve it. Consequently everybody, no matter what his original work had been, was pressed into administrative service. Major J. R. L. MacDonald, who had come to Africa to survey a route for the East Africa railway, became, for lack of anyone else on the spot, Administrator in Uganda. Joseph Thomson, though known only as an East African explorer, was called to Nigeria by Sir George Goldie to make treaties with the northern Emirs. Mackenzie, familiar with the Bechuana tribes through his missionary work, was appointed Commissioner of Bechuanaland. Alfred J. Swann, employed by a mission society, provides an example of how the work of empire took priority over other commitments.

Our routine of life at the London Missionary Society Station was again disturbed by the arrival of a special envoy from Consul Johnston requesting me to make treaties with the chiefs at North Tanganyika on behalf of the Government. . . . I had a long consultation with my comrades, but they declined to have anything to do with Johnston's request, stating as their reason that it was impossible to depart from the Society's rule which forbade interference in politics. . . . It was a dilemma. On the one hand an opportunity presented itself of hoisting our flag over a people for whom so much had been spent. . . . On the other hand, I had to face this refusal of my comrades to take part with me, and possible censure from the directors if I made the treaties. I decided to take the responsibility as it seemed to me that no one could possibly object to my helping to secure for the British Crown tracts of country. . . .[11]

The importance of missionaries diminished as political officialdom took command in their areas. The first concern was empire, and the kingdom of God had to move in to second place. The general opinion was that the missionaries should confine their activities to religion and education. In many areas, by the time government officials appeared on the scene, missionaries, with long tenure and in good standing with the native chiefs, had often assumed the role of political arbiters. At the arrival of officials the missionaries were expected to relinquish this role and never to resume it or to interfere in any way in political matters. This came as a hard blow to many, and numerous accounts detail the ensuing conflict between the political and religious guardians of the Africans.[12]

As a rule, the officials were lukewarm on the subject of missionary activity. Even when they tolerated the missionaries in their area, they doubted the value of such legitimate missionary enterprise as proselytizing and education. They felt that missionaries were too soft with the Africans and encouraged "native cheekiness." [13] However, not all missionaries advocated mildness in dealing with the Africans, and Lugard praised those who understood the need for force.

He is a first rate fellow, a strong, sensible man without any hyper-pious nonsense about him. . . . If only more men of the strong-willed sensible type came out, instead of the "turn-the-other cheek also" stamp, missionary enterprise would succeed much better, for the first essential to a negro is to have a strong *respect* for the white man.[14]

The missionary's success with the Africans may have depended upon his powers of persuasion, upon precept and example. The administrator, however, saw no need to abjure the use of force, and it was even more commonplace in this period than it had been before. Every Englishman in Africa saw himself as the embodiment of the principle of White Supremacy and British power, and thus entitled to treat the Africans as his personal subjects. Grogan asserted that "the Boer method of treating niggers as vermine is after all the only one they deserve." [15]

Many of the English were by this time indignant at the mere suggestion that they pay to pass through a chief's domain, or even to wait for his permission. In truth, the African chiefs no longer had the power to compel patience or gifts. They either had to submit gracefully to domination, or, in attempting to counter it, lose to superior force.

Though the use of force was common in dealing with the Africans and was thought to be unavoidable, it was not considered an ideal method. Thoughtful officials and observers held that respect was the inevitable response to proper administration and believed that resorting to physical coercion represented administrative inadequacy. Hence, what was required was administrators with the natural ability to command obedience without coercion. The British firmly believed that such qualities were most likely to be found in gentlemen. H. Rider Haggard and Lord Lugard voiced a widely held conclusion that *only* gentlemen could make good colonial officials.

> Also if white men are set over Zulus at all, they should be gentlemen in the position of government officers, not successful adventurers.[16]

> Select a gentleman for the command of an expedition, and one who will remember that in all times and places he *is* an English gentleman.[17]

It was even thought that no one but a gentleman had any business in Africa. Trader, settler, and missionary as well as official should be gentlemen by birth and breeding. Johnston is one of many writers who held this opinion.

> I have been increasingly struck with the rapidity with which such members of the white race as are not of the best class, can throw over the restraints of civilization and develop into savages of unbridled lust and abominable cruelty.[18]

Any Briton who failed to maintain the vitally important social distance between himself and Africans was not only self-destructive, but would be weakening the fabric of empire. Histories of such Englishmen read like cautionary tales. A Mr. Stokes, forsaking loyalty to "his own kind," became a mercenary, selling his services to the highest bidder. Even worse, he openly married an African woman, and was altogether too comradely with his in-laws. Stokes, of course, came to a bad end; he was hanged by Belgian authorities. The writers of this sad saga were wrathful that the Belgians should have taken it upon themselves to punish an English subject, gentleman or not, but they state that Stokes deserved his fate.[19] Another case was Mr. George Fenwick, who, dismissed from the service of the Church of Scotland mission, turned to trade. His imprudent and overfamiliar behavior with the natives not only caused his death, but became the cause of a war between the Makololo and the English.[20] It was distressing that native-born Englishmen could "let the side down" so badly. British honor and prestige suffered from such derelictions, and writers said that these renegades lessened British authority in native eyes.

The issue was not British supremacy alone. At stake was the whole issue of white supremacy, which could only be maintained, it was felt, by upholding the standards of European life and the prescribed social distance from the Africans. In this particular the Portuguese were considered grievously at fault. They were too little concerned with these issues to suit the English. They openly cohabited with African women and recognized their half-breed children, even placing their sons in official positions. In short, the Portuguese did not behave like gentlemen and were considered poor specimens of European colonizers.

Whatever the faults of the Germans, overintimacy with Africans through bland ignoring of race was not one of them. They, said the writers, placed the proper value upon the principle of white supremacy according to the British standard and upon Teutonic supremacy in particular. For this, if nothing else, the Anglo-Saxon British gave their co-Teutons highest marks.

The parallels between India and Africa, tropical countries with non-white populations, organized under local rulers, seemed obvious, especially to those with previous experience in India. And many British "India hands" came to Africa to assist in building the new empire. Their services were thought to be particularly valuable since previous experience enabled them to deal with familiar problems in Africa.

There was, at this time, confidence that British rule in India was an unparalleled success. J. R. Seeley, though skeptical of the ultimate value of Indian empire, nevertheless asserted that "our Government is better than any other which has existed in India since the Mussulman conquest."[21] Hence, India was held up as the model by which Africa should be ruled. Winston Churchill envisioned a future princely state in Uganda quite like "its great counterparts among the native States of India."[22] Lugard stated that a native African army, from its table of organization to the type of pack saddles should follow the pattern of the Indian army.[23] It was further suggested that the emigration of Indians into Africa would provide civilizing models for the Africans.[24] And the missionary, Ashe, appealed to the conscience of England to "do for Africa what she has so triumphantly effected for the people of India."[25]

The African experience had gone on long enough to produce its own experts—"old Africa hands"—like F. Courtenay Selous, Swann, Stanley, Johnston, and Lugard. Their on-the-spot experience and special knowledge gave them inside advantages in dealing with the problems of Africa, and they were often enraged by the government at home for ignoring their informed advices. They felt that government was not as fully committed to empire in Africa as they were themselves, and the journals bristle with charges of vacillation, "fossilized apathy," lack of understanding, and unwise penury. Basil Worsfold, though not himself a "man on the spot," expressed his sympathy with their difficulties by citing Sir George Grey's plea for confidence in the "man on the spot."

> Can a man who, on a distant and exposed frontier, surrounded by difficulties, with invasions of Her Majesty's territories threatening on several points, assumes the responsibility . . . be fairly judged of in respect to the amount of responsibility he assumes by those who, in the quiet of distant offices in London, know nothing of the anxieties or nature of the difficulties he had to encounter?[26]

The old Africa hands had all played a vital part in the domestication of the continent. They had permanence in Africa; indeed, for many, it was the only home they knew. The hitherto-untamed land had become part of Greater Britain, and those who came to work or settle there now had a stake in making their surroundings as homelike as possible. Whole areas of the Dark Continent were transformed into small islands of home, complete with cricket grounds, tennis courts, English gardens and cozy bungalows. The domestication of British Africa was progressing at such a rate that trouble with porters was being replaced by trouble with house servants as a refrain in the literature.[27]

The clearest indication that the British were now at home in Africa was the ubiquitous presence of the ladies. Previously there had been settlers' wives in South Africa, but they did not write of their lives, and it is only from the accounts of some of the early missionaries' wives that we learn something of the Englishwoman's situation. They were expected to share the work, hardship, and discomforts; they lived (and often died) with the fewest amenities, as transients in the wild land. By the end of the century, however, administrators, traders, and even travelers were bringing their wives to Africa. The land was considered sufficiently tame for lady tourists to travel on safari. What had so recently been real dangers gave way, even for the tourists, to the problems of maintaining accustomed standards. Thus, Mrs. Pringle on safari laments the lack of proper eggcups! "We were not a little amused to find . . . that no use could be made of the eggs for the want of egg-cups." [28]

The lack of eggcups would never have deterred the indomitable Mary Kingsley from eating eggs. She ate whatever was edible by whatever means was available. Miss Kingsley was a scientist, traveling alone in West Africa where the conditions of travel were always difficult. Never abandoning lady-like standards, or her long, full skirts, she nonetheless camped out in a very sportsmanlike fashion, suffering rain, heat, hunger, and thirst with unfailing humor and courage.

With the empire the lady writers became more numerous, although they do not provide any uniquely feminine point of view. In fact, the women wrote as if they were typical British gentlemen

—and gentlemen of action to boot. They were as interested as the men in sport and as vigorous on safari. A comment from the safari journal of Mrs. Mary Hall indicates that she dealt with recalcitrant porters just as a man would.

. . . my men were unusually troublesome. When I wanted my machila dried and the tent taken down, not any one of them was forthcoming . . . at last I had to take matters into my own hands. With giant strides, and stick in hand, I went towards the shed. The moment they saw me coming they knew the game was up, and fled before me like the wind. . . . I felt like Hercules clearing the Augean stables, and I am sure he did not do it more thoroughly.[29]

Certainly Mary Kingsley echoes the sentiments of her male colleagues almost precisely in her statement of how to deal with the Africans.

It is not necessary to treat them brutally, in fact it does not pay to do so, but it is necessary to treat them severely, to keep a steady hand over them. Never let them become familiar, never let them see you have made a mistake. When you make a mistake in giving them an order let it be understood that that way of doing a thing is a peculiarly artful dodge of your own . . . and if it fails, that it is their fault.[30]

Whether it was due to the process of self-selection or to the result of a literary convention, the Victorian Englishwoman in Africa was always depicted as a fit counterpart of the man of action. None of the ladies swooned or clung; they were all good sports, vigorous and plucky. Lionel Declé's admiring portrayal of Mrs. Colenbrander, wife of the agent of the East Africa Chartered Company, will serve as a prototype.

I could not help admiring the pluck of Mrs. Colenbrander; a most remarkable woman, fearless of danger, a splendid rider, a capital shot, and possessing the knack of doing what she liked with the natives, most difficult to handle . . . many a time I have seen her, in her husband's absence, turn out two or three stalwart natives, drunk and most threatening; more than once she had to seize her gun and threaten to use it. It was a pleasing sight to see these savages who rather despised most white men, quail before this plucky British lady.

She had considerable influence over Lo Bengula. Often when she visited him she used to sit boldly on his throne . . . a sacrilege that would have cost any man's life. But the old African chief used merely to laugh.

"What funny people you white men are," he used to say, "to bend before a woman. If you were my wife," he used to add, turning to Mrs. Colenbrander—

"Well," she usually interrupted, "if I were your wife I should make you do what I liked. I should be the King of the Matabele, and you —well, you would be my husband."

Then Lo Ben used to roar, and grant what she came to ask for. Through her, many a difficulty was smoothed down that might otherwise have become most serious.[31]

It was probably just as well that not all the English ladies in Africa were as formidable as Mrs. Colenbrander, but for the most part they were women of purpose and character. Wives of officials were not usually as overbearing as Mrs. Colenbrander, nor would Victorian propriety easily permit such outspokenness. But all of them were at the very least dutiful chatelaines and interested helpmeets of their husbands. Lady Flora Lugard, although we know little else about her from her own writing, was sufficiently interested and involved in her husband's work to write a scholarly history of the colony over which he was High Commissioner.[32] Mrs. Constance Larymore considered her role as wife of the Resident in Northern Nigeria predominant over any personal considerations. She graciously accommodated to every situation, no matter how bizarre, in order to help her husband. Her sense of obligation and duty stemmed not only from wifely devotion, but at least equally from the fact that she considered herself part of the British official family, for the ladies were not one whit less patriotic than the men.[33]

Whenever they could, the English wives created homes that were duplications of upper-middle-class homes in England, complete with garden, furnishings, and accustomed household routine. The increasing number of such homes was one of the most striking signs of the domestication of the continent, and visitors to British Africa could be fairly certain of invitations to stop over where they might enjoy true British hospitality and comfort, if not always the elegance described here by Declé.

What struck me most was the simple elegance and good taste reigning in this pleasant household. Pretty services of china appeared at meals; spotless, well-washed, and embroidered table-linen, all so clean and well kept that you could hardly believe yourself in the heart of Africa.[34]

It is also very clear that the insistence on maintaining British standards in these homes was a response to Africa itself. The very Englishness of the home made it a needed refuge and escape from the alien qualities of the Dark Continent. Mrs. Larymore is explicit in this regard, and as the first, and for a long time, the only, Englishwoman in Northern Nigeria, she expressed her determination to resist Africa by creating a small island of home.

. . . no English housewife in West Africa—if she is "worth her salt" —will spare herself in the endeavour to, at least, turn "quarters" into "home," even if only for a few months . . . no one, I think, could resist a pathetic appeal for a pretty sketch to carry away into far Africa! And, indeed, it is a joy sometimes, when the temperature is unpleasantly high, little worries abounding, and *Africa* asserting itself unduly, to be able to glance occasionally at a sketch of some English woodland, or a corner of a picturesque village.[35]

Wherever the British were in Africa, they were now in British territory. Order was maintained by British law; personal safety was secure. Servants were trained to run British households and to speak English. The continent and its savage population was being run in British fashion. The "darkness" of Africa was being dispelled by the civilizing light of a British administration and British values.

The White Man's Burden

The new challenges and tasks of colonialism in Africa wrought changes not only in the British self-image but in their image of the continent. The former image of Africa made it the setting for a drama of personal heroism, yet it conferred upon Africa some status as an entity, however hostile and dangerous. In the new view, the continent was merely raw material to be molded skillfully into a colony that would provide a market, resources, and room for settlement. This was its challenge and its *raison d'être.* The image of Africa had been transformed from a land to be conquered into a territory to be exploited.

The writers continued to describe the physical surroundings as they had earlier; such detailing had by now become an integral part of the tradition. But there was an additional emphasis on potential. Terrain was not purely for mapping or marching over, but was to be studied with an eye for utilization and for settlement. Landscape descriptions in the flowery language of Victorian prose abruptly shift to business-like appraisal of potential worth. In the following passage on Uganda, it almost seems as if Sir Harry Johnston the artist began, only to be replaced by Sir Harry the practical administrator.

> After the hot sunshine, which has played on the traveller's back as he toiled up the hill, with its red soil and very green grass, the plunge into the cool depths of forest, with their innumerable palms, wild bananas, and soaring trees with white trunks, gives a delightful sense of relief, and he is sorry when the pretty causeway of white sand comes to an end, and he must toil once more up the opposite bank of red clay. I am afraid the country being of this nature it will prove extremely expensive to construct a railway across it, though a short railway from the coast of Uganda to Ruwenzori and the south end of Lake Albert would be of immense value. . . .[1]

The literary justifications of empire in Africa were primarily directed at the British taxpayer to convince him of the worth of the new dominion. Thus the new possession was portrayed as a salubrious, picturesque, and valuable adjunct to the British Empire. The English had been writing this way about South Africa since the beginning of the nineteenth century, and it might simply have been, at the height of empire, a continuation of this earlier literary convention. It seems, however, to be more clearly an advertisement for empire, and is almost startling to find in certain descriptions of West Africa. For example, Thomas J. Alldridge, the Governor of Sierra Leone, suddenly and incongruously transforms the White Man's Grave into a new Zion where the Englishman might take his ease.

> Lounging in my most comfortable rokhee chair, chatting with pleasant companions, while taking the beauty of the scenery, it was really quite delightful; so that . . . we felt contented and at peace with all mankind and affectionately inclined towards the West Coast of Africa, which . . . is able to provide us with enchantingly beautiful scenery, pure air, and most needful repose.[2]

It is impossible to ignore the factor of vested interest in the use of this particular image. Most of the writers who stressed the advantages of Britain's new colonial acquisition had serious personal commitments to Africa. Emphasis on the difficulties could only contravene their own strenuous efforts to build an empire. There is not the slightest suggestion of dishonesty in their outlook; it is more a matter of self-delusion.

The image of Africa as a new Zion had a short life, lasting only so long as the initial excitement about the new African colonies; even during that period many writers continued to use the older and more enduring image of the Dark Continent. For them, as for the writers of the twentieth century, it was a land of mystery and danger, a crucible for testing character. Though such depictions were neither frequent nor elaborate, they cropped up often enough during this period to indicate the persistence of the earlier image and to adumbrate its use in the twentieth century.

> Africa always claims its forfeits; and so the four white men who had started together from Mombasa returned but three to Cairo.[3]

> . . . the West Coast of Africa . . . is a Belle Dame Sans Merci.[4]

> . . . the vacant look upon our maps, which tells how long this mysterious land has kept its secrets.[5]

> . . . Africa proves a man, and he who issues unscathed from that furnace is pure gold indeed.[6]

Presently one of the liveliest conventions is that of Africa as a preserve, and it took shape in the literature of the height of empire. Partly rooted in the already familiar convention of the sportsman's paradise, it also reflected the new possessive attitudes toward the land. Conservation was the new theme: to preserve for the civilized world those features of Africa which were unique. Some writers, though rather atypically, deplored the excessive slaughter of game for fear it disappear and lessen both the beauty and the value of the colony. Aside from the promotion of settlement and tourism, the preservation of natural wonders was considered essential if Africa was to retain its most appealing qualities. What would Africa be without its herds of wild game, its dense forests, or its savage population? [7]

These were also the very features that many of the writers evoked as vestiges of primordial times. They saw Africa as a reservoir of antiquity. Churchill referred to Africa's "primeval chaos," "primary religion," and "primordial nakedness";[8] Bryce, discussing social evolution, suggested that Africa was preservative of ancient forms.[9] It is left, however, to Sir Harry Johnston to state the theme most explicitly.

> The European, in fact, feels, consciously or unconsciously that he is out of his element and his age, that, as in Mr. Wells's suggestive story "The Time Machine," the wheels of time have been reversed for him, and he has been transported back to a past epoch in the earth's history, before this planet was fitted in its atmosphere and surroundings for the presence of modern man.[10]

This theme is congruent with the basic image of the Dark Continent in its emphasis on inordinately great age and primitivity. It also related to the widely accepted evolutionism which placed African cultures at the very bottom of the ladder of Progress and Civilization. Yet now that Africa was part of the British Empire it was unthinkable to the empire-builders that it be left there. The vigorous exponents of Victorian values fully intended to lift Africa from its "primeval chaos" to civilized order.

Britain's new imperial status in Africa also brought about significant changes in the image of the African people. As the land was a resource to be developed, the people were subjects to be governed and labor to be utilized—"the white man is the brain and the black man the muscle." [11] The final outcome—one that was confidently anticipated—was a profitable colony inhabited by a contented and hard-working people, moving ever toward Progress and Civilization. Whatever reservations there were about this outcome concerned the extent to which the Africans were improvable, and even these doubts were overridden with the optimism typical of the times. If the Africans were not inherently capable of attaining a higher civilization themselves, they could, as adequate and docile workers, do their bit for the general advancement of mankind.

The fulfillment of this imperial vision involved first, pacification of the territories, by treaty preferably, by arms if necessary. It was thought that military action would not be called for save against Arabs and the few intransigently militant tribes. And in these cases the British would be delivering oppressed peoples who would clearly prefer the just and humane rule of the British. Such people would reward British efforts on their behalf with open arms. In his accounts of British campaigns in Nigeria, Seymour Vandeleur described the heartwarming welcome accorded Goldie after he had defeated the Fulani overlords of the area.

> . . . Sir George Goldie . . . received quite an ovation. He was met by about 2000 people, and the chief and leading people threw themselves on their knees before him, and thanked him for having rid them of their oppressors. The women and children emitted shrill shrieks of joy as each white man passed, and seemed very glad to see us. . . .[12]

In the same vein is Lugard's description of the poignant anxiety of the Toru of Uganda at the possibility of British withdrawal.

> The people of Toru . . . were most eager to come under our protection. . . . Others asked me if we had come to stay; for if we should desert them as the Egyptian garrisons had deserted the people of Northern Unyoro . . . only massacre and slavery would await them. . . . I replied—how could I do otherwise?—that these countries were ceded to the British by the nations of Europe, and that the British flag never went back.[13]

Portrayal of Africans as innately servile people who had to be rescued and protected was an older convention stemming from the historical conditions of the slave trade. In the imperial tradition, however, the primary issue was not one of slavery, but of political and social subjugation. Since the African's "natural servility" made him a willing and perennial subject, it was up to the British to protect and liberate him from all exploitive despots. There was no doubt that the Africans had to be governed; they could not be left to govern themselves, and indeed, they would not want to. In this, as in other things, they were, points out Lugard, totally unlike the English (Teutons).

In Africa, moreover, there is among the people a natural inclination to submit to higher authority. That intense detestation of control which animates our Teutonic races does not exist among the tribes of Africa.[14]

The new subject status of the Africans called for a reworking of some of the older stereotypes; the Africans were now to be evaluated in terms of subordination and incorporation into a colonial system. The British were thus concerned with African docility, cooperativeness, industriousness, bellicosity, or any other characteristics pertinent to colonial efficiency.

Much more attention was paid to tribal characteristics. The generalizations about "the African" and "the Negro" were still used, usually by those with limited experience in Africa. For example, Mrs. Hall, a temporary visitor to Africa, wrote as if there were no distinction at all between one African and another; all Africans were the same, and all were innately "childlike." [15] Others who may have been far more aware of tribal differences saw them as qualities or characteristics of everyone in the tribe.

Though at first there were some differences of opinion among the writers as to what particular tribal qualities were,[16] the descriptions soon became set. In Arthur S. White's summary of African geography, resources, and people, the Africans were described only in terms of these stereotypes. White presented each tribe through a sketch of tribal character, directed toward an evaluation of the tribal role in the development of empire—their special abilities or defects, the problems they might present in the creation or maintenance of a colony. Most patently the governing of the "unstable Bechuana" and the "vigorous and independent Kaffir" would require entirely different methods, and neither would do at all for the "Jews of Africa, the enterprising and shrewd Fula." [17]

The Baganda were described by Lugard as "extremely clever in artisan work . . . and the more civilized methods of agriculture." [18] Both Johnston and Churchill called them the "Japanese of Africa" for their politeness and elegance of demeanor; and Churchill went on to say that they were "docile and intelligent, an island of gentle manners and peaceful civilization." [19] Such a depiction of the Baganda could only have been written at the end of the century. Before that they were consistently described as one of the bloodier kingdoms of Central Africa, torn by constant civil strife, ruled by a savage and bloodthirsty despot.

Since an African army was required to serve the needs of empire, tribes were appraised in regard to their military fitness. Vandeleur, himself a professional soldier, volunteered the Hausa as "sturdy-looking men and excellent marchers . . . the best fighting material in Africa." [20] Robinson knew the Hausa well, and he fully concurred in this opinion, suggesting further that the Hausa were such "splendid soldiers" because they were superior in character and temperament to the "degraded savages" of Dahomey, Ashanti, and Benin.[21] While in partial agreement with these opinions, Lugard nevertheless plumped for the Sudanese as the best soldiers; "they are brave, extremely amenable to discipline . . . having the instincts of a soldier in routine duties." [22]

African rulers, no longer possessing the power to hinder empire, were evaluated solely in terms of their potential usefulness to colonial administration. The policy of indirect rule required cooperation from native rulers, so this was the quality upon which they were judged. If the chief proved amenable and efficient in carrying out British programs he was a good chief; otherwise, he was bad.

The attitude toward the chief did not differ from that toward all Africans. The chief required some special treatment, perhaps, but only because of the usefulness of his office, not because of the deference customarily due a ruler. The descriptions of African rulers often evince contempt, sometimes politely veiled, and at other times explicit. Mary Kingsley here leavens her contempt for a West African chief by her customary jocularity.

> . . . strange and highly interesting function of going to a tea-party at a police station to meet a king—a real reigning king—who kindly attended with his suite . . . Tachie (that's His Majesty's name) is an old, spare, man with a subdued manner. His sovreign rights are acknowledged by the Government so far as to hold him more or less responsible for any iniquity committed by his people; and as the Government do not allow him to execute or flagellate the said people, earthly pomp is rather a hollow thing to Tachie.[23]

If permitted to rule without government supervision the chiefs would merely perpetuate savage customs—trial by ordeal, cannibalism, human sacrifice, infanticide, and certain forms of marriage and property rights—all designated as targets for reform. Yet these very customs are given so much attention in the literature that it is clear the British were at least as fascinated as they were horrified by them.

A new fillip was added to the beastly savage conventions by many sensational tales of cannibalism. There had been, earlier, minimal interest in the subject, though it had been occasionally reported. William Snelgrave, Robert Norris, and Archibald Dalzel in the eighteenth century had referred to the cannibalistic practices in Dahomey. It was reported from West Africa in the early nineteenth century, but there is little reference to cannibalism in the literature on South Africa in that period. Exploitation of the theme began in the mid-nineteenth century. Stanley was carried away in his zealous horror of anthropophagy and repeated every tale of cannibal tribes that he heard in addition to creating quite a number of his own. Winwood Reade sprinkled cannibals about West Africa rather like raisins in a cake. Other mid-century explorers mention certain tribes as cannibalistic, relying on older reports or hearsay.

In the imperial period writers were far more addicted to tales of cannibalism than the Africans ever were to cannibalism. Its prevalence was taken for granted, and no actual evidence was required to establish that a tribe was notoriously anthropophagous. Lady

Flora Lugard postulated the existence of a "belt of cannibalism . . . across the whole breadth of Africa."[24] Grogan, almost always more sensational than judicious, wrote his eyewitness account, only a small part of which is quoted here, of the aftermath of a purported cannibal orgy in Mushari, a district inhabited by the Bateka tribe.

> Mushari, lined with grain and torn skins, relics of those unfortunates who had been caught; and dried pools of blood, gaunt skeletons, grinning skulls and trampled grass, told a truly African tale . . . about 3000 square miles in extent had been depopulated and devastated. I do not believe that 2% of the thousands of inhabitants have survived.[25]

Modern anthropology casts considerable doubt on the extent of cannibalism in Africa. The evidence would seem to indicate that the practice of cannibalism was extremely circumscribed, and occurred only within the context of sorcery and witchcraft.[26] But the writers of empire were clearly predisposed to find cannibalism even where there was no evidence.

Besides the political value of the theme as a justification for colonialism, the commercial value of literary sensationalism cannot be ignored as a motive for its perpetuation. Cannibal stories were titillating enough to insure increased sales of books, and few writers were averse to exploiting the theme. European readers are accustomed to cannibalism as a literary theme. It is an integral part of the fairy tales and nursery rhymes, and adults still respond with avid interest to tales of cannibalism especially when presented as one of the "realities" of African life. So valuable an adjunct to the literary tradition was the theme of cannibalism that it remained one of the most persistent conventions.

The most important contribution of the cannibalism theme to the entire literary tradition is that it provides a vivid new variation of the beastly savage image of the African. It underlines in a most dramatic fashion that African behavior is a negation of European values.

All descriptions of Africans throughout this period emphasized traits thought to be indicative of inferiority. Ascriptions that had been made at an earlier time to the Africans of thicker skulls, harder heads, and insensitivity to pain were all continued in the imperial tradition. Hitherto there had been only an occasional mention of any distinctive African odor. The literature of empire, however, frequently refers to the "bouquet d'Afrique." Johnston thought it of sufficient interest to discourse "scientifically" on the nature of the "peculiar foetor." [27] A new group of stereotypes concerning the excessive fecundity and sexuality of the African appeared at this time. James Bryce and Johnston remark on these.

They are more prolific than the whites, and their increase is not restrained by those prudential checks which tell upon civilized man.[28]

. . . the concentration of their thoughts on sexual intercourse . . . is the negro's greatest weakness. Nature has probably endowed him with more than the usual generic faculty. After all, to these people almost without arts and sciences and the refined pleasures of the senses, the only acute enjoyment offered them by nature is sexual intercourse.[29]

The writers also ascribed a host of mental and moral failings to the Africans. They were ignorant as well as incapable of any intellectual attainment. They lacked any sense of time; they could not reason or think in abstract terms; and since they were without the gifts of invention or creativity, they were innately imitative. As for emotions, Africans were described as lacking all the finer feelings such as gratitude, pity, or true love, and in general they were emotionally unstable. Morally, too, they were very short of the mark since they were lazy, liars, thieves, cowards, and bullies.[30]

Underlying these attributions was the still unequivocally accepted racial determinism of mid-century, and now it was strongly supported by the doctrine of evolution. Popularized versions of Darwinism were apparently so congruent with the temper of the times as to require no amplification, defense, or argument. Evolution provided a tailor-made and facile explanation of the Africans' place in nature and in society.

The typical late nineteenth-century statement concerning the evolutionary position of the African placed him on the lowest rungs of the evolutionary ladder. Bryce's evolutionary scheme posited secure pigeonholes for all varieties of mankind—tribe by tribe—and if some African tribes were more advanced than others, all ranked well down on the scale.

> As their religious customs were rather less sanguinary than those of the Guinea Coast negroes, so the Kaffirs themselves were somewhat more advanced in civilization. Compared with the Red Indians of America, they stood at a point lower than that of the Iroquois or Cherokees, but superior to the Utes or to the Diggers of the Pacific Coast.[31]

Bryce's scheme contains more literary than scientific merit, but it, at least, has the virtue of retaining the Africans within the confines of humanity. Others believed that the Africans had not yet, or only just, come down out of the trees, and were far more akin to monkeys and apes than to man. Grogan even discovered an entirely new and improbable tribe of

> . . . ape-like creatures . . . quite distinct from the other peoples. . . . Their face, body and limbs are covered with wiry hair and the hang of the long powerful arms, the slight stoop of the trunk, and the hunted, vacant expression of the face made up a *tout ensemble* that was terrible pictorial proof of Darwinism.[32]

Nineteenth-century theories of Social Darwinism, racism, and biological determinism provided justification for the initial conquest and subsequent domination of Africa. According to the tenet of "survival of the fittest," which was, for the layman, the most outstanding aspect of evolution, conquest was self-validating. The innate inferiority of the conquered was demonstrated by the fact that they *were* conquered and could be accounted for by their unfitness in the evolutionary contest. The inevitable concomitant of these assumptions was developed in colonial policy—the European had to assume responsibility for the governing and welfare of the inferior peoples.

The evolutionary schemes propounded by the writers of empire were grounded in racism. Differences in culture, history, language, and behavior were confounded with biological differences, and even when they were able to distinguish among them, the writers attributed all differences to the crucial factor of race; thus evolutionary development, too, was seen as a function of racial difference. Restatements of the biblical concept of the Negroes' descent from Ham do not appear in the literature of empire as frequently as they had earlier, but theories of polygenesis flourished, most of them indicating that the Negro belonged to an entirely different and lesser species. This is the substance of Mary Kingsley's comment that ". . . the difference between the African and [the European] is a difference not of degree but of kind. . . . I feel certain that a black man is no more an undeveloped white man than a rabbit is an undeveloped hare." [33]

The rationalization of empire and white supremacy was predicated upon the assumption of vast differences between the British and their African subjects. The philanthropic-minded among the British may have been concerned that the gulf between them was so great, but nowhere was it altogether denied, and for the most part it was considered inevitable, permanent, and even essential. Bryce was one of many who believed that even the Africans accepted it as the natural order.

> . . . the black man accepts the superiority of the white as part of the order of nature. He is too low down, too completely severed from the white, to feel indignant. Even the few educated natives are too well aware of the gulf that divides their own people from the European to resent . . . the attitude of the latter.[34]

Westernized Africans represented some lessening of the disparity between the two cultures and hence were seen as a source of disruption of the natural order. They were viewed with suspicion and hostility; the British seem angered at what amounted to African presumption at having attempted to bridge the gulf. Emotion and theory parted company at this point; the Africans were to be guided toward progress, but at the pace and under conditions dictated by the British. It was too soon for any visible signs of progress, and the Westernized African represented too quick a leap. A frequent concomitant of the attitude of hostility toward the Westernized African was a nostalgic expression of preference for the simple savage, untouched by progress. Thus Lionel Declé comments.

> Black gentlemen . . . were to be met with in the grog shops, the headquarters of the Salvation Army and the gaols . . . they served only to show the result of the devolution of a fine savage into a degraded, European-dressing, hard-drinking, work-hating . . . black-looking villain: for such is the free-born, dark-skinned citizen loafer of the Cape Colony, the proud and respected owner of a vote.[35]

It is paradoxical that the agents of progress and civilization should have expressed such a preference for the "fine savage" untouched by their influence. The paradox can be resolved by recognition of the nature of British attitudes toward subject peoples in general and toward the Negro in particular. The Westernized African contravened the clear-cut distinctions the British had drawn and intended to maintain between themselves and the Africans—ruler and subject, white man and "nigger," civilized and savage. The British had vested political, economic, and psychological interests in maintaining these contrasts.

The Westernized African was an ever-present reminder to the British that the disparity might be overcome in a single lifetime. They viewed the acculturated African as a threat to their prerogatives and to the established social order. Their response in the literature was to make him a target for ridicule and censure; it was sometimes humorously phrased, but always contemptuous. In Vandeleur's comments on Westernized Liberians, the contempt outweighs the humor.

> The Liberian Government is quite a farce; all the members are styled right honourable, but notwithstanding this they have proved quite unable to govern themselves. . . . The Liberians have a very great opinion of themselves and the influence of their state on the affairs of the world, though their knowledge of history is rather vague, as will be gathered from the following story:—A senator met a Frenchman one day in the street, who knocked up against him, when the former in an indignant manner, turned round and said, "You d——— Frenchman, what for you shove me? What for we give you at Waterloo?"[36]

A different set of responses were the reiterated emphases on the innate moral and intellectual failings of all Africans, which placed them outside the pale of civilization, if not forever, at least for a very long time. Johnston firmly stated that it would take over three generations for the native Africans to acquire anything approaching a civilized condition, and his was a more modest estimate than many.[37]

At any rate, the quality of African mentality was believed to be of such a nature that any manifestation of civilized behavior was believed to be superficial and tenuous, since sooner or later the African would revert to savagery. Besides, in becoming Westernized, the African could only become corrupted, since his ignorance and immorality always prompted him to adopt Western vices rather than virtues.

We first encounter the widespread use of the term "nigger" during this period. Some writers, like Grogan, saw the Africans only as "niggers"—he used no other term. No issue was taken with the word or its use at this time, though some in positions of administrative responsibility, clearly aware of its pejorative content, eschewed its use. In this connection it is interesting to note that in his earliest writings, Johnston occasionally lapses into using the word, but discreetly, hemmed in by quotation marks.[38] Later, when he became Proconsul of British Empire in Africa, he did not use the term at all.

As for much of the rest of empire-building, the use of "nigger" was borrowed from the Indian Empire. The word was in use there much earlier than in Africa, and the transformation of the Africans to subject peoples equated them in this, as in other aspects, with the Indian subjects. Having already acquired derogatory and tendentious connotations elsewhere, it made a useful label for the new stereotypes and the new image of the Africans.

Fiction of Empire

Surveys of the literature of empire contain bibliographic references to a substantial body of fiction.[1] Many of these novels are still obtainable, and some are still widely read; others have not survived the changing literary tastes and can be obtained only by sustained search.

Novels about Africa had strong appeal for the turn-of-the-century reader. Morton Cohen, the biographer of H. Rider Haggard, suggests that the Victorians were surfeited with the all-too-familiar realities of the domestic novel, and that stirring tales of adventure in exotic locales provided a most welcome change.

> For too long the reader's attention had been trained on London slums, prison houses, artists' attics, Manchester mills and village vicarages, and King Solomon's Mines was one of the books that offered a "way out." It let the reader turn his back on the troublesome, the small, the sordid; and it took him on a journey to the Empire's frontier to perform the mighty deeds he could believe in.[2]

In addition, the fiction was generally more exciting than contemporary nonfiction because the novels echoed the thrilling journals of the great period of African exploration at mid-century. Even the few novels of mid-century had been dull reading beside the verve of the explorers' accounts. Novels at the end of the century, however, recaptured that excitement that had been so much a part of the mid-century journals of exploration.

A number of the novels of empire were books for boys. G. A. Henty's *Young Colonists*[3] marched and fought bravely with General Buller to Natal and with General Roberts to Pretoria—glorious scouting adventures, undertaken with high moral purpose and designed to appeal to the young. The battle scenes were described in detail so that a boy might reconstruct the entire encounter with his lead soldiers.[4] Youngsters could readily identify with the young heroes of *Jock of the Bushveld*[5] and *Prester John*.[6]

Sandwiched between incidents of pure adventure were items of deliberate pedagogy: discourses on natural history, British history, and British character. More frequently the instruction was less explicit, but the values were undisguised, presented in high relief. First and foremost, this was a manly literature, relating the deeds of brave men in sport and war, travel, and empire-building. It was, moreover, a highly moral literature which laid great stress on the glorious deeds of idealized British heroes. It was considered by the Victorians to be the right kind of literature for young boys.

These didactic-cum-adventure novels were considered to be of the most elevated moral tone since they were almost entirely sexless in plot. Haggard, for example, guaranteed that in *King Solo-*

mon's Mines "there is not a petticoat in the whole history."[7] Other novels of this sort do not contain even one feminine character.[8] But there are love stories in others (and we may assume these were not for boys) in which the romance was either the central or a peripheral plot, and it was always in terms of the Victorian ideal: sentimental, moral, and always subordinate to the adventure.[9]

Often these Victorian novels were highly sexual in overtones and implications, though conforming superficially to the morality of the times. *King Solomon's Mines* may have lacked "even a petticoat" but *She* and *Allan Quatermain* quite made up for that lack. Cohen points out that modern psychological interpretation would make "Ayesha the projection of Haggard's unconscious idea of the ideal love . . . and *She* a beautiful allegory of the penalty attendant on our yearning to return into the womb."[10] Repressed sexuality finds its way into many of these novels by indirection and innuendo.

Haggard is undoubtedly one of the most significant figures in the tradition. He assembled into his fiction the greatest number of themes from the earlier tradition and most directly influenced the later tradition as well as the fiction of his own period. The Haggard stamp appeared on almost every one of the hundreds of exotic adventure tales that were written after *King Solomon's Mines.*

Bertram Mitford, like Haggard, wrote of the Zulus in the same blend of pseudo-scholarly and biblical styles, idealizing Zulu chivalry and courage in battle.[11] The Matabele uprisings at the end of the century provided the background for a number of novels by Mitford and others.[12] These are all tales of energetic adventure, but unlike the best of Haggard they lack the quality to capture the imagination of the modern reader. Their style and content are dated and of so little interest that now they are forgotten, while Haggard's most successful novels have become minor classics.

Rudyard Kipling, too, had a pervasive effect on the fiction about Africa, though he wrote very little about Africa himself.[13] His few African stories are about the Boer War and contain little reference to either Africa or the Africans. His African travel essay is only tangential in pertinence since it deals mainly with his journey in Egypt and along the lower Nile. Yet his stories of the every-inch-a-Briton, public school, empire-builders in India were models for much fiction about Africa. Edgar Wallace's *Sanders of the River*[14] might have been borrowed directly from Kipling, as might the British officials portrayed in the African novels of Mitford and John Buchan. The "great game" of espionage and international intrigue central to Kipling's *Kim* is also the predominant theme of *Prester John* and *Sanders of the River*.

In his Indian stories, Kipling developed the idea that the colonies were the most admirable school for character building of young Englishmen. This theme was totally taken over by the novelists of Africa. G. A. Henty's *Young Colonists,* the Boy in *Jock of the Bushveld,* young David in *Prester John,* and Drury in *The Fossicker* all emerge from their African ordeals strengthened and ennobled, ready to face the responsibilities of manhood. Allan Quatermain, Sanders, and John Ames demonstrate the characterological virtues of the British gentleman in the face of Africa's challenge.

Africa thus provided the arena and the external stimulus for either the making of man or his destruction. But very few of the Englishmen portrayed in these novels of empire had the fatal character flaws which might entail their destruction. The heroic self-image was too pervasive and the concern with national prestige too great to depict Englishmen who lacked the basic virtues of loyalty, courage, and above all, strong moral fiber. Even in these novels, however, there is the occasional weakling who is destroyed by the African trial, and his failure as a man and an Englishman is even more striking because it is so rare. Yet he, too, serves the same function as the ideal hero, since his failure enhances the hero's success. W. Somerset Maugham's description of such a weakling in *The Explorer* indicates that he could not withstand Africa as a stronger man would.

> But the effect of Africa was too strong. Alec had seen many men lose their heads under the influence of that climate. The feelings of authority that seemed so little limited over a race that was manifestly inferior, the subtle magic of the hot sunshine, the vastness, the remoteness from civilization, were very apt to throw a man off his balance. It needed a strong head or a strong morality to avoid the danger, and George had neither. He succumbed.[15]

This sort of character delineation was completely within the Kipling ideal. Kipling's most important influence, however, was not so much in plot or characterization, but as the Bard of Empire. Rhodes was his great hero, and British imperial prestige his great concern. He bitterly denounced the home government during the Boer War only because it had failed to achieve the ideals of his imperial dream; of these ideals he was uncritically jealous. His work was a stentorian paean of praise to the empire which set the tone for the fiction about Africa at the turn of the century and for a long time after.

Maugham's novel *The Explorer* probably survives only because of his later reputation. It is a pretentious and wooden piece, relating the life of Alec Mackenzie, the soldier-explorer par excellence, whose major concern was to "add another fair jewel to England's crown." [16] Stanley was Maugham's avowed model for the super-life-sized hero, but the ideology of the novel was Kipling's. Thus, Alec Mackenzie feels "pride in the great Empire which had sprung from that small island, a greater Rome in a greater world." [17]

The novels of this period were all pro-empire, many actively defending it, others taking it quite for granted. As works of fiction they were free to surround empire with romance, ignore its bitter realities, and invest it with the mystique of the Anglo-Saxon mission to civilize. The British characters understand and willingly shoulder the task of bearing the "white man's burden." In *Prester John,* Buchan simultaneously thrusts maturity and awareness of responsibility upon his young hero.

> I knew then the meaning of the white man's duty. He has to take all the risks, recking nothing of his life or his fortunes and well content to find his reward in the fulfillment of his task. That is the difference between white and black . . . the gift of responsibility, the power of being in a little way a king; and so long as we know this and practice it, we will rule not in Africa alone but wherever there are dark men who live only for the day and their own bellies. Moreover the work made me pitiful and kindly. I learned much of the untold grievances of the natives, and saw something of their strange, twisted reasoning.[18]

As in this Buchan novel, justification of the British historic right to dominion and power was usually expressed in terms of racism —the rights and duties of the white man in regard to the inferior blacks. Again it was Kipling who was the leading exponent of this ideology; he firmly believed with his contemporaries, Rhodes and John Ruskin, that only the Anglo-Saxon approached God's ideal type, and that the British were divinely ordained to fulfill the great mission of colonizing Africa.[19]

Olive Schreiner's fiction, especially *The Story of an African Farm*,[20] is, for this period, a literary anomaly, differing in several points from its contemporaries. Neither "manly" literature, adventure, nor a novel of empire, it was the first novel about Africa written by a woman, expressing a feminist viewpoint. In an age of imperialism, the prevailing note of humanitarianism in Schreiner's novel is uncommon. It is, however, a humanitarianism that recalls most sharply the writings of John Barrow and Thomas Pringle in the early nineteenth century. She shared with them a deep compassion for the Africans, and though not actually disapproving of the Boers, she viewed them with a keenly realistic eye. She depicted the inarticulate misery of the African servants on a Boer farm in late nineteenth-century South Africa with pity, but this compassion was only part of her grander ideology of egalitarianism, which was primarily directed to woman's rights. The Africans caught only the sentimental backwash. She perceived very few Africans as individuals; for the most part they are downtrodden, though shadowy, background figures. Schreiner's protest was not so specifically pro-African as it was pro-underdog.

Englishmen did not fare well in Schreiner's book. Of the two that are portrayed, one was an opportunistic scoundrel, and the other a fickle and callow youth. But the English heroine is beautiful, virtuous, kind, and awesomely intellectual. She is the sharpest contrast to the "naked, sullen ill-looking Kaffir woman with lips hideously protruding."[21] Schreiner may have had some revolutionary notions about the status of Victorian women and compassion for the similarly enslaved Negroes, but her basic perception of Africans did not depart from the tradition; she referred to them as "niggers" and held to the traditional conventions concerning their place in nature and society. They were inferior beings whose "race must melt away in the heat of a collision with a higher," and who were "the vestige of one link that spanned between the dog and the white man." [22] Yet it is the general tone of humanitarian protest that Olive Schreiner is remembered for, and in this she was the forerunner of the modern novels of protest concerning race relations in South Africa.

Of all the fiction about Africa written at the turn of the century, only the work of Joseph Conrad stands out as great literature. Conrad wrote but two pieces on Africa: a novella, *Heart of Darkness,* and a short story, "An Outpost of Progress." [23] Both were based on his own experience in the Congo. Though he was one of the major forebears of the twentieth-century tradition, Conrad's influence upon the literature was not apparent until the 1930's; unlike Kipling and Haggard, he had no immediate followers or imitators.

Conrad was also unlike Kipling and Haggard in that he was keenly aware of the moral ambiguities of empire; he was critical of its exploitiveness and profoundly pessimistic about its consequences. He described imperialism as "robbery with violence, aggravated murder on a great scale," and as "conquest of the earth . . . taking it away from those who have a different complexion or slightly flatter noses than ourselves." [24] Yet his indictment was more a condemnation of society than of empire, and his pessimism was directed more toward the inner corruption of mankind than at the evils of colonialism.

Conrad did not abjure the conventions of the imperial tradition in his writing; he was perhaps unaware that he was using them. The Africans seemed to him pitiable, but they were nonetheless "niggers" and "ferocious savages," victimized quite as much by their own stupidity and ignorance as by European brutality. He accepted the mission to civilize as a redeeming "idea and an unselfish belief in the idea," [25] and he idealized the role of the British adventurers and conquerors of Africa as "messengers of the might within the land, bearers of a spark from the sacred fire." [26] He questioned the right and the morality of exploitive colonialism, but he nowhere questioned the superiority of the civilized European, the inferiority of the Africans, nor the British imperial role in Africa.

Conrad's major contribution to the literary tradition was the psychological orientation that is now the mainstay of African novels. Conrad's Africa was the macrocosmic psyche, the very soul of man, the heart of darkness in which the European was compelled to come to terms with himself, there to search out his strengths and weaknesses, to discover the deepest meanings of existence. His journey into Africa was the journey within himself, the penetration of the psyche for self-knowledge. In *Heart of Darkness,* Kurtz's ultimate knowledge was of his own lack of moral resources, and this knowledge spelled his end.

> . . . there was something wanting in him . . . whether he knew of this deficiency in himself I can't say. I think the knowledge came to him at last—only at the very last. But the wilderness had found him out early. . . . I think it had whispered to him things about himself which he did not know, things of which he had no conception till he took counsel with the great solitude—and the whisper had proved irresistibly fascinating. It echoed loudly within him because he was hollow at the core.[27]

In a sense Conrad was using the familiar convention—Africa as the testing ground of character—that was typical of the work of his contemporaries. But the convention was transmuted by Conrad; the heart of darkness was Central Africa, but it was also the dark mystery that lay coiled about the very soul of a man.

The fiction at the turn of the century stressed two contrasting and equally important conventions. West Africa was still the fever-ridden white man's grave of the earlier literature, and the novelists wrote of it as the hostile land of darkest mystery. Edgar Wallace said of it, "There are many things that happen in the very heart of Africa that no man can explain . . . a story about Africa must be a mystery story."[28] And Conrad describes the land through the eyes of the two Europeans in "Outpost of Progress."

> . . . they felt themselves very much alone, when suddenly left unassisted to face the wilderness; a wilderness rendered more strange,

more incomprehensible by the mysterious glimpses of the vigorous life it contained . . . the great silence of the surrounding wilderness, its very hopelessness and savagery seemed to approach them.[29]

There were, however, more novels written about South and East Africa than about the west during this period. They were the areas of greatest imperial concern and of colonial settlement. Here was the vast land of free, open space, where a man might have sufficient room to act out his heroic impulses. England, though the beloved homeland, induced only claustrophobia; it was constraining and drab.

The charm of a life of freedom and complete independence—a life in which a man goes as and where he lists. . . . Not back to the cage. Anything but that! [30]

Already I can hardly bear my impatience when I think of the boundless country and the enchanting freedom. Here one grows so small and mean, but in Africa everything is built to a nobler standard. There the man is really a man. There one knows what are will and strength and courage. You don't know what it is to stand on the edge of some great plain and breathe the pure air. . . .[31]

The novelist was limited by the existing conventions in creating his African setting. Even those totally imaginary locales in the Haggardian novels were sufficiently conventional to seem authentic. Beneath the romantic thriller, the writers wove a strong and intricate web of seeming realism. Readers were often convinced that what they were reading in *King Solomon's Mines* was a true story told by a real person, a white hunter named Allan Quatermain, and the places he told of could be pointed to on the map of Africa.

The self-image of the Briton in the novels paralleled the extravagant contours of his preconceived Africa. He may have come on a quest for health or fortune, for adventure or soldiering, but once in Africa he was bound to establish his own, and British, supremacy. His sphere of action in Africa was the microcosm of empire, and he, on the mission of empire. As in the nonfiction, all the British behaved as if they were personal representatives of Her

Imperial Majesty. Each Briton exemplified his nation's dominance, assured of his acceptance and of his superiority, expecting deference, and demanding it when it was not immediately forthcoming. The British insisted that all Africans defer to them. Mitford's hero, John Ames, makes this point succinctly. "A nigger's a nigger, even if he is high class; all of them should show proper respect to a white man." [32]

The fictional administrators were modeled upon Kipling's Indian administrators—and what men they were!—resourceful, wise, and brave. Each of them knew the natives of his particular district better than they knew themselves, and he governed them with skill, zest, good humor, and even with affection.

Cohen, in his description of Allan Quatermain, has summed up the ideal image of all the British protagonists in this fiction.

> The real protagonist is . . . an experienced wise, gentleman . . . an excellent person of unimpeachable honour and genuine feeling. . . . He is clear minded in all situations, prudent, practical, strong-willed, decisive, humble, ingenious, resourceful, sporting, and a devoted friend, a kind master, and of course, an expert rifleman. He gets on with most men very well, regardless of their colour or nationality. . . . But he is an Englishman staunch and steady, and England is his home. He is, in fact, the Englishman of Empire, the Crusader who takes England's divine mission to heart and carries the white man's burden of spreading Christian love and Anglo-Saxon justice to the four corners of the world.[33]

When, in the novels, attention was turned to the Africans, they were seen through the distorting lens of empire. They were always inferior by virtue of their race and their low position on the scale of civilization. The same hallmarks of inferiority that distinguished the beastly savage in the nonfiction of the period were present in the novels.

The term "nigger" appears in all the fiction; the outright imperialists employed the term liberally, but it was so much a part of the contemporary British perception of non-whites that it is even present in the work of Conrad and Schreiner. While it was clearly disparaging, the frequent and almost offhand use of "nigger" leads one to suspect that it was normal usage for all non-whites. And to the British for whom "niggers began at Calais," the term undoubtedly included all non-Anglo-Saxons as well.

The novelists describe the acculturated African with even more distaste than do thc writers of nonfiction.

> . . . a Sierra Leone nigger . . . spoke English and French with a warbling accent, wrote a beautiful hand . . . and cherished in his innermost heart the worship of evil spirits.[34]

> . . . the cheap swagger of the convert to the new civilization.[35]

> . . . a Christian Kaffir was an impostor, a bastard and a hypocrite . . . not to be trusted under any circumstances.[36]

Such exaggerated emotional reactions to the Westernized African may have been partially due to the nostalgic trend that was typical of the literature of these times. Often the writers in their "out of the cage" mood conceived of civilization as an insidious poison, corrupting the wild, free Africa and the simple, natural (though savage) African. However, it seems more likely that the issue, in this time of stepped-up empire-building, concerned the Africans as natural subjects rather than as natural men. While the empire-builders might wax sentimentally nostalgic over the game and the land, they could not afford the luxury of being too explicit about the people. Africans bearing any of the trappings of civilization merely confused the issue for the English as portents of things to come. Perhaps, too, they provided a mirror in which the British, however reluctantly, perceived the ambiguities of their self-image and of their entire role in Africa.

The half-caste was as difficult and uncomfortable a by-product of empire as the Westernized African, and the novelists were as censorious of him. There is neither humor nor sympathy in the portrayals, rather a shuddering withdrawal as from something repulsive and disquieting. The "taint of the tar-brush" was a stigma, eliciting the same reaction of hostility as the Westernized African, and for the same reasons. In regard to the half-caste there was an additional factor involving the racist imperative to maintain the purity of blood lines. Miscegenation, besides being immoral, lowered British prestige. Perhaps the major reason for derogation of those of mixed blood was that they muddied the sterling view the British had of themselves. Ernest Glanville describes a half-caste as a "thorough bounder as all of his ilk." [37] Watty, "the half-caste Kaffir lad" in *Fighting the Matabele,* was a braggart, a thief, and most signally a "chicken-hearted fellow"—all of which failings were the direct consequence of hybridization.[38]

In his *Kaffir Stories,*[39] William Charles Scully depicts a half-caste girl whose "Aryan blood told." She was intelligent, loyal, and kind, but she is scarcely an exception to the general trend since "the Aryan element manifested itself mainly in force of character and ability; for in her tastes and desires, as in her physiognomy, she followed her mother's race." In the end, of course, her "African blood" won out; she ran off with her African lover and lived and died in the bush with him. Thus the bloodlines maintain their integrity, and racism provides the answer.

Scully's book is one of the few novels of this period in which Africans have more than a minor role. Highly conventional in all other aspects, in this regard at least, *Kaffir Stories* broke some new ground. Haggard, following the pattern set earlier by Stanley and Thomson in their "all-African" novels, wrote *Nada the Lily,*[40] in which all the characters are African. Scully's Africans were stereotyped, but placed in a realistic context; Haggard's Zulus in *Nada the Lily* were noble savages in never-never land. Published in 1892, *Nada the Lily* is anachronistic in its harking back to the noble savages of mid-nineteenth-century fiction. This is not a convention which is typical of or congenial to the fiction of empire.

Turn-of-the-century approximations of the noble savage were stereotyped depictions of "loyal" savages or "warriors." They were viewed with sympathy and even liking, but described in terms of the single dominant and traditionally phrased quality. The "loyal" Africans were the very best of subject peoples and they were described with humor and affection. Gert, the Hottentot hunter and servant in *The Fossicker,* is distinguishable from Khiva, the Zulu guide in *King Solomon's Mines,* and Pukele, the Matabele gunboy in *John Ames,* only by details of dress and appearance; their characters are almost identical. All were keen fighters, trackers, and faithful to the death to their white masters, whom they died defending. In such cases, the only noble savage obviously had to be a dead one!

An even clearer echo of the noble-savage romance is the idealized portrayal of Zulu warriors. Admiration for the Zulu seemed almost mandatory for the novelists of empire.

Like all Zulus, the aristocrats of the native tribes, they were lithe and well-formed, with the stamp of war upon their faces. Their intense pride of birth and contempt for all others were visible in the poise of their heads and their dignified bearing.[41]

Jim was one of the real fighting Zulu breed . . . and they were always ready for a fight and would tackle any odds when their blood was up.[42]

And now, behold, Umslopogaas, I know thee for a great warrior of the blood royal, faithful to the death. Even in Zulu land, where all men are brave, they called thee "the Slaughterer," and at night told stories round the fire of thy strength and deeds.[43]

Although the British identified with and admired the brave, warlike Zulus, they qualified their admiration by depicting them also as the wildest of savages, uncontrollable berserkers, lacking any restraint when their blood lust was roused, ". . . the savage with all self-control flung to the winds." [44] Haggard said that when the Zulu was roused "he is like a fiend." [45] In this regard the Zulu personified the complete contrast to what was probably the most highly valued British trait, the restraint of aggressive impulse.

The warrior who displayed physical courage, loyalty, and who fought fairly was an exemplar of the British code of honor. These same values were projected onto certain of the domestic animals in the novels. *Jock of the Bushveld* is an eponymous tale of a noble hunting dog who personified all the virtues attributed to the Zulu and to the British themselves. He possessed the qualities of "courage, fidelity and concentration" that marked nobility of character. In the same novel there is an exceedingly virtuous horse.

Tsetse was also an old soldier, but he was what you might call a gentleman old soldier, with a sense of duty; and in his case the discipline and honour of his calling were not garments for the occasion, but part of himself.[46]

Apparently the British did not require human intellect to achieve the status of gentleman or soldier. The noble animals served a distinct and unique literary function, for in addition to personifying British virtue, the writers projected onto them an overt hostility toward the Africans that they would not and could not admit of themselves. As dedicated "Crusaders" of empire, the British were to help, to educate, even to fight the Africans, but never to exhibit hatred. A true gentleman could openly admit only to feelings of protectiveness and affection for his savage charges, but his dogs (also gentlemen) instinctively hated them, and lacking the human qualities of self-control, exhibited hostility by growling, barking, and openly attacking Africans.

In general, the novels of empire expressed the British devotion to country and dedication to the civilizing mission in Africa. They expressed as well the characterological virtues which reflected British values. In these respects they were similar to and supported the contemporaneous nonfiction. Nor did the major themes of the novels differ from those of the factual accounts; in both the descriptions of the land, sport, beasts, and people were the same. Where the novels differ from the nonfiction was in affording greater literary freedom to elaborate on the mystique of Africa and to proliferate all the images. Most significantly, the fictional embellishments presented even more dramatically the case for empire.

CHAPTER IV

The Tradition in the Twentieth Century

THE British Empire in Africa, so arduously acquired in the nineteenth century, was lost in the twentieth. The Boer War (1899–1902) marked both the apogee of the empire in Africa and the beginning of its decline. It resulted in the consolidation of large and desirable territories, but at the same time it exposed crucial areas of weakness. The mere fact that so much time, effort, men, and materiel had to be expended in the "little war with the Boer Republics" [1] weakened British prestige and self-confidence. This, the first in a series of White Men's wars fought on African soil, disrupted the united white front which had, however tenuously, been maintained throughout the partitioning of Africa.

World War I, demonstrating how tenuous the united front had been, hastened the decline of African colonialism. The postwar fate of the German colonies was a portent: it was the first European empire in Africa to end. Outright imperialism yielded to mandated trusteeship. The British policy of the Dual Mandate had always assumed responsibility for the welfare of subject peoples, but the newer principle committed the European trustees, at least in theory, to foster African self-determination. Italy's invasion of Abyssinia in 1935 ran sufficiently counter to the new concepts so that the League of Nations invoked sanctions. Empire-building was now deemed aggression, rather than the expression of "manifest destiny," and the whole idea of empire was in bad odor.

Economic crisis and social unrest marked the period between the two world wars. The spread of Marxist thought and the rise of fascism were responses to the difficult times and both were hostile to Great Britain's imperial rule. Ideological attacks on the empire,

Britain's own economic plight, and unrest within the colonies, particularly in India, further diminished British faith in empire.

The rise of Nazi Germany involved Great Britain in a second world war. The challenge of nazism had to be met, and Great Britain responded to totalitarianism by reaffirming liberal, democratic values. Racism, always opposed by humanitarians, had to be refuted as the ideology of the enemy. Modern science had exposed the fallacies of racism, and scientific opinions were now publicized to discredit Nazi propaganda.[2] Racism joined imperialism and jingoism as obsolescent ideologies.

The years between 1910 and 1960 saw radical change on the continent of Africa as well. Roads, railways, airports and modern communications linked regions within Africa and Africa with the world. New knowledge and techniques in medicine and hygiene attacked the problems of disease. Industrial developments led to concentrations of population, creating an increasingly urban mode of life. The new African elite, trained and educated by the West, was impatient with colonial status and anxious to test its new powers. It was from this group that new political leaders arose, to spearhead movements for national independence. Great Britain, impoverished by two world wars, her imperial impulse spent, could not or would not summon the force to retain colonies that demanded sovereignty. Beginning with Ghana in 1957, one by one the African colonies were granted independence. In the short time span since the Berlin Conference in 1884, the status of Africa underwent a remarkable change: from booty to be parceled out among the European powers it became a land of sovereign nations.

The literature of the first decades of the twentieth century lagged behind the events. The British still wrote as if Africa were a colonial possession which they held in the full confidence that this state of affairs would go on forever. And, indeed, in the early years of the century the surface of British-African relations seemed undisturbed. In this period of relative quiescence the literary conventions and stereotypes formulated during the height of empire became the fixed pattern for all the literature to follow.

The long careers of certain writers form the most obvious link with the literature of the past. Sir Harry Johnston began his work with the account of his exploration of the Congo in 1884 and ended it almost fifty volumes later with the publication of *The Story of My Life* in 1923. Lugard's writings dated from *The Rise of Our East African Empire* in 1883 to 1945, when his last articles appeared. For both of these architects of empire little seemed to have changed. Their later works are entirely consistent with their earlier.

Time stood still as well for novelists like John Buchan and Edgar Wallace, who wrote from before World War I until the 1930's. During twenty-one years of service Wallace's hero, District Officer Sanders, achieved the rank of Commissioner and managed to learn the drum language, a skill that as a young officer he had considered impossible for a white man. That is the sum and substance of change in Wallace's novels. Buchan, too, depicts Africans in 1936 almost exactly in the same terms that he did in 1910.

> I heard a sound which I had not heard since the Matabele Rising, the deep throaty howl of Kaffirs on the war-path . . . this outrage of their sacred place had awakened their manhood. Once they had been a famous fighting clan and the old fury had revived. . . . Also there were scores of them, the better part of a hundred lusty savages, mad with fury at the violation of their shrine.[3]

> . . . a mob of maddened savages surged around me. They were chanting a wild song and brandishing spears and rifles to its accompaniment. From their bloodshot eyes stood the lust of blood, the fury of conquest—all the aboriginal passions . . . a wave of black savagery seemed to close over my head.[4]

The twentieth-century biographers of the builders of empire do not discredit either the empire or its architects. For the most part they are in sympathy, if not full agreement, with their subjects. Their accounts reiterate their heroism and idealism as well as the imperial view of Africa.[5]

The proconsuls of empire, Lugard and Johnston, have a long line of literary descendants, some as recent as 1958. Whether journal or memoir, accounts by government officials in Africa are in the Lugard-Johnston vein. There are few differences in basic attitudes, perceptions, and concepts, but changed conditions of work and travel modify the narratives. Modern transport, for example, obviates the long, often exasperated, chapters devoted to organization and conduct of the safari. Capture of Mau Mau leaders—facilitated by jeeps, planes, and bombs[6]—makes an altogether different story from the military actions in the nineteenth century. British courage never goes out of style, but modern cpportunities for its exercise are diminished.

The improved communications made for greater administrative efficiency. The price of efficiency was, however, often seen as the loss of independence, self-reliance, and individuality. The modern British colonial officer was, however reluctantly, a bureaucrat and had little of the rugged individualism of the empire-builders which often led one to wonder whether they were agent or incarnation of England. The outstanding difference is that the early officials were writing of the job to be done, and the later officials discuss its accomplishment. The former presented the case for empire, making commitments and justifying their plans and activities; the latter defend the programs, stating that, in retrospect the commitments had been fulfilled and the empire vindicated. Sir Charles Dundas, former Governor of Uganda and colonial official of long experience, writes.

> Today the word Empire is taboo; we may not speak of subject races, they have become backward peoples; colonial rule has become "trusteeship." . . . A chapter of world history has therewith been closed. Whether another chapter of comparable benefits to the human race will be written may be questioned. Certainly more was done for backward mankind in the era of British colonial rule than in any previous age, and if colonialism is now discredited I believe that its passing will nevertheless be mourned by the simple people of one-time British colonies as the end of a Golden Age.[7]

All the autobiographies, whether or not directly concerned with colonial administration, uphold the values and concepts of imperialism and consequently project the standard images. It is perhaps natural that those who wrote about empire should write in the idiom of empire. What is more significant is that this idiom should have dominated so many other writers on Africa. Traders, settlers, prospectors, and tourists tended to be equally imperialist in sentiment. It is as if the nineteenth century never ended for them, for they cling to the Kipling notion of the "little brown brother" even though they may have given up hope of empire along with the solar topee.

The production of novels placed in an African setting increased markedly after the turn of the century. The bibliography of the period since 1910 contains approximately four times as many works of fiction as that of the entire preceding three hundred and fifty years. Like the nonfiction, the novels and short stories have their prototypes in the earlier literature—namely in the work of Haggard, Conrad, and Kipling.

The themes of the modern fiction fall into two major categories: one emphasizes action and the quest for adventure; the other stresses psychology and the quest for identity. In contemporary writing some interweaving of these themes is fairly common. Tales of the encounters between dauntless heroes and ferocious beasts or savage natives were more typical of the first decades of the century. The simple adventure novel is now out of date; adventure must be weighted with introspection. However, neither the adventure nor the introspection stray very far from the lines laid out by Conrad and Haggard.

The works of Conrad and Haggard are not only prototypes; they have been incorporated into the mystique of Africa. It has become standard literary practice to cite them as if the mention of their names added authenticity and heightened effect to the account. Haggard is regularly invoked as if he were a minor deity, and some writers, Peter Viertel, for example, create the appropriate atmosphere by summoning Conrad.

> When he said "Africa" he seemed to give the word a greater meaning than it had ever had for me. . . . I had the spontaneous feeling of darkness and evil. Everything Conrad had said in thousands of words about the black, stagnant river where Kurtz had died was echoed in Wilson's pronunciation of the name of that continent. I saw twisted trees and jungles and black rivers. . . .[8]

Kipling is not explicitly invoked because he is out of fashion as a writer and because, having written little about Africa, he is not identified with Africa. His stories of the empire in India, however, remain as prototypes for African novels in which colonial administration is the dominant theme and the administrators the major characters. The recent novel *Jimmy Riddle*, by Ian Brook, follows the Kipling model so closely that the band of clever young colonial officials might have stepped right out of *Stalky & Co.*

Joyce Cary is probably the most significant of the twentieth-century British novelists to write about Africa. In view of the low esteem in which Kipling has been held, it may seem like heresy to link Cary to him. But not only are their writings similar in theme and content, they also share to some extent a commitment to empire and a serious concern with its problems. In writing of empire as the arena for the interplay of moral forces, both authors emerge as idealists, advocates of moral purpose rather than power politics. They are sensitive to the ambiguities inherent in British morality and values, to the clash of cultures in the imperial venture and its reflections in human expenditure. Of course, Cary is a modern; his patriotism is muted, his tone ironic, and he shrills no clarion call for empire. Cary, unlike Kipling, is totally lacking in racism. None of his characters can be comfortably categorized as Negro or white, civilized or savage. Every one is a highly idiosyncratic individual. Yet, his portrayals of individuals, African and European, are built out of the traditional conventions by a process of subtle selection.

Cary is not an uncritical advocate of colonialism. He makes his position explicit in his nonfictional work, *The Case for African Freedom*. Scarcely what its title indicates, this book does not support African independence. It is a critique of British colonial administration and a plea for reform and a more enlightened policy.

Certain of the twentieth-century novels are truly anticolonial.[9] Winifred Holtby, Evelyn Waugh, and Gwyn Griffin attack the whole notion of British competence to rule. But even in these novels the portrayal of Africans is entirely conventional. Anticolonialism has little effect on their depiction of Africa and the Africans, for they tend to stress the futility of the attempt to civilize savages. These novelists direct their criticism at the decadence of British culture, and anticolonialism becomes the vehicle by which they express their discontent with the state of the modern world.

A distinct genre of fiction of social protest exists in modern novels of South Africa. The works of Doris Lessing, Nadine Gordimer, Alan Paton, and Dan Jacobson represent some of the most distinguished and widely read fiction about Africa. They exhibit a slight family resemblance to the earlier work of Olive Schreiner in their prevailing humanitarian and egalitarian outlook. Their egalitarianism, however, belongs to the twentieth century and is explicitly antiracist and anti-imperialist. These novels seem irrelevant to a discussion of the British literary tradition about Africa because they are concerned with problems of the multiracial society and not with the image of Africa or the British in Africa.

Doubt and disillusion predominate in much of the recent literature, and they are usually expressed quite apart from any reference to colonialism or race relations. The writers have shifted from the domain of social problems and public issues to the narrower sphere of the individual and his psyche.

Whether the literary approach is based upon the Victorian certainties or upon modern uncertainties, the formal aspects of the tradition are constant. The stereotypes and idioms may have undergone some evaluative revisions, but they remain as the same contrastive conventions. The narrative still emphasizes the confrontation of civilized values with their savage negation.

As fashions in attitudes have changed at least some of the details in the tradition have changed too. Growing secularism has outmoded any concern with the African as "heathen." The Africans are no longer described as ugly, a frequent judgment during the more parochial nineteenth century. A new sophistication has led to appreciation of the beauty of exotic people, and the Africans have come in for their share of admiration.

In general there is an increased awareness of cultural variation among the Africans manifested in frequent and accurate use of ethnographic detail. In a sense the literature reflects the coming of age of anthropology, since the authors pride themselves on the authenticity of their descriptions of tribal customs and history. But modern anthropology only adds detail to the fundamental conceptions which remain traditional.

Alan Scholefield's recent novels about South Africa in the early nineteenth century [10] are precise in their ethnography and history, as well as meticulously preserving the feeling and ethos of the period. The very vocabulary of his characters evokes the time and place with economy and elegance. But the characters themselves are stock figures, familiar through long acquaintance. We meet again the "loyal Bushman boy," first encountered in Pringle, the Zulu berserker, obviously kin to Haggard's Umslopogaas, as well as a duplicate of his venomous old hag who smells out witches. The European characters are also old friends: the young Scottish protagonist seeking his fortune ever deeper in the interior, at peace only away from civilization; the humane old doctor whose passion is specimen-collecting; survivors from the wreck of the *Grosvenor;* and Boers, some patriarchal and others brutal.

Scholefield's novels demonstrate the literary value of the tradition which provides the ingredients for lively novels: the stock characters are nevertheless striking figures, the incidents are exciting, and the setting colorful. In contrast there are some recent novels that have bypassed the tradition. That they are set in Africa is a matter of geographical interest only. Eric Ambler's recent thriller, for example, and a few detective stories are set in an Africa without mystique and incidentally without much interest.[11] In view of the lackluster Africa of the tradition-free novels it is not surprising that writers continue to mine the accumulated riches of the tradition.

Continued conformity to the tradition is not without its problems. Contemporary disapproval of racism forces some alteration in twentieth-century writing. Outright racist ideas are scarcely respectable, and the writers avoid their direct statement. Since they are governed by the tradition, however, they are constrained, despite themselves, to racist evaluations. The authors try to avoid racism while conforming to the conventions by feats of literary gymnastics. For example, Dr. Grantly Dick Read's attempt to combine science and the tradition seems erudite on the surface, but science is defeated by the conventional racial determinism.

> . . . but we must accept again the argument that although environment is one of the strongest influences in the development of the mind, it can never supplant or change the fundamental characteristics of an individual. The environment of the "cultured" European is entirely different from the hereditary environment of the African, but the genetic constitutions of the two peoples remain unaltered.[12]

In attempts to resolve the dilemma caused by the discrepancy between the new attitudes toward race and the exigencies of the literary tradition, authors cite hearsay and anonymous authorities. Stuart Cloete's "doctor" is nameless, but under the guise of scientific authority he provides the writer with seeming validation of the old racist stereotypes.

I had an interesting talk with the doctor who has been eight years in the Congo, about some of the differences between the white man and the black. . . . Actually the differences have not been sufficiently studied, but some believe that the brain and nervous system are as different as the body and organs from those of the white man. This would suggest that the African's development would follow different lines even if he becomes Westernized. The doctor considered that the tribal Africans were satisfied with eating, breeding, fighting and dancing.[13]

Belief in Social Darwinism as explanation of British superiority has collided with the newer doctrines of psychoanalysis. Freud also assumed evolutionary stages of human society, but cast doubts upon the idea that civilization and progress are unequivocally worthwhile. Victorian morality is transmuted into unwholesome repression, religious faith into an illusion, and civilization is marked more by discontent than satisfaction. The literature on Africa translates these concepts into a neo-primitivism that stands the conventions on their heads. The savage African is simple and content, close to nature and the eternal verities. Progress has led only to the destruction of essential human values. The British still find themselves at the top of the evolutionary ladder, but their position there is rapidly becoming unbearable. These concepts have influenced the current shift from social and political issues to psychological concerns. The thread of psychoanalysis which runs through modern writing on Africa is the new significant element in the tradition.

The twentieth-century modifications of the tradition can scarcely be described as revolutionary. They do not alter the basic images of Africa. The most striking feature of all the literature is still the continuity within its governing tradition. The influence of nineteenth-century writing seems to have so shaped concept and preconception of Africa that even the innovations of new ideologies and of highly creative writers are but further elaborations of the tradition rather than departures from it.

By far the most significant development of the tradition in the twentieth century is its formalization. All the elements of the tradition as it appears in current writing were present in the literature of the nineteenth century. Yet the conventions, metaphors, and stereotypes used to describe Africa, the Africans, and the British were unstructured and diffuse. All these separate elements coalesced to become the highly complex and integrated series of images that dominate the twentieth-century literature.

The chapters which follow present an analysis of these images and their interrelations. Each image in the series expresses only one aspect of the total contrast between Africa and England and between the Africans and the English. Each image, however, is an entity in its own right. The depiction of the continent as the setting for the narrative is usually the first and most obvious indication of the particular image the author will establish. It seems expedient, then, to categorize the entire image by the metaphor describing the continent.

CHAPTER V

The Abysmal Gulf

THE fundamental theme in twentieth-century British writing about Africa is that Africa constitutes a world apart. All its features—the land itself, the people, the animals, and the vegetation—are viewed as too alien to be encompassed within the normal rubrics of civilized understanding. Exaggerations of the differences between Africa and Europe make the two continents appear entirely discrete phenomena, lacking any similarity or continuity. Attempted explanations of the cause for this disparity attribute to Africa a unique geology, biology, human history and, indeed, a unique soul. Europe and Africa are envisioned as separate worlds with a deep and abiding gulf between them, and their differences are so irreconcilable that the gulf can never be bridged.

The conventions of this image of the continent focus upon its great antiquity, its formidable size, and its resistance to domestication. These qualities make the essential contrast. Ancient, vast, and wild, Africa is the opposite of small, cozy, industrialized England. These are, to be sure, old and familiar elements of the tradition which now become preconditions for the modern attitude that the Briton is out of his element in Africa. He is intimidated by the foreboding that he and his works will be annihilated.

The notion of Africa's great age recurs in a variety of phrasings and as part of several of the images. The land, the people, the fauna, and the flora are presumed to be relics of some remote era. In this image of the Gulf the convention reinforces the singularity of Africa; no other continent is so old.

Geologically the shield of Africa is old, but not older than other continental shields. The ancient shield of Canada produces literary clichés about Canada's lusty youth. Obviously geological dating has little relevance to the chronology assigned by literary traditions. In fact, geology, like other sciences, simply provides grist for the mill of literary metaphor.

> . . . I begin with the earth of Africa. Now, Africa is old in the longest measure of time on earth. It is old in a way which makes the lovely white mountains in Switzerland not solid immovable matter but waves curling and breaking in the storm of time, wherein even Everest is but the ghostly spume of spray torn by an angry gust from curling breakers. Long before vegetable, organic, or biological matter were in being, the rocks and earth of Africa as we know them today were already formed.[1]

In this passage, Laurens Van der Post grants Africa an inordinately great age and further implies that it has remained throughout time as it was at the beginning. Africa is thus not only old, but unchanging as well. For the modern writer, Max Catto, as it was for Sir Harry Johnston, Africa is a time machine by which to enter the world of antiquity.

> It was all as primitive as the brontosaurus. Life swarmed savagely and voraciously down there, as nakedly ravenous as in those past ages when Africa was formed. . . . "—Go into that forest, I'm telling you, it's like walking back into the beginning of the world." [2]

A world that has endured without change for countless ages does not yield readily to any attempt at alteration. There is a refrain throughout the writing that the British in Africa are out of place and time, temporary intruders, unable to make even a small imprint to mark their passage. Richard Wyndham recounts, "I felt for the first time the fear which a civilized being must experience in a landscape that has not changed since the world began." [3]

Africa's great size, quite real enough, is overstressed in the literature. This exaggeration of size bolsters the idea that it is an unchanging and unyielding land; sheer mass overwhelms man's efforts and sheer space dwarfs him and his ambitious schemes to insignificance. Elspeth Huxley in the following passage seems to have further augmented the oppressive size of Africa by adding to it the Indian Ocean and even India.

. . . Robert . . . stared into the darkness that concealed the vast interior. A hundred, a thousand miles and more it stretched, bush and jungle and desert, away beyond imagination to the swamps of Chad, to forests of the Congo, beyond that again to the headwaters of the Nile, the Mountains of the Moon and the land of the lakes, to reach that ocean which lapped the Indian shore. Confronted with such immensity, his irritation seemed petty, even the elation of the morning absurd. How could one man's foot shake the earth of such a continent.[4]

Vast and ancient, Africa seems impervious to the most strenuous British efforts; it will not permit any inroads of their civilization. Reflecting twentieth-century political changes, the British now write of their feelings of transiency, intimidated by the land over which they had formerly been the confident masters. They see themselves not as conquerors but as trespassers on the alien continent. Many writers echo Lady Packer's cry, "This isn't our place." [5]

The image follows through to its logical culmination; British entry into Africa was fruitless. The gulf is too great, and attempts to bridge it are futile. The artifacts of civilization—buildings, roads, bridges—everything will be obliterated, for they are ephemeral in the face of Africa's permanence.

Conquerors have come and gone. Africa has swallowed them.[6]

How soon would . . . western civilization be devoured by the atavism of the Dark Continent? [7]

Do you realize that quite soon *we* shall be the past? And what will there be to show that we have ever existed? We shall be swallowed up like everything else in a dreadful, sunny limbo.[8]

The land wore these flashy gew-gaws of civilization slightly askew like a comic mask which was always falling down, cracking up, the plaster splitting as the ants and the sun and the roots of the palms and the baobabs and the acacias pushed and ate and gnawed and nagged away at this little pancake of the Western world.[9]

Africa has negated the very spirit of British progress. The optimism of the empire-builders is gone. The British protagonist seems defeated almost before he starts in his attempts to pit himself against the unyielding perdurance of Africa. All the energy, all the will toward change that he brings with him from Britain cannot prevail against the immutability of the Dark Continent. He feels a boundless frustration in his encounter with "that enormous reserve of inertia with which . . . Ethiopia confounds Europe."[10]

The population of Africa, across the fathomless abyss, is as antithetical to the English as the continent itself is to England. The Africans are too alien, too different even to be understood. Their languages, their cultures, their mentality belong to an entirely different order of humanity. No Englishman, despite long residence in Africa and close contact with the people, can hope to comprehend them. Those who believe they do understand the Africans are deluding themselves, for the core of African character is so enigmatic that it is simply unintelligible to the European. Statements to this effect occur in almost every modern book on Africa.

If the Africans are a mystery to the British, the British are equally inexplicable to the Africans. According to John Rowan Wilson, for example, they find the British utterly bewildering and understand nothing of their behavior or their point of view.

> He was a phenomenon totally incomprehensible to them . . . what can he have represented to men to whom the last 2,000 years, which had produced him, were totally unknown? They could not dispute with him. When he tried to explain what he was doing, they stood before him, understanding nothing. . . . There was no judgement available to them but that of their emotions, primitive, amorphous; no weapon but that of force. . . .[11]

The literature frequently alleges that the very thought processes of the African and the British are of a different nature. There are solemn discussions which describe the "round mind" of the Africans, proferring as evidence their predilection for the curved line —round houses, curvilinear designs, winding pathways, and irregular plowing. Numerous statements aver that Africans are unable to do anything in a straight line, and this is interpreted as indicative of the strangeness and inferiority of African mentality.

Because of his "round mind" the African is forever barred from attaining full participation in straightforward, right-thinking Western civilization.

Culturally determined motor habits and styles are thus defined as innate inadequacies. In reality, not all Africans are biased in favor of curved lines. In West and Central Africa the houses are rectangular, and straight-line designs are common. The problem, in any case, is not one of the "African mind," but rather refers to a cultural tradition which conditions the manner of all perception and execution.

The writers ignore the factors of cultural conditioning. They base the lack of mutual understanding on the accepted myths of immutable inherited characteristics. Their facile reliance upon heredity indicates that biological determinism is still a bedrock of the twentieth-century tradition. Culture, character, and temperament are still taken to be inherent traits carried in the "blood." Anything from craftsmanship to violence to superstition can, at the author's discretion, be attributed to the blood line. Augustus Collodon's statement on the genetics of cannibalism differs from the similar statements of others only in its blatant absurdity.

> These two boys came from cannibal stock. In their blood was the hereditary taint that no civilization or education could eradicate. When a cannibal instinct came to the surface, we were shocked, horrified, disgusted and revengeful—but really the fault was our own. If we had treated them all along as cannibals we would have known what to expect. It was because we ourselves invested them with a higher-than-cannibal mentality that they disappointed us so dreadfully. . . . You can't turn a horse into a camel.[12]

Apparently "blood" is not only a cause, it is the only cause. Cultural conditioning, life-experience, and sheer chance count for little. Despite the widespread interest in psychology, there seems no need to refer to any of the other factors that shape personality. The highly individuated psyches of the Europeans often receive a rather tender regard. The Africans, however, share a tribal psyche, and the conventional stereotypes of tribe and race suffice to portray and to explain the individual. Membership in a tribe confers upon the individual his talents, virtues, and vices; his traits and those of the group are one and the same. Deviation from the tribal stereotype, when given any recognition, is explained by mixed blood lines. Thus, Isak Dinesen entirely discounts the effects of both maturation and learning in favor of heredity.

> Kaninu [a Kikuyu] presented Kabere to me in a jovial manner, but at heart he was a little frightened of his recovered son. He had reason to be so, for the Masai had had from the farm a small lamb and now gave us back a young leopard. Kabere must have had Masai blood in him, the habits and discipline of Masai life could not in themselves have worked the metamorphosis. Here he stood, a Masai from head to foot.[13]

Rather fanciful excursions into history are undertaken to provide appropriate mixed ancestry for tribes that cannot be made to fit the racial stereotypes. Since only base and simple qualities are thought to be indigenous to Africa, the more subtle traits and the more admirable characteristics must have originated elsewhere. Richard Llewellyn, for example, enamored of the Masai, finds for them an ancient Roman ancestry. Stuart Cloete provides northern Nigerians with Chinese forebears. Lineage-hunting is a popular literary sport. The blood mixture that occurred in a long-ago, imaginary past is apparently the only interbreeding that is viewed favorably. Actual interbreeding between Africans and Europeans, past or present, can have only deleterious effects, for in the genetics of the tradition vices are dominant traits and virtues recessive.

From a biological point of view, interbreeding is an obvious mechanism for creating intermediate linking types, but in the literature it is not permitted to serve as a bridge across the gulf. African and European are far too disparate to produce wholesome offspring, and the hybrid is seen as a biological failure. Should the half-breed possess admirable qualities he is still considered an anomaly, something of an unnatural phenomenon. The essential wrongness of a mixed union surrounds its issue with an aura of either tragedy or pathos. The writers no longer evince the active distaste toward the hybrid so typical of the imperial period. They now write of him more in sorrow than in anger.

The differences between the Africans and the English can no more be overcome by education than by race mixture. The writers are convinced that the African should learn to behave like an Englishman. They are equally convinced that he is inherently incapable of doing so. The long period of contact has resulted in African acculturation and a new Westernized elite. Nevertheless, the idea that acculturation is spurious and superficial remains a secure tenet of belief.

The tradition assigns the African to a lower order, one dominated by instinct and by inability to reason or to cope with abstractions. So inferior a being can never master the subtle complexities essential to civilization, although he may acquire the outward trappings—clothing, adornments, and gadgetry—of Western culture. Thus attired, bedecked, and equipped, he is but the caricature of a civilized man. Graham Greene found the behavior of the acculturated Creoles of Sierra Leone to be a painful travesty.

> . . . they were expected to play the part like white men and the more they copied white men the more funny it was. . . . They were withered by laughter; the more desperately they tried to regain their dignity, the funnier they became. . . .
>
> It would be so much more amusing if it was all untrue, a fictitious skit on English methods of colonization. But one cannot continue long to find the Creoles' playful attempts at playing the white man funny; it is rather like the chimpanzee's teaparty, the joke is all on one side.[14]

The simple African is satisfied merely to ape white man's behavior. He believes that mimicry of speech and manners makes of him a civilized man, but he can have no comprehension of the underlying concepts and codes. Without these, there is no civilization. There is but a shoddy facsimile, a veneer over the essential savage.

The writers admit that certain aspects of civilization have been accepted by the Africans. They go on to say, however, that the qualities that mark these as civilized are somehow lost in the very process of acceptance. African adoption of any European institution reduces it to their level of savagery. By far the most striking accounts of such debasement are related as the transformation of Christianity into what amounts to no more than a bloody juju. Elements of Christian ritual are unmistakably retained, but their meaning is lost. The theme of Christianity corrupted is an important component of Joyce Cary's *Aissa Saved* and Elspeth Huxley's *Red Rock Wilderness.* The most sensational episodes in *The Tribe that Lost Its Head* by Nicholas Monsarrat depict such debased rituals.

> . . . the crowds lining the sides of the fish emblem fell silent. The old man . . . lay down upon the cross unasked and stretched out his hands to suffer the nails. The priests chanted in time with the pounding of the wooden mallets; presently the cross was raised up, and either side of it the two smaller crosses with the "thieves," the goats that were also dying. . . .
>
> When he was quite dead, the head priest took command, and directed the cutting and sharing of the body . . . all the tribe now gathered close; the small slices of flesh were passed round, and they spoke the hallowed words which had come down to them from misty times: "eat this in remembrance of me." They had long been taught that this was the very strongest part of the magic.[15]

The African is victimized first by his piecemeal acculturation and then from the fundamental conflict between the values of European and African cultures. The cultural disparity is more profound than mere difference in customary patterns of behavior. The tribal culture of the African is innate, the result of genetic transmission. The Westernized African is seen as doomed to profound frustration because he is, in effect, trying to operate against his own grain.

> . . . he [the Western-educated African] is himself completely entangled in this intermixture of opposing cultures. He remains truly a man of two worlds, anxiously absorbing all things new, feverishly groping for the white man's "know-how," yet never quite able to free himself from the compelling forces of his environment and the dark inheritance of his fore-fathers.[16]

In a number of novels the disastrous consequences of Westernization for the individual is a major theme. The best known is probably Joyce Cary's *Mister Johnson.* The protagonist's bafflement in the face of the two cultures isolates and finally destroys him. Mr. Johnson's predicament can seemingly be traced to his ebullient temperament and lack of sophistication, but in another of Cary's novels, *The African Witch,* a brilliant Oxford scholar returning to his tribal home suffers a similar confusion resolved only by death. One of the heroes of the more recent novel, *The Brothers M* by Tom Stacey, is a MuGanda, completely at home in an English university, learned, popular, and aware of his marginal position. Yet his awareness cannot protect him from the clash of cultural values, and he, too, goes insane and dies.

Westernization is more often seen as corrupting, rather than destroying. And this is a convention carried over from the height of empire without change. European vices, apparently more attractive than European virtues, are more readily acquired. The tribal African, however savage, was secure in his society and, more important, subject to its disciplines. With the adoption of Western ways, he rejects tribal custom, and freed from customary discipline, the detribalized African becomes little more than a bundle of vices.

It is, then, apparent that Westernization, like hybridization, fails as a means to bridge the gulf. Since only "horrid hybrids," "caricatures," and "corrupted savages" result from attempts to overcome the differences, such attempts should never have been made. That the uncivilized, racially pure savage is more acceptable to the Europeans is evidenced by a current literary trend toward a diluted neo-primitivism. If the unacculturated African is not depicted as a noble savage he is, at least, shown to be superior to the acculturated African. The "bush" African has remained a savage, yet he is a whole man; as his tribe is intact so is his own identity. Greene and Cary present the generally held view that an integrated and intact savage, no matter how childish or brutal, is better than a confused marginal man.

The Englishmen here didn't talk about the "bloody blacks" nor did they patronize or laugh at them; they had to deal with the real native and not the Creole, and the real native was someone to love and admire.[17]

> I, too, preferred the naked savage to the mission boy, with his scraps of second-rate knowledge, his attempts to copy the white man. . . . I, too, said "European civilization, so called, is the ruin of these people" . . . ten minutes in a company store could change a warrior fit for a Parthenon pediment into a nigger minstrel. . . .[18]

Probably the greatest virtue attributed to the "bush" African is his acceptance of his subordinate place in the scheme of things. This scheme had been the social order envisioned by the imperial British in which, properly reflecting the natural order, the inferior African and the superior British played out their complementary roles. Such a social structure requires the maintenance of social distance between the superordinate and the subordinate. Insistence upon the Gulf is a device which keeps the separation intact. The Westernized African is a contradiction to the validity of the social order and the reality of its supporting myth. The expedient response is to deny the success of his acculturation.

The image of the unbridgeable Gulf, though it rationalized colonialism, ran counter to the ideology of the Dual Mandate. The Dual Mandate was not committed to the preservation of a static imperialism, but rather to the principle that the British were in Africa with the mission to civilize. The British took upon themselves the responsibility of elevating the Africans to their own level. This policy posed the insoluble problem of reconciling the attempt to create equality with the necessity of maintaining inequality. The dilemma is made vivid by this literary image which phrases the problem as the question: How can one civilize the uncivilizable? And resolves it with an unequivocal statement that it can not be done and should not have been attempted.

Throughout their history in Africa, the British thought of themselves as benefactors. If they could not bring enlightenment to the African, then the role of the British in Africa was a purely exploitive one. They resist seeing themselves, even in retrospect, as self-seeking conquerors. The question then to be faced is what had they been doing in Africa at all. The answer provided by the image of the Gulf is pessimistic and disillusioned: they have been and are in Africa for nothing. They have profited neither themselves nor the Africans. It has all been a waste, their efforts futile, their works evanescent.

CHAPTER VI

The Dark Labyrinth

THE Dark Labyrinth is the modern extension of the Dark Continent that gives the old synonym a new psychological dimension. The older classical image reflected geographical ignorance which fantasy filled in with marvels and monstrosities. Although the map is no longer blank, Africa is still presented as a strange and mysterious land. So unfamiliar, so utterly alien, seems the continent on the other side of the gulf, that the Briton must grope his way as though he were in a maze.

Like the ancient Cretan labyrinth the African maze conceals a mystery at its center. The "heart of darkness" holds the answers to the questions which perplex the modern Theseus: questions about his own identity and the meaning of life and death. Elspeth Huxley writes that where once Europeans were drawn to Africa to unravel its geographical mysteries, they now seek there revelations about themselves.

> Older explorers went to seek the source of rivers and to map their tributaries. Today one seeks the source of human conduct and tries to map the course of history.[1]

The lure of Africa is its mystery—once geographical, now psychological. The map of Africa itself carries enchantment. It is never merely a geographical chart; the writers project upon it personal imagery expressing mystery and threat, and their fascination with both. They seem pleased to find astonishing blanks and inadequacies even in modern maps, and each blank or error exercises a pull toward the unknown. Thus Greene describes the maps of Liberia.

I could find only two large-scale maps for sale. One, issued by the British General Staff, quite openly confesses ignorance; there is a large white space covering the greater part of the Republic, with a few dotted lines indicating conjectured course of rivers (incorrectly I usually found) and a fringe of names along the boundary. . . . The other map is issued by the United States War Department. There is a dashing quality about it; it shows a vigorous imagination. Where the English map is content to leave a blank space, the American in large letters fills it with the word "cannibals." It has no use for dotted lines and confessions of ignorance; it is so inaccurate that it would be useless, perhaps even dangerous to follow it, though there is something Elizabethan in its imagination. "Dense forest"; "Cannibals"; rivers which don't exist . . . one expects to find Eldorado, two-headed men and fabulous beasts represented in the Gola Forest.[2]

Greene is reluctant to give up "the imaginative Elizabethan quality" in African cartography. In his most recent book on Africa, he rejects the scientific filling of the blank spaces and remains committed to the older inadequacies. Africa is each man's unexplored continent which he alone must discover; no one else may interpret it for him: ". . . Africa will always be the Africa of the Victorian atlas, the blank unexplored continent, the shape of the human heart."[3]

From early times the lure of Africa has been a staple of the tradition. The lure is paradoxical, however, in view of the present image of the continent; for it is as sinister and evil as it is mysterious. Cullen Gouldsbury hints that Africa offers fulfillment of a wish for death, and this promise is a potent part, or perhaps even the essence of the lure.

Perhaps indeed, it is from this very terror that the charm, deadly as it is, proceeds. Think of the death-roll of the early years—from 1875 onwards, let us say; reckon up the number of those invalided from the ranks of officials and missionaries alike. How many men have succumbed to the sinister influences of the country? And yet, many a man invalided through black-water or some similar cause has crept back again to the country to die. . . .[4]

The call of Africa is the insistent voice of the "dark gods."[5] No experience of disaster is sufficient to quell the fascination; the "dark gods" do not relinquish their hold. They are omnipotent, awful, almost satanic in their power, and are the symbols of the malevolent forces of Africa. They have not been driven out by Western civilization, but have merely withdrawn into the shadows of mystery to await their own inevitable return. Raymond Tong depicts the approaches to Benin in these terms.

The better we came to know Benin and its forests, the more we felt that they were a fitting background for the machinations of dark and cunning sylvan gods. Sometimes we came upon patches of bush where every shadow seemed to harbour a mysterious, malevolent shape. Often even a slight trembling in the undergrowth was enough to suggest the presence of strange, unseen powers. Long before we knew the names of the gods, it seemed that we had made their acquaintance.[6]

The image of the Dark Labyrinth in the main refers to the tropical rain forest and swamps. As the "White Man's Grave" they were invested by the earliest writers, and ever after, with a sinister and terrible quality. The hot, moist lowlands were unwholesome and uncongenial, causing more distress to the English than any other environment. The misery, discomfort, and disease they suffered are projected upon the continent: Africa is evil.

When the landscape impresses the writers with beauty or grandeur, its very beauty is presented as the crowning touch of horror, since the fair surface treacherously masks underlying evil. Under the placid exterior there is a pullulating life which feeds on itself —devouring or being devoured. Death and violence emanate from the very atmosphere of such a land.

Violence is what you might call indigenous to this soil. It is part of the landscape. While you slept the jackals were hunting, the antelope dying and the ants have been out scavenging the mess. It's blood that fertilizes this soil.[7]

This excerpt from a Catto novel underlines the violence of Africa and serves to introduce the convention of the "blood-soaked soil of Africa." It is one of the key conventions of the Dark Labyrinth and has been sensationally exploited by many writers. So much blood has been shed in the course of Africa's long history, they say, that the land is polluted with blood. This image also plays upon Africa's great age, so that Monsarrat says it is "perhaps the oldest country in the world, old as the oldest bones of foully murdered men, old as sin itself." [8]

The "blood-soaked soil of Africa" serves as a basic premise for the literary reconstruction of African history. Richard Wyndham asks in all seriousness: "What was happening in Wau several thousand years ago? Was it some obscene sacrifice, some unbearable torture that gave this place its name?" [9] Wyndham's pun merits consideration only because it is an example of the traditional tendency to seize upon any item, no matter how innocuous, and convert it into something bloodcurdling. A simple place name, a stone ruin, the twisting course of a river—all conjure up a bloodstained past. The writers create a gruesome pseudo-history which feeds upon and, in turn, reinforces the nightmare aspects of the image.

> Everything except for the garishly painted front of the ju-ju house was plain and simple. There was nothing to get hold of except that, in spite of the bright sunshine, the place was sinister. What had taken place on this clean-swept, leaf-dappled yard? What else was there in those huts that we had not seen? Human skulls hidden in the thatch or dangling from strings almost certainly. But how old were they? [10]

In this passage the illusion of the sinister overshadows what was actually observed. Cloete saw "the painted house," the "bright sunshine," and the "clean-swept leaf-dappled yard." From there on, preconception and fantasy take over. He perceives the sinister in what he does not see and then speculates on its age. Cloete is not unique in such imaginative powers; many writers see that which is invisible and impute evil to what is not there. Apparently evil, like beauty, is in the eye of the beholder.

The Dark Labyrinth epitomizes the savagery of untamed nature, and the native inhabitants of the Labyrinth are fittingly depicted as the human counterpart of nature in the raw. Thus Winifred Holtby writes of the cruel savagery of both man and nature in Africa.

He might wake up one night and find himself ill and desolate, utterly alone in a savage land and horrible place, where men killed and hated and tortured each other, where nothing tender nor green nor beautiful had life, and where even Talal, the man he had called his friend, touched him with cruel, blood-stained fingers.[11]

In describing the Africans, the writers frequently refer to the "tribal mind," but the Labyrinth permits neither tribe nor mind. What is really meant is animal instinct and racial memory. The pan-African "tribal mind" is as dark, as labyrinthine, and as filled with assorted horrors as the continent. The African is dominated by instincts which make him sensual, cruel, bloodthirsty, unthinking, and fear-ridden. All behavior is the expression of these instincts, and all African culture consists merely of such behavior in institutionalized form.

Certain African customs were particular stimuli for British fantasy, since they seem to best exemplify the workings of "savage instinct." The writers seize upon aspects of religion and art and detach them from their cultural matrix and their actual significance. Ritual elements such as sacrifice, cannibalism, drumming, and dancing are removed from their context and so overblown that they are made to represent the totality of African life.

Earlier in the century, writers had occasionally witnessed human sacrifice, and even then less frequently than their writings would indicate. Modern writers have never seen it but, relying on the older accounts and hearsay, give it undue significance. Human sacrifice is admitted only as an isolated element, not as an element of ritual within a total religious system. So its cultural significance is ignored and its meaning sensationalized into a literary fantasy of savage blood lust.

Whenever African religion is discussed, it is presented primarily as phallicism shot through with fear. The "tribal mind" has created religions, rituals, and gods in its own fear-ridden image. Cloete sees African religion as a fearsome package of blood, fertility, and destruction.

In the mind of the African there exists a curious area where propagation—the fertility of men, beast and field is mixed up with the blood of sacrifice, ritual murder, cannibalism and the gods and spirits of his ancestors, any of which, unless propitiated, will destroy him.[12]

Not only religion, but all African life is permeated with fear. It inevitably accompanies blood lust and cruelty, and the Africans appear as the cowering victims of their own terrible instincts. In the view of many writers, fear is the predominant emotion which colors all African behavior. For example, Ronald Hardy states that the Africans have "Minds peopled with shapes and horrors beyond our conception. Negroid minds, Negro blood running straight out of a past thick with violence, and fear and death." [13]

The capstone to discussions of cruelty and blood lust is the perennial topic of cannibalism. The literary play upon this theme reached its apex during the height of empire and has since diminished little, if at all. The extent of cannibalism in the literature, even now, gives the impression that it is a major industry, and that human flesh was once, if it is no longer, a staple in the diet of most Africans. Of all the writers, only Talbot Mundy seems to have appreciated the effects of the law of diminishing returns. In *The Ivory Trail* he indicates that a whole tribe of ferocious cannibals had to turn to vegetarianism since they had eaten up everybody in the vicinity.[14] Unwilling to relinquish a pet theme, the writers continue to find cannibals everywhere. Modern authors tend to be self-consciously broad-minded about it, attributing anthropophagous tendencies to basic nutritional needs for salt, sugar, or protein, rather than to a depraved taste for human flesh. In some cases cannibalism is dealt with in a jocular manner; in others it climaxes the accounts of African instinctive blood lust. Whether comical, sensible, or horrible, cannibalism provides an ever available sensational embellishment to a narrative.

Neither reason, intellect, nor learning are thought to play any role in African life. Over and over again the Africans are described as unable to think in abstract terms, as lacking any notion of time or of the relationship between cause and effect, symbol and object. Griffin goes so far as to indicate that the African is almost without capacity for true language.

Simon found the English language infinitely difficult and complex. He was always at a strained attention to catch the meanings of sentences;

for his own unwritten tongue, a crude series of grunted monosyllables was used only to express the most direct and concrete things. Abstractions and propositions were as much beyond his grasp as the most delicate irony or subtle wit.[15]

The conventional literary treatment of African arts is a striking negation of intelligence and creativity, for the African artist is supposed to produce art only out of the wellsprings of race and instinct. Since the writers see no evidence of purposeful design, esthetic canon, individual talent, or training, they are, in effect, denying the existence of any creative art in Africa. What passes for art is but the expression of innate Africanism that, as Elspeth Huxley points out, mirrors the nightmare tribal mind.

The Palm Wine Drinkard is a folk tale, full of the queer, distorted poetry, the deep and dreadful fears, the cruelty, the obsession with death and spirits, the macabre humour, the grotesque imagery of the African mind.

African art, if it is genuine, is never comfortable, noble, or serene; perhaps for that reason it may never reach the heights—rather will it explore the depths of fear, torment and intimidation, with a relish of humour. It is possessed by spirits and the spirits are malign.[16]

A few writers such as Geoffrey Gorer, Graham Greene, and Raymond Tong have a healthy respect for the artistic merits of African carving and sculpture. They are aware of variation in form, materials, and style as well as the skill and talents of the individual artist. But they are exceptional, and for the most part the writers perceive the masks and figures only as grotesque or gruesome cult fetishes. Thus relegated to the realm of superstition and witchcraft, they are withdrawn from the purlieu of art. Music receives considerably more attention than do the plastic arts, but it, too, cannot be considered an art form, since the authors always describe it as the spontaneous outpouring of a particularly African instinct. For example, Catto indicates that "there is something about the African that preconditions him to rhythm," and that all Africans sing "because it was natural for black men to sing in the sun." [17]

Of all the arts, African drumming seems to have most captured the imagination of the British writers. They have transmuted the sound of the drums into the voice of Africa itself; "the throbbing of the Black Giant's heart," "the authentic sound of Africa," "the real voice . . . of the forest." [18] Huxley feels that the drums evoke the dark and terrible nature of Africa, for the beat of the drums

> . . . throbs in the blood like an old wound. It dries the mouth and weakens the bowels. It is something that has come down to us from our ancient origins in forest and swamp, and that still keeps its power over man in the darkness, and in danger and alone.[19]

Africa's role in the traditional literature has always been as stimulus for European response. This is nowhere more evident than in descriptions of African dancing. In the literature of the past the British were amused or appalled spectators, detached, if disapproving. The modern British writers are anything but detached. They dismiss the dance itself as instinctive, an orgiastic shake and shuffle, but they dwell on their own reactions to it. They are, indeed, responsive, and somewhat taken aback to find that their responses are intensely sexual. Unexpectedly the British participate in the sensuality they have attributed to the Africans.

> . . . the deep drum voices little hands in her belly, breaking down her European guard, the cold withdrawn planning of the correct thing, the respectable word and deed. She wanted to run about, spin, shake, laughing in release as the thunder shook her.[20]

The most striking modern development of the literary tradition —the transformation of the Dark Continent into the Dark Labyrinth—came about in the 1930's as a result of modern psychological orientation. The writers in this genre use the contrastive conventions to illuminate the nature of humanity rather than to focus upon British superiorities. This trend derives from Conrad and was further stimulated by the influence of psychoanalytic theories. On the continent the influence of Conrad was felt somewhat earlier than in England. In France, André Gide's *Voyage au Congo* and *Le Retour du Tschad*, and in Germany, the novel *Das Reise ins Innere*, by Kurt Heuser, both bearing the mark of Conrad, were published in the 1920's. In England the first, and still the most outstanding, writer in the Conrad tradition is Graham Greene—many other writers, among them David Caute, Gwyn Griffin, Gerald Hanley, Richard Llewellyn, Tom Stacey, and Laurens Van der Post (since the publication of Greene's *Journey Without Maps* in 1936) have become heirs of Conrad.

The transformation adds a new dimension to the image of the Africans; the brutish African is now cast in a universal role. He symbolizes the essential brute inherent in all mankind. This use of the conventions gives a different meaning to the term "brute" than it had earlier. It is not now merely pejorative, something to be expunged, exploited, or changed, but a basic component of all human nature. In this sense the African symbolizes the vitality and strength more than the horrors of animality.

The positive values presently attached to brute savagery correlates with changes in the British self-image. The Briton is no longer the adventurous emissary of civilization, certain of its values and his own. The modern British traveler in Africa is a rather shaky Theseus wandering forth, estranged from his homeland and from himself. His malaise with civilization has propelled him to Africa, where human nature is still undisguised. He journeys into the labyrinth in quest of renewed contact with the sources of his own being. The following passages are from Greene's travel book, *Journey Without Maps,* but the ideas are central to his novels about Africa as well.

Today our world seems peculiarly susceptible to brutality. There is a touch of nostalgia in the pleasure we take in gangster novels, in characters who have so agreeably simplified their emotions that they have begun living again at a level below the cerebral. We . . . are living after a war and a revolution. . . . It is not that one wishes to stay forever at that level but when one sees to what unhappiness, to what peril of extinction centuries of cerebration have brought us, one sometimes has a curiosity to discover if one can see from where we have come, to recall at which point we went astray.

I thought for some reason even then of Africa, not a particular place, but a shape, a strangeness, a wanting to know. . . . I have written "a shape" and the shape, of course, is roughly that of the human heart.[21]

The books which are oriented around the image of the Labyrinth depict civilization as a repressive or even destructive force, and civilized men as its crippled and suffering victims. In contrast, the African represents the natural, undefiled man. He is not cerebral; he does not repress sexuality or any other instinct. He is able to maintain a firm faith in his religion and, above all, is inextricably one with nature and his society. The instinctive African affirmation of life, says Van der Post, is to be envied.

> One fact alone which seemed to me of an inspired significance was that, no matter how grim the fate or circumstances, no matter how meagre the scrap of living allowed to him, life was always worth it and worth fighting for to the end. Such natural aristocracy of the spirit alone, I would have thought, should commend attention in an age which, despite its advantages and comforts, has seen such a lowering in the human beings' sense of the value of life that he is increasingly inclined to take his own.[22]

Formerly despised characteristics of the Africans have become the object of the British quest. Contact with the elemental in Africa is sought as a means of resolving the problems of the anomic protagonist. The heart of the narrative is always the quest for reaffirmation of self and faith. Modern biographers have even reinterpreted the motivations of the nineteenth-century men of action, so that their explorations in Africa are now seen as a search for personal and universal meaning. Moorehead, writing in 1960, transforms Livingstone's "geographer's itch" into a psychological quest.

> . . . perhaps now in his loneliness the river had begun to assume for him a religious significance. This last effort was to be more than a journey to the lost fountains. It was to be a revelation and a justification of everything he had lived and prayed for, a proof of himself and . . . his faith.[23]

The journey through the labyrinth results in a confrontation with ultimate truth. The final knowledge may hold no hope, help, or comfort. It may be a truth too horrible to be endured, as Kurtz tragically encountered in *Heart of Darkness*. A similar revelation proved the undoing of the heroes of Huxley's *Red Rock Wilderness* and Stacey's *Brothers M*. The essential confrontation with disillusion is expressed in the following poetic passage by Powys.

> Africa, like one of her own blackmaned lions, laps up the life-blood of all the delicate illusions that have for so long danced before the eyes of men and made them happy. Truth alone is left alive. What was subjective in Europe is made plain here: at the bottom of the well of life there is no hope.[24]

Despairing climaxes do not make for happy reading, so that even when Conrad's basic theme is followed, it is not the usual literary practice to follow it all the way. In Greene's novels, for example, the heroes' deaths are accompanied by transfiguration, but more often the modern Theseus emerges alive from his encounter in the African labyrinth, a new and better man.

The uncertainties which beset modern men are very clearly reflected in discussions of African magic and witchcraft. Loss of faith in Christianity and dissatisfaction with science leave the way open for a willing credulity about African supernatural powers. Most English writers report that they feel themselves compelled to suspend disbelief in the efficacy of African supernaturalism. There is a tacit gratification that belief is thus compelled, an implicit groping at the coattails of any kind of manifestation of faith and an envy of the Africans whose belief seems secure.

Thus European doubts and vulnerabilities are projected onto Africa, the new map of the unconscious. The journey, the quest, the venture into Africa are converted into explorations of the psyche. To Greene, the African journey is the substitute for the analyst's couch.

> The method of psychoanalysis is to bring the patient back to the idea he is repressing; a long journey backwards without maps, catching a clue here and a clue there, as I caught the names of villages from this man or that, until one has to face the general idea, the pain or the memory. This is what you have feared, Africa may be imagined as saying, you can't avoid it . . . you can't turn your back, you can't forget it, so you may as well take a long look. . . .

But what had astonished me about Africa was that it had never really been strange. . . . The "heart of darkness" was common to us both. Freud has made us conscious as we have never been before of those ancestral threads which still exist in our unconscious minds to lead us back. The need, of course, has always been felt, to go back and begin again. Mungo Park, Livingstone, Stanley, Rimbaud, Conrad, represented only another method of Freud's, a more costly, less easy method, calling for physical as well as mental strength. The writers, Rimbaud and Conrad, were conscious of this purpose, but one is not certain how far the explorers knew the nature of the fascination which worked on them in the dirt, the disease, the barbarity and the familiarity of Africa.[25]

The writings of Laurens Van der Post deserve special consideration, since he has given the most vivid portrayals of Africa and the Africans since Haggard. He has recaptured the wonder of the Africa of the early explorers. Africa is his homeland to which he feels deeply committed, and Van der Post sees it with heightened awareness. Other writers in this genre describe Africa mainly as a catalyst for European renascence. The Africans, though envied for their instinctual life, nevertheless remain in their customary role as background figures. But Van der Post gives Africa and the Africans new significance by his metaphor of the "mirror" in which the European must look to find his other self, the African. Thus he reworks the conventions of the subcerebral brute to confer upon the African a new status, that of the European Id. The African is transformed from an incidental figure in the landscape to the embodiment of the racial childhood and the racial Id of all men.

. . . he gave these children of African nature, the consideration and affection he would have liked to give his own, dark unfulfilled self, only centuries of so-called English civilized values prevented him from doing this. We all have a dark figure within ourselves, the Negro, the gipsy, an aboriginal with averted back, and the nearest many of us can get to making terms with him, is to strike up these vicarious friendships with him through the black people of Africa.[26]

For most of the psychologically oriented writers Africa is the Labyrinth, and at its center is the African who represents the lost, natural self. Once contact with that self has been made and accepted, transfiguration frees the European from Africa. His need for it is over and he may continue his life, though with renewed self-acceptance, away from the scene of his quest. Van der Post, on the other hand, maintains that the contact and awareness of "the dark figure within ourselves" must be an enduring relationship, and the European can no more be free of Africa than he can be detached from his own Id.

The new wine of psychology has been poured into the old bottles of imperialist conventions. For as the African is converted into the European's Id, he is as ever the contrastive figure. The European, though no longer the superior individual, is, however, the personification of the human ego and superego. Stripped of Jungian concepts, Van der Post echoes the well-intentioned apologists for empire; the European owes the African the benefits of his own enlightenment, and the African needs and welcomes the guidance of the civilized white man.

> There is a whole natural language of the spirit that we have lost and can no longer receive or read. . . . I believe one way of rediscovering that language is for us to honour the primitive man in our societies; not to reject him any longer, but to lend him the light of our own reason and the shelter of our own conscious knowledge.[27]

> . . . I think the initial readiness of the black man to serve the white man was perhaps because, unconsciously, he had long waited for someone like the white man to come and bring him something which only the white man could provide. So, when he did come, it was as if it was in answer to some dream far back in the African mind and in response to some deep submerged hope that Africa had of the future.[28]

The difference, however, between the older imperialist view and the new psychological orientation lies in the concept that the white man also needs the African. The path to salvation lies not in repression but in awareness of the Id and full acceptance of the African as its symbol.

CHAPTER VII

The Strange Woman

ANOTHER twentieth-century image stemming from that hardy perennial, the Dark Continent, personifies Africa as a woman. In it is expressed the quintessence of the lure of Africa, for the continent appears as an irresistible woman, but one whose beauty is a snare and an enticement to destruction. Like "the strange woman" of the Book of Proverbs, "many strong men have been slain by her. Her house is the way to Hell." Sex has enlivened the old image almost out of recognition. The following passage from Marguerite Steen's best-selling novel, *The Sun Is My Undoing*, demonstrates the metamorphosis.

> Africa is a woman, a dark devastating witch of a woman, coiling herself around you like a snake, making you forget everything but her burning breasts. . . . Listen to the drums of Africa . . . reminding every man of things he forgot—when he left his mother's womb.[1]

English idiom readily suggests parallels between acts of conquest and of sex, between the conquered country and the raped woman. It is, therefore, not surprising that one of the frequent metaphors should depict Africa as the ravished dark woman. Although Margery Perham and Jack Simmons are scholarly writers, in their introduction to *African Discovery* they follow the literary tradition in the use of this image.

> Africa is allowed at times her beauties but the general impression . . . is one of caprice, of treachery, of violent extremes, and of hostility to men, which combined with the allure which held them, has suggested the dark slave, ravished, beautiful but untameable.[2]

It is commonplace enough to personify a land as feminine, most often in terms of a nurturing earth-mother. When, however, Africa is described as generatrix it is hardly a maternal image. Most often the personification stops short with reproduction itself. She is not the fertile mother, but the fecund womb which spawns rather than gives birth. What is spawned is as monstrous as the mother. Steen writes of ". . . the black African womb that now prepared, with its expansions and contractions, to usher into the world some unspeakable foetus implanted by one of its antique gods."[3] Cloete makes something truly terrible of the fecundity of Africa.

> This was the womb of the world her dark, moist womb. This was a breeding place, a spawning place, lush, dark, hot, fetid—a place where tremendous mushrooms grew in a night; where flights of locusts blackened the sky . . . where everything was strangled by its own fecundity. Lianas choking the trees with their thick brown arms, garroting them; where orchids in a scentless decadent surrealism clung to dying trees.[4]

Whether mother or mistress, Africa is never gentle or cherishing. Love for Africa is fruitless, for her charms entice only to thwart. The lover remains under her spell despite intimidation and frustration, enthralled even as he awaits his impending destruction.

The women of Africa are incorporated into the fantasy, and they, in turn, become symbols of what is projected upon the continent. Cloete, for example, shifts directly from a metaphor about the continent to a blunt comment about the women.

> One is suddenly aware of the immense fecundity and sexuality of Africa. Many of the women were beautiful once you became used to African beauty. One could see why white men took them as housekeepers. They were all woman. They were, in a sense, without souls. . . . They were bold and without innocence. They said with their dark eyes: We are women. You are a man. We know what you want.[5]

The British have had minimal contact with African women and hence have little firsthand knowledge of them. The writing displays almost no awareness of the complex nature of the social roles of women within African societies. The women of Africa are stereotyped as creatures that are all body, without mind or soul. This delineation results from a convergence of independent stereotypes, that of the mindless, instinctual African and the Victorian (and still viable) concept of women in general. Once the icing of Victorian gentility is removed from that stereotype, what remains is the concept of women as the inferiors of men. Being passive, without intelligence, narrow in interests and understanding, women are fit only for the subservient roles of housekeeper and breeder.

The subordinate status of all Africans obviously precludes the possibility that an African woman may ever be considered a lady. She is, then, thought of as the embodiment of the inferior qualities of womanhood, compounding the mindlessness of women with the mindlessness of Africans. This notion Joyce Cary very deftly conveys in the following passage.

> The girls and women know that the speech is none of their business. They will do what they are told. They fix their sleepy eyes on the speaker and allow their usual train of feelings to continue.[6]

What is observed of women in African villages appears to be limited to their seemingly continuous labor: working in the fields, marketing, carrying loads, tending babies, and arduously preparing food. The rarely more than casual observer takes these to be all there is to a woman's life. The assumption that she is nothing but a drudge, completely subjugated if not actually enslaved, is reinforced by superficial knowledge of the bride-price and polygyny. These institutions are only half understood. The bride-price, for example, is interpreted as evidence that women are bought and sold like chattels and that only the strong worker commands a good price.

The true significance of the bride-price is well described by Edwin W. Smith and Andrew Dale in their ethnography on the Ba-Ila of Northern Rhodesia. Their description applies to almost any African group in which this custom obtains.

The goods given by or on behalf of the bridegroom to the clansmen and parents of the bride are called the chiko. . . . To us it may seem to be a matter of buying and selling but the Ba-Ila would repudiate any such ideal. . . . The woman is not bought. Her husband does not acquire . . . proprietary rights in her. . . . The chiko is more properly regarded as a compensation to the girl's clan, a return to parents and guardians for the expense they have incurred in her rearing, the seal of a contract by which she is to become the mother of the man's children, and a guarantee of good treatment . . . a woman among the Ba-Ila has a certain pride in the amount of chiko given by her husband, because it is an indication of her worth in his eyes. The chiko is an acknowledgement that the marriage is an honourable one. . . .[7]

The popular literature interprets polygyny as further evidence of the exploitation and abuse of women. The writers apply the Western values of exclusive sexual possession and a romantic concept of marriage and rail at what appears to be the ignominy of polygynous marriage. Such marriages are unhappy and the women deprived only when one insists upon viewing them through the eyes of the West. In African societies there exist clear definitions of the rights and duties of every member of the household. It is customary for each wife to have her own house within the compound in which she and her children live, her own garden plot, an assigned share of the livestock, and her own secure status as a co-wife. Her duties to the combined household are delimited, and the husband's obligations to each wife are equally well regulated and understood by all. Most African women want to have co-wives for companionship, help in the work of the household, and as a sign of their husband's prosperity. Certainly, the wives are jealous of their prerogatives and of the interests of their children. They have their ways of bringing pressure to bear upon the husband to obtain those rights. Smith and Dale describe the Ila husband's trials in a polygynous household in the following terms.

. . . the life of a polygynist is not always a rosy one; if he wishes to preserve domestic peace he has to exercise considerable tact . . . he must be careful to show no marked favour to one wife at the expense of another. . . . While they fight among themselves they will in case of necessity unite against the husband. . . . On the other hand many polygynists are very devoted to their wives and live happily.[8]

According to the literary conventions, however, as one of several wives, all bought and paid for, the African woman cannot command the respect and love due a wife and mother. She is valued only for her capacities to work and bear children, and her life is limited to these activities. She is a beast of burden with the intelligence and humanity of just such a beast. Passages in *One Man's Africa* by John Seymour and *Out of Africa* by Isak Dinesen describe the African woman literally as some kind of domestic animal.

. . . the women were still completely tribal. They were treated as little better than beasts of burden. Their heads were (and are today) terribly deformed by the tump strap, a piece of rawhide which goes around their foreheads to support the heaviest loads, their earlobes were enormously distended by great discs, their clothes were untanned ox-hide, copper wire and beads. And they were sullen like overworked oxen.[9]

It was a curious thing to see my old Kikuyu women in beds with white sheets to them, like seeing an old worn-out mule, or other patient beast of burden, there; they themselves laughed to me at the situation, but sourly, as an old mule might do. . . .[10]

Childbearing is but another function of the female beast of burden, who drops her young like any other animal. Even the integral relationship between reproduction and motherhood has been slighted. There are virtually no descriptions of the relationship between an African mother and her child, other than the very young infant. The child is delivered, carried about, suckled, and then as far as the literature is concerned, seems to disappear.

Within the image the alternative stereotype to the beast of burden is one which limits the woman to a purely sexual function. In either case the image of the African woman is never that of a whole woman. Whether drudge or sex-object, the literature reduces her to physical organs. As a worker she consists of hands and feet and a strong back; as sex-object she is the receptive vagina; and as a mother, the expelling uterus.

The significant difference between the alternative stereotypes lies in the responses to them. The drudge, the chattel of African men, is to be pitied, but otherwise arouses little literary interest. The sex-object, however, the British writers find very interesting, and the sexuality of African women is a well-worked theme. There is prevalent a notion that all women of the tropics are precocious and hypersexed. Both the warm climate and the darker skin are believed to create hot-blooded women. What seems unusual in the fantasy when applied to African women is the passivity attributed to them. They are sensual but lack volition; they are available but lack initiative.

The emphasis upon the sexuality of African women can be partially accounted for by the social distance maintained between British and Africans. An Englishman neither marries, employs, nor befriends an African woman. The only possibility is a *sub rosa* affair, making sexuality the only basis for any relationship at all. Such a relationship is likely to be temporary, without emotional involvement or social commitment. Sometimes the purely sexual encounter leaves much to be desired. The woman, as writers such as Robert Shaw and Gerald Hanley indicate, cannot satisfy the complex emotional needs of her lover.

> Certainly in Africa his needs of women had to some extent been met. Well, affection, yes, passion, yes—nobody could smile more affectionately than Syoni—an exciting smile, a passionate smile—but not what you'd call sharing.[11]

> Shalonga was not anybody. She was a part of this place, a child of the fierce sun and the bloody ceremony from which he had bought her. She did not and could not give him comfort for that strange deserted feeling which he experienced when he thought he might one day die here.[12]

The very lack of commitment, on the other hand, often proves to be a source of great satisfaction. Freedom from social and moral restraints is the essence of one aspect of the literary fantasy about Africa, including sexual freedom. The African woman will satisfy an Englishman's sexual needs without limiting his freedom. At home he is contained by the demands of society and the responsibilities of family, class, and country. Africa represents a dream of sexuality without attendant obligation or responsibility.

I was interested to find the number of men right through Africa who asked me if I had ever slept with a native woman. The idea had no appeal for me as the charm of the black woman—sex without involvement—is the very opposite of my taste. But for those who wanted it that way nothing could surpass the African.[13]

He was one of those white bachelors who preferred a black bint whom he could control and who lost nothing of his own personality as he would have done in marriage. . . . It explained all the liaisons between white men and black women. It gave them freedom and supplied the body's solace. . . .[14]

This attitude distinguishes the English fantasy from that of certain French and American novelists who envision some ultimate sexual experience to be found only in Africa. The British, on the other hand, less concerned with heightened sexuality, project a desire for freedom and a withdrawal from the importunate demands of marriage, of women, and of love itself.

Stories about Englishmen who did become emotionally attached and committed to African women always end unhappily. The ill-considered liaison creates a general scandal and leads only to personal tragedy. The man is considered to have removed himself from the pale of accustomed behavior, upset the straightforward pattern of dominance and submission, and broken the charmed circle of British civilization so precariously maintained upon the Dark Continent. By abjuring all that British society values, the unfortunate man has destroyed himself.

According to the literature, sexuality is a disruptive force, one which must be either repressed or else safely channeled into inconsequential affairs, or even more safely into marriage. Marriage, of course, provides the socially sanctioned outlet. Ideally, it should be a union between members of the same class who share the same values. Thus, the marriage would be permitted to claim but a small portion of the Englishman's time, energy, or interests. Neither sex nor marriage should ever be interposed between a man and the real businesss of life. That is a masculine business which may range from sport to the establishment of an empire. Hanley's virile white hunter states that "Women are for those who need them, chum, for the weaklings who want their three meals on time and to be canceled out from the real living." [15]

The English wives depicted in this literature are engaged in a valiant effort to remain unaffected by the alien environment by creating a pleasant English home and maintaining the standards of English life. Such tenacity accentuates both their Englishness and their lady-likeness. The ladies share the values of their husbands; they provide comfort and loyal support without any undue demands. They, too, seem more interested in sport than in sex. Lady Dorothy Mills gives the following explanation for the success of the English wife in Africa.

> The English girl is not given to "nerves"; by habit and taste she's often suited to an outdoor, even a rough life, to the exercise so necessary to maintain health and morale in the tropics. She is more given to active hobbies, to an intelligent interest in her husband's job; in other words, she is less exclusively feminine, and consequently makes a happier and more "all-round" partner to men in rough places.[16]

The English lady, who does not flaunt her sexual attractions or draw any attention to them at all, is an extreme contrast to the image of the blatantly sexual African woman. For the most part, the English women remain coolly English to the core, untouched by the hot, lush environment. Though perhaps not consciously aware of Africa's sexuality, they assume an attitude of defense. They hold themselves aloof from anything that brings Africa too close.

Some English women are portrayed as being drawn into the pervasive sensual *ambiance* of Africa. They become intensely aware of their own hitherto unrealized sexuality which they are no longer able or willing to repress. In most cases such women engage in love affairs with other Europeans, but a few recent books recount, with a light, almost comic touch, affairs with Africans.[17] Women who are sexually awakened by Africa appear often enough in the literature to confirm the over-all sexuality of Africa which can so transmute the British character.

The British attitudes toward sex, as they are expressed in this image, are curiously contradictory. On the one hand, intimacy with women and sex itself are devalued; they should be kept carefully compartmentalized, separate from the more important areas of life. To regard sex as a major satisfaction, to engage in its pleasures too freely or too enthusiastically, is to yield to one's baser instincts. Granting that the needs of the body must be met, the British do not regard sex as a vital aspect of life, let alone as the wellspring of psychic energy. They can apparently take sex or leave it alone, but it will certainly never replace the more manly sports.

Yet the image of the Strange Woman contravenes this devaluation of sex. The image of Africa as a dangerously alluring woman may reflect current discontent with the British attitude toward sex, a feeling that sexuality cannot be merely shunted aside, and that a more spontaneous yielding to the emotions might be preferable. As in all the modern images the earlier surety, the unwavering conviction of the rectitude of Victorian values, seems shaken.

CHAPTER VIII

The Land in Amber

OF ALL the images, only the Land in Amber is a whole-hearted expression of British love for Africa, free of any hostility or ambivalence. The Africa of this image is beautiful, open, sun-drenched—a golden land that preserves ways of life now but a memory in Britain—a nostalgic fantasy that, born of a distaste for the present, glorifies the past. The nineteenth-century writers on South Africa laid the groundwork of the image in their depiction of the southern veldt as a region where the British could enjoy the active, outdoor life so dear to their hearts and so increasingly difficult to obtain at home. The modern image still refers mainly to South, Central, and East Africa, but at times it is extended to include the entire continent and to span centuries as well. It may have initiated in real geography, but its true province is in the British imagination.

The older British values are unquestioned: discipline, physical courage, loyalty, and respect for social hierarchy are universal absolutes. Modern society, in which these values seem to have become incongruous, is rejected. The writers are disenchanted with progress, for it has resulted in a dreary life where the human spirit is diminished and belief dimmed. This literature is a long litany of complaint against the false values of modern life: its materialism, its vulgarity, and its ugliness—"the world of money, whores, lies and crippled greatness." [1] The innocence of Eden, the gallantry of medieval chivalry, and the glories of the height of empire are all encapsulated in the image. The British coming to Africa are presented as knights-errant in quest of values no longer to be realized at home.

In one aspect of the image the dawn of human history is replicated. Africa is a primal land of great beauty and grandeur, inhabited only by animals. In this Africa without Africans the British protagonist feels himself to be the first man to set foot upon its soil. Like Adam in the Garden of Eden, he delights in this first springtime and finds joy in his sole proprietorship.

> There is no feeling like being absolutely alone with creation, even perhaps the first man to stand upon this particular rock and set eye on this particular scene, with nothing spoiled or sullied or abused.[2]

> Always it was there as I have described it, alone with itself, its grass, flowers and animals and no people except us. Every morning we rose early . . . and made our way until sunset across a new tract of our own exalted land.[3]

The Briton has left behind him the cage of a civilization gone soft and tame to discover a world of unlimited opportunity. In Africa the only true resources and the only limits of the individual are his own abilities, and only here can his powers of enterprise and daring be realized. The hero of Huxley's novel, *The Walled City,* "felt that he carried his future with him in his bare hands."[4] In this image, as in the nineteenth-century literature, the call of Africa is the pull toward action and adventure. The envisioned freedom of Africa provides the excitement of challenge, the thrill of a brush with danger and even death. Here is a true affirmation of life in contrast to the half-dead existence in Britain.

Even more than freedom or the promise of fortune, the sense of being fully alive constitutes Africa's great gift to modern men, as it had to their Victorian predecessors. Van der Post concludes that it was personal challenge that had kept an "old Africa hand" in Africa.

> "I found all I wanted here, and here I'll stay until the end." But what had he wanted. . . . A personal challenge and call to individual battle. . . .
>
> There is deep within him a sense of heroic quest; and our modern way of life, with its emphasis on security, and its distrust of the unknown and its elevation of abstract collective values has repressed the heroic impulse.[5]

At no time does an Englishman feel more fully alive than when he is risking his neck in an encounter with the cosmic and elemental forces of nature. Against their surrogates, the big game of Africa, a man may pit himself to fulfill his "heroic impulse." To Peter Viertel's white hunter the very sight of the animals seems to test his manhood.

I saw elephant and rhino and it was like seeing our world thousands of years ago and asking yourself, "How the hell would I have stood up then, with just a piece of hide hanging around my loins and a spear facing some huge animal, and testing my strength and my wits against him." [6]

Hunting is the sharpest demonstration of mastery over one's self and over nature, the ultimate answer to the challenge of Africa. The writers continue to give the impression that the hunt is a major preoccupation for all the British in South and East-Central Africa. Africa as the hunter's paradise is still so exploited in the literature that there is almost automatic association between Africa and big-game hunting. When, in one of Gerald Hanley's novels, a young newcomer to Africa acquires a gun, the very name of Africa becomes for him "a word of magic again as it had been in boyhood such a few years before. Without the rifle it had not been quite Africa" [7]

Twentieth-century writing no longer emphasizes the sport as a symbol of status; interest has shifted to the profound emotional satisfactions to be found in hunting. Dinesen phrases it that "hunting is ever a love affair . . . and the hunter is infatuated with the head of game." [8] Robert Henriques describes the hunt as a transcendent experience.

. . . it is not death which brings these moments; it is the death of a noble animal. . . . Accomplishment lies in the destruction of some superb male specimen, full of the pride of life and his own strength and magnificence, a fitting antagonist, a fitting quarry. . . .

I hunt big game frankly and brutally because not otherwise can I find the same disappointments and reverses, the same excitements, the same antagonists, and the same exhilarating rewards. . . .

Above all, I get from it a moment of triumph and of pure emotion which I have never found elsewhere.[9]

Many of the books describing Africa as a hunter's paradise or as the Garden of Eden, ignore the existence of the Africans except for passing mention of servants or gunboys. The context of a primal land, however, does lend itself to an idealization of the savage. Accordingly, when the African is described it is as simple, child-like, at one with nature and his tribe. In the expression of a basic dissatisfaction with civilization these traits acquire positive value. This parallels, but is not identical with, the image of the Africans in the Dark Labyrinth in which the African symbolizes the positive values of the instinctive vitality of the brute. In the Land in Amber, the African is the happy child of nature who has integrity in his simplicity and virtue in his innocence. Closeness to nature makes him wise in essentials, and from unity with his society he gains certainty.

As a corollary, the introduction of civilization into Africa is deplored. The issue is not the failure to civilize, but the failure of civilization itself. Civilization is destructive of basic human values as yet intact in the primitive world. Huxley questions whether the mission to civilize can bring any thing other than corruption.

It becomes continually more difficult to sustain a conviction that the introduction of money, literacy, taxes, votes, the doctrine of work and the religion of materialism; that the suppression of cattle-raids, magic, dancing, sacrifices and indigenous justice; that the end of contentment and the beginning of *angst;* that all these aspects of civilization have made life happier and fuller for the tribesmen. When they have turned their arrows into duodenal ulcers, their *Kokwet* councils into political parties, their virgins into strip-tease artists, will they be better off? [10]

Another phase of the image of the Land in Amber idealizes imperial Africa, and the conventions of that period are almost identically restated. Nostalgia for an idealized Victorian class structure accompanies nostalgia for an idealized empire. The writers castigate the modern social order which has seemingly weakened British class structure. They are nostalgic for a past when, presumably, the country was well ruled by its natural leaders—men of unquestioned loyalty, courage, and discipline—the products of a ruling class born and bred to its position. Then Great Britain was ruled by gentlemen, and Great Britain ruled the world.

Class stability and privilege and national power are inextricably bound together in this picture of the past. In the African colonies this ideal social and political order was epitomized, clear-cut, and intact: there was no blurring of the social hierarchy; the British were masters, the Africans subjects. To those British for whom the modern situation spells impoverishment and an unwonted loss of prestige, Africa, by virtue of the anachronism of the image, still holds the promise of retention of their status. The contemporary novelist Gwyn Griffin underlines the overwhelming value of this promise to the new poor.

Like most of their class their lives were spent in contriving somehow, to hold on at least the outward appearance of their social position, and their greatest fear . . . of forfeiting their precious gentility. . . . It is inevitably such people who, as young men go out to fill the most thankless positions in the least attractive of British colonial territories in the knowledge that however questionable their social situation in England, once they are east of Suez they will habitually be addressed as "lord"—even if only in exotic synonyms of "sahib," "bwana," or "tuan." Out they come, pinkfaced, pink-kneed, pathetically eager to hunt big game, trek endlessly through vast open spaces, rule savage tribes. Out they come as assistant district commissioners, assistant superintendents of police, second-lieutenants of third-rate native levies, or junior overseers on plantations of a dozen varieties of tropical produce. For such occupations are generally considered to offer "a gentleman's life" and most of those who undertake them, would, perhaps, accept the job of shoveling coal in hell if they believed it to do the same.[11]

Africa appears as the special preserve of the British upper classes. The colonial administrators and settlers, even the transient visitors, are distinguished for their blue blood, their old school ties, and a predilection for the outdoor life, especially for the more active, violent sports. Such men were considered the fit rulers of empire. In his foreword to H. M. Jackson's work on the Sudan, Lord Vansittart extols their qualifications.

I have never wavered in my conviction that the Sudan Civil Service was the finest body in the world. . . . They were all picked men, scholars and athletes. . . . Look at their credentials! A former Rugby football captain of Oxford and Scotland, an ex-captain of the Cambridge University soccer XI, a racing trials man, [etc.]. . . . This was a typical intake, chosen not by examination but by shrewd judges of capacity not only to survive in but to administer huge wild districts.

Entrance went by character and the strength to bear early responsibility. These traits are typical of the British at their best.[12]

Memoirs of the "old Africa hands," as well as modern accounts, make very clear the satisfactions of British life in Africa. They concentrate on its freedoms, opportunities for sport and companionship, the plentiful, cheap servants, and they discount the difficulties of climate and isolation. In short, the life of the colonial officer and settler was an idealized counterpart of British county life in the "good old days." Lord Cranworth recalls the luxury, so inexpensively procured, of his African estate.

We spent some of the happiest years of our lives at Chiromo, and never before or since have I been so rich. We had the best car in the Protectorate, the best civilian house, three ponies and a goat carriage, a first-class Goan cook . . . a spacious and most beautiful garden, and syces, domestic servants, and gardeners without stint. Our total expenditures on these was about £1200 a year.[13]

This literature of reminiscence is a valedictory to empire that stresses the unselfish motives of the British. Their dedication to the ideals of responsible service outweighed any desire for self or class aggrandizement. Just as the picture of good living is an important facet of the literature, even more is the depiction of devoted and arduous labor.

The valedictory to empire is made with a clear conscience; the zeal, the devotion, and the self-sacrifice were justified by their results. In short, it was "a golden age," but according to the literature it was as much the golden age for the British in Africa as for the Africans.

The African is depicted as the willing and grateful recipient of British beneficence. He is a child—not the child of nature as in the image of primal Africa—but the untutored child in the nursery. He is by nature subservient and responsive to a kind, but firm regime. The relationship between Briton and African resembles that between parent and child. Any coercion used in dealing with the Africans was not aggression; it was, rather, akin to the discipline of children—for their own welfare. A. C. G. Hastings, a former colonial official, phrases it as being administered in the "spirit of correction and eventual good." [14] As children ought to do, the Africans accepted just correction from authority without resentment. The British sentiment that force does not vitiate benevolence is presumably established by the reports of African loyalty, trust, respect, and even love for their British masters. The British mandate to rule was thus validated by African acceptance.

The loyal African servant is a stock figure in both fiction and nonfiction. Whatever faults he may have are redeemed by his devotion to his master. That this should be an overriding virtue reflects the British (or perhaps human) desire for love and approbation. The loyal servants, however, are significant figures, for they are the only Africans who elicit love from the British. This love seems the only bridge to span the gulf. Haggard writes that it even reaches beyond the grave.

> Or if my Mazook should be dead, and if there is any future for us mortals, and if Zulus and white men go to the same place—as why should they not?—then I am quite certain that when I reach that shore I shall see a square-faced, dusky figure seated on it, and hear the words, "Inkoos Indanda, here am I, Mazook, who once was your man, waiting to serve you." For such is the nature of the poor despised Zulu, at any rate towards one whom he may choose to love.[15]

For some writers the "Golden Age" preserved in the Land in Amber is medieval Europe rather than Eden or empire. Feudalism represents a social order in which an individual was secure in his identity and his social role. Furthermore, it permitted a gentleman by birth and by breeding to live by the code of honor. A number of writers attempt to recapture that chivalry long lost in Britain by projecting it onto Africa and certain groups of Africans. Dinesen, thus, makes a true "gentleman" out of her Somali servant, Farah, along with the Somalis in general.

In our day the word "gentleman" is taken less seriously than before. . . . If the word may be taken to describe or define the person who has got the code of honour of his period and milieu in his own blood, as an instinct—such as the rules of the game will be in the blood of the true cricket or football player to whom it would not be possible in any situation to throw the ball at the head of his adversary—Farah was the greatest gentleman I have ever met.[16]

The idealization of feudalism in this literature carries with it an idealization of warfare. Final validation of oneself as a man and a gentleman is achieved primarily through combat, for the chivalric code of honor is essentially a warrior's code. Warfare is a completely masculine activity by which a man can absolutely validate his manhood. Sheer physical courage—the willingness to face death in battle—is the essential virtue.

Modern civilization is decried because it lacks an equally ready definition of a masculine ideal. The incredibly destructive and dehumanized nature of modern warfare renders the older ideal of the gallant warrior meaningless. With increased mechanization there is opportunity for neither gallantry nor honor, and the bonds of good fellowship are replaced by the bonds of shared misery and fear. The writers turn from this reality to glorify the warrior who fought like a man and died a hero.

The ideal of manliness, exemplified in the warrior, transcends differences in race, language, and culture. The writers are still ready, along with Kipling, to "give the certifikit" to the "Poor benighted 'eathen who's a first class fighting man." The mystique of the warrior culminates in the almost worshipful British attitude toward the Masai. Some officials became so enamored of the Masai that their administrative effectiveness was impaired. It occurred often enough to be designated as the disease of "masaitis," and those infected with it were transferred to other posts. "Masaitis" is not limited to colonial officialdom; it permeates the modern literature. Respect for the Masai is mandatory, even if the author has had no more than the routine tourist glimpse of them. Grantly Dick Read implies that recognition of the worth of the Masai can serve as an index of the worthiness of the British. "We clearly understood why the best type of white man holds them in such high esteem and even real affection." [17]

One can understand the cult of Masai worship only by recognizing that the bases of British perception rest upon a concept of aristocracy partly defined in terms of feudal values and partly in those of nineteenth-century gentry. Aristocracy becomes associated with a somewhat curious syndrome of traits: disdain for the tradesman, impassioned interest in domestic animals, appreciation of the value of pedigree for man and beast, disciplined self-possession as well as marked self-assurance, and above all, a chivalric preoccupation with warfare.

British adulation of the Masai is based on their seemingly upper-class attitudes. The Masai do little work, aside from tending the herds (and even here much of the labor is done by boys). They generally have little interest in farming, trade, and crafts—an indifference which matches the standards of a feudal nobility. As they move about with their herds they seem free of ties to soil, job, or any of the mundane economic preoccupations. To the Europeans who ignore the iron necessities of Masai life—grass and water for their herds—this seems like the freedom of a man with a private income.

> The Masai, a brave, proud, handsome race are admired by all travelers. Nobody likes the idea of such a people settled, tamed and commercialized.[18]

> These fierce six-footers, burnished with grease, are far too proud to work as farm hands and one is forced to draw on inferior stock from the agricultural tribes. . . .
>
> They are aristocratic and are quite conscious of it.[19]

The Masai physical type is also much admired. They tend to be tall, slightly built, with slender hands and feet, aquiline features and thin lips. These traits are found praiseworthy not only for their esthetic appeal but also as the hallmarks of aristocracy. Roderick Cameron praises both Masai beauty and breeding.

> Physically, they are extraordinarily beautiful, with slender bones and narrow hips, and the most wonderful rounded muscles and limbs. So delicately built are they that they look more effeminate than the

women. But their beauty is entirely masculine. Their breeding shows in their finely-cut nostrils and the precise chiselling of their lips.[20]

The great admiration for the cultural and physical characteristics of the Masai is overshadowed by the esteem given them as outstanding warriors. Historical evidence hardly supports this reputation; as fighters they were not in the same league as the Zulu, the Matabele, the Ashanti, or the Dahomeans. Masai warfare consisted primarily of cattle raiding, which was scarcely full-scale war. The pattern of raid and harassment continued on into the European regimes, causing enough disturbance to require police action by Europeans, but not any serious fighting.[21]

Though raiding was undoubtedly rewarding and perhaps even necessary, this is discounted in the literature. Masai warfare is written of as if it were an end in itself and combat the Masai's only true career. Only by a display of personal valor could manhood be validated, so that when there was no warfare, lion hunting took its place. Their need to protect the cattle from lions is played down, and both warfare and lion hunting are described as expressing the same bravura sportsmanship. Just as British writers overlook economic motives, so they tend to overlook any brutality in Masai raiding. They choose only to see that the Masai fought like gentlemen, gallantly, but without hate or economic necessity. Since the British never had to engage in full-scale warfare against the Masai, and suffered no major losses at their hands, they can afford to see only the elegance and panache of the beautiful young *Moran*, the noble young warrior, playing the game of war. The Masai seem to embody the chivalric ideal of warfare as a sporting contest of brave young men.

The Pax Britannica put an end to Masai forays, but the organization of the youths into warrior groups continued; the *Moran* still paraded in full panoply, and the free life of the pastoralists remained relatively intact. The anthropologist Melville J. Herskovits states that the Masai, like other East African pastoralists, were particularly conservative and resistant to Westernization.[22] The British admire this as proud self-sufficiency. Masai cultural rigidity thus takes on value as part of the fantasy; Cameron sees it as the pride which so befits a noble warrior.

> But it is not for their aggressiveness, nor even for their prowess in war, that we admire them today. It is for their beauty, their sense of fair play, and their pride. No Masai will deign to work for a white man. They obstinately refuse to be civilized.[23]

The much-vaunted arrogance of the Masai automatically commands respect, for such supreme confidence in one's own superiority has always been the sign of aristocracy. Many Moslem tribes also elicit Western admiration for the same reasons; they seem unalterably and serenely sure of themselves. The Moslems are not susceptible to European influence, at least to that of the missionaries, and their resistance to Christianity is taken as an index of assurance, integrity, and pride, which is in itself reinforcing evidence of their nobility.

On the surface it seems strange that Islam should be given such prestige by Christian writers. But Islam as a religion and a way of life which elevates warfare, assigns women to the obscurity of purdah, and is altogether male-oriented has had undiminished appeal for the British since the 1850's.

> Although himself a stout Christian, Hereward had no wish to attract members of the subject races into the fold, but rather resigned them to the Prophet, whose views on discipline, strong drink and women he considered very sound.[24]

The African literary tradition merges with another important literary tradition about the Bedouins and other pastoral Moslems. Strong interest in the Moslems during the nineteenth and early twentieth centuries is evidenced by the overwhelming success of Burton's Arabian studies and explorations, the works of Charles M. Doughty, T. E. Lawrence, and Gertrude Bell, to say nothing of the novels of Ethel M. Dell. Such writers depicted the Arabs as the romantic and dashing horsemen of the desert. The Moslems of Africa came in, even if only by the back door, for their share of homage on this wave of Arabophilia.

It is consistent with the image of the Land in Amber that the Africans to whom any attention is paid are all admirable. Either they are the unspoiled children of nature dwelling in a primal

Eden, loyal and devoted subjects of empire, or the proud warriors resisting the inroads of Westernization. None of these are tainted by modern civilization, but the most conservative are the most admired. Perhaps this fact explains why Zulu stock is presently lower than it had been in Haggard's day. The Zulu, unlike the Masai, adapted to Western culture; many became Christian; and the warriors were transformed into miners and laborers. None of this is in accord with the nostalgic fantasy of the Land in Amber.

Of all the images this one is the clearest and most consistent reflection of British discontent with modern life. It differs from the Dark Labyrinth in that the dissatisfaction is not based on uncertainty about values. This image expresses great certainty; the writers are very sure that modern civilization is all dross and that true worth is to be found only in the past. The British have created utopian settings in Africa wherein are reconstituted the lost values of earlier times.

CHAPTER IX

The Antagonist

CONFRONTATION between the British and Africa is, in the image of the Antagonist, formulated as conflict with a formidable adversary. The metaphor of Africa as a personal antagonist is a staple of the tradition. It is an old figure going back to the explorers' accounts where, Margery Perham and Jack Simmons point out, "the continent plays such an active, and indeed violent part, as to fill something like a distinct role in the drama, certainly that of the villain." [1]

The people of Africa are the merest adjuncts to the central conflict with the continent. At most, the Africans are but the passive objects of British endeavors. As subjects to be governed, ignorant people to be taught, heathens to be converted, patients to be treated, they almost always belong to the faceless, nameless category of "the natives."

The literature since the 1940's has, however, added another dimension to the image of the Antagonist. As the Sleeping Giant, the new aspect complements that of the Antagonist, for it focuses all interest on the Africans. They are the source of Africa's power, and it is their hostility which makes the Giant so threatening a figure.

The older version of the image which relegates the Africans completely to the background, dramatizes the British protagonists more vividly than any other image. So highlighted are the British that any Englishman who can retain his identity and can adhere to his customary code of behavior is acting like a hero. What is merely conventional in England requires courage in Africa, and even the most routine activities, such as serving tea or riding on a train, seem gestures of defiance.

The image of the Antagonist derives from the records of the

early explorers and travelers. The modern literature reinforces it with elaborate accounts of tropical discomforts. Insects, endemic diseases, heat, and loneliness all contribute to the general misery. Unlike their predecessors, the modern Britons appear oversensitive, excessively vulnerable, and prone to interpret every unpleasant experience as an attack upon themselves. Thus, Huxley comments on an African storm that "There's something personal, vindictive, inexorable, about these tropic storms, as if a great mindless beast was out for your blood." [2]

Whatever the irritants are, they are taken as intentional expressions of Africa's hostility. The very first intimation of discomfort confirms the expectation of an all-out attack. This is the self-fulfilling prophecy with which the Englishman makes his own blood run cold. So deeply engrained is this preconception that even where there are no overt manifestations of enmity they are expected, and Africa is seen as "Too careless or too treacherous to threaten . . . with an impassive air that seemed to mask the very claws of danger." [3]

The hostility of the continent is sometimes thought of as defensive, and Africa has consequently erected barriers to ward off intrusion. The hazards, the discomforts, every difficulty the British encounter in Africa are cunningly laid impediments in their path. Van der Post, in the following passage, describes Africa's masterly defense against invasion.

Her coastline, no matter how the sea nibbled at it, kept its defences intact and, when it gave way, retreated in good Macedonian order. To this day the coastline of Africa not only offers no convenient harbours, but most of it, together with the interior, is raised above the water level and the rivers come tumbling out of it in swift, churning, angry torrents that make navigation impossible. Where the earth was not so raised this ancient land threw up vast seas of desert which could be crossed only by a few initiates at their peril. Also, as if to make quite sure that her defences completely sealed Africa off from the outer world, nature developed the most redoubtable champions in the mosquito and tsetse fly and other minute parasites, all able to strike down any invader with a wonderful selection of deadly diseases, from sleeping sickness, malaria, dysentery, and typhoid to leprosy and the bubonic plague. One day I hope to persuade my fellow Africans to put up a monument to the despised mosquito and tsetse fly for discharging so well this task of defending Africa against invasion.[4]

The image depicts the British engaged in perpetual conflict with a powerful enemy. They feel that they can never acclimate to Africa or become inured to its attacks. Eventually all their efforts will be defeated, and Africa, as Greene predicts, will emerge victorious.

. . . they were living here for a short while on the surface of the land, but Africa has the last say, and it said it in the form of rats and ants, of the forest swallowing up the little pits the Dutch prospectors had made and abandoned.[5]

Win, lose, or draw, the conflict with Africa is seen as the crucial test of the true worth of a man's character. The theme of British trial by African ordeal is central in a number of recent novels. In some of them the African experience is the equivalent of ceremonial initiation into manhood. Africa sets the trials which the youth must undergo and the endurance of these vicissitudes makes a man of him. In Hardy's novel, *The Men from the Bush,* two adolescents undergo the ordeal of an African adventure; one is ultimately exposed as a cowardly bully; the other develops into a strong and good man. Even a little boy, the hero of the W. H. Canaway novel, *Find the Boy,* achieves manly strength of character. In *At Fever Pitch* by David Caute the making-of-man theme is painfully literal; a young homosexual, transfigured by his African ordeal, achieves a fully heterosexual experience. Other novels concerned with the testing of character deal rather with the restoration of manhood.[6] The remedial value of African experiences is a popular theme in modern fiction. Ne'er-do-wells, men who have never found themselves, and defeated men all come to Africa—"the cure for the sick heart" [7]—submit to the ordeal, and achieve renascence.

I see a remarkable change in your face. . . . There is something different. I see authority and confidence in your eyes. . . . For every man there comes a testing time that one way or another utterly changes his life. . . . That is a man's critical moment. You will harden, Dennis . . . you will have discovered wonderful new depths in yourself when you finally come through.[8]

In some instances the literature stresses the abrasive effects of Africa that divest a man of his civilized façade, exposing his essential character. In Africa men are "like plucked chickens losing a feather at a time, who would soon find themselves naked before each other with every defect of character plainly visible and beyond disguise." [9] This concept of an abrasion that lays bare all a man's passions and idiosyncrasies is the key to the descriptions of the British settlers in the Kenyan highlands of East Africa. They appear to be singularly eccentric, engaged in a "cult of unconventionality." [10] The Kenyans, Alastair Scobie tells us, "developed a strange 'bush happiness'; let their eccentricities have full rein; and their hair well down." [11]

The suggestion is made that the Highlands, perhaps all the British colonies, are reservoirs of eccentricity, having drained off the deviant members of British society. In this view self-selection partially accounts for the difference between the unconventional colonials and the restrained and orderly society at home. The abrasive effects of Africa only exaggerate pre-existing eccentricities, and it is appropriate in this context to see Africa as the natural refuge for those who are misfits in Britain. Dundas claims that there is "truth in the remark" that the family black sheep can always go to Kenya.[12]

People lacking true strength of character should never have come to Africa. At home they might have lived out their lives securely laced in British conventions, but in Africa they lose their civilized veneer, and with the façade gone nothing remains. The literature recounts numerous tales of men who "went bush," became insane, took to drink, or committed suicide. These cases all demonstrate the consequences of defective character, for, as Hanley sums up, "Africa beat them. It was the kind of place which puts its finger into a man's weakness more swiftly than all the bloody infantry attacks of the war." [13]

Neither the value placed on character nor its definition seem changed since Victorian times. The significant component is still self-discipline. Impulse and spontaneity must be held in constant check, and vigilant social conformity is both means and measure of that control. Confrontation with Africa confirms the value of discipline which alone enables the British to survive intact.

Not all the British engage in open conflict with the Antagonist. The responses of some are defensive, and they attempt to protect themselves by some sort of insulation. Although the insulation takes various forms, all have the express purpose of excluding Africa from their awareness. By means of a precariously maintained nescience they try to negate the presence of the continent.

The oversensitized Englishman resorts to a number of devices to anesthetize himself. The anodynes commonly relied on are made familiar by much usage: drink, flirtations and love affairs, petty intrigue, gossip, and an exaggerated interest in the small change of daily life. The tight little community of beleaguered Englishmen live in a hothouse atmosphere of forced intimacy, depending upon each other for personal relationships, and exploiting each other's personalities for distraction. John R. Wilson's novel, *Double Blind,* conveys the idea that Africa itself enforces such behavior upon the British.

> I could imagine the British residents sitting out on their terraces on these soft summer nights, filled with a restlessness that they could not express. It was no wonder they drank too much, that they engaged in listless flirtations with each other's wives. It was almost as if the landscape itself expected it of you.[14]

The pretense that Africa does not exist, seemingly at the root of all the defensive techniques, demands the refuge of a reasonable facsimile of English life. The literature from the mid-nineteenth century on describes the British attempts to re-create small islands of home in "darkest Africa." Up through the imperial period each small replica of Britain was to have been a center for diffusion which would eventually spread light to all the continent. In the twentieth century hope for the spread of civilization has faded, and the British community is only a little clearing in the jungle. By contrast, the surrounding darkness is intensified, while Africa maintains "its habitual vigilance on the frail outposts of the invaders." [15] The only security lies within the British enclave where life goes on much as it would in Britain, and Africa is seldom permitted to intrude. Yet, Hardy writes, it cannot be entirely forgotten.

The room had been painfully English with chintz cushions, a Victorian bureau and a sheaf of mimeographed missionary tracts, a few sepia portraits of solemn cricket teams, curtains out of Manchester cloth. The Lauries had shut the country out. There were no spears or tree-drums or devil-masks on the walls, no carved African figurines, no ebony heads or miniature elephants. "We bake our own bread," Mrs. Laurie said. They could see the panic at the back of her eyes.[16]

The Victorians took for granted their ability to behave as Englishmen wherever they were. It was not considered especially meritorious, but quite simply the natural, inevitable consequence of being English. The modern writers consider that success in carrying on as Englishmen is a triumph of British character. It apparently takes a singularly British form of gallantry to serve tea properly or to grow an English garden in Africa. In the face of Africa, the gesture is made to seem pathetic.

There were drinks, but beyond that there was a tea-table lavishly spread as only the English can spread them. I have sometimes thought since of the Elkington's tea-table round, white, standing with sturdy legs against the green vines of the garden, a thousand miles of Africa receding from its edge.[17]

. . . in Africa, the vision of an English lawn flies over the exiled British imagination like colours nailed to the mast of an out-gunned, sinking ship of the line. The lawns impinged on borders which grew European flowers of a sickly and outraged appearance . . . the African zinnias . . . seemed to be sharing a jibe of their own at the patient, determined nostalgia of the gardens about them.[18]

Whether the British respond directly to the challenge that Africa offers, or retreat from it through evasion and insulation, there seems no doubt that the African experience is preconceived as painful. Against the enmity of Africa the British rely chiefly on the bulwark of British character, either in the personality of the individual or in the maintenance of English forms of behavior. The only defense against the African Antagonist is British character, and the only victory is its vindication.

The complementary image of the Sleeping Giant stresses the antagonism of the people rather than of the continent. It is a new synthesis of conventions in response to the present political situation. The literature has always put emphasis on the vastness of Africa, but this image refers rather to the size of the African population. The older convention of the excessive fertility of the Africans is taken up to become the basis for a new theme. The expanding African population poses the terrifying possibility that the world will be overwhelmed.

> As for the people: they pullulate . . . the population will double in 30 years.
>
> The implications are frightening. Adam's instructions were to multiply and replenish the earth, not multiply and despoil it.[19]

The population explosion as a world problem has been sufficiently publicized to make such prognostications seem reasonable to readers. It should be borne in mind, however, that Africa is a far-from-crowded continent. In 1962 the historian, Donald Wiedner, described the demographic facts of Africa as follows:

> These more crowded areas (the West-African coast, between the Senegal River and the Cameroons; around the Great Lakes and along the Kenya-Uganda Railway; and in the eastern and southern parts of Southern Rhodesia and the Republic of South Africa) compare roughly to the density variations within France, Ireland or Virginia, but the greater sub-Saharan area has a population about as scattered as that of northern Sweden or the American plains.[20]

The power of the Giant is still unrealized, for Africa has not yet fully awakened. It has only now begun to rouse from its sleep. The conventions that Africa is both ancient and changeless have been revamped, and the many thousand years in which Africa remained unchanging are rephrased as the sleep of the Giant. So the writers speak of "the long trance of African history," [21] "the long sleep of centuries in the sun," [22] "where time made no cross but the present paralleled the eternal," [23] or "a savage land which had sat silent and sick on the edge of history since time began." [24]

Africa had no history, since the passage of time was unmarked by any change. Basil Davidson points out in *The Lost Cities of Africa* that this pervasive concept of an eventless African past even invades the scholarly writing on Africa. His book was written at least partly to counteract the conventional approach which he summarizes as follows: "Nothing with them, as many Europeans thought, could have changed since the age of apes and stone." [25] Elsewhere in the book another passage reads.

> The Negro, many have believed, is a man without a past. Black Africa—Africa south of the Sahara desert—is on this view a continent where men by their own efforts have never raised themselves much above the level of the beasts.[26]

This concept of African history stems from the parochial assumption that Europe alone changed throughout the course of time. It is, in fact, a form of solipsism—that Africa had no history because the Europeans played no part in it, and even more were unaware of it.

In place of this relatively unrecorded and little-known history, the writers substitute all the stereotypes of African culture and behavior. Africa existed unchanged, its people in a primal condition and their cultures preserved relicts of the first men in the world. The tribes were presumed to have been isolated not only from the events that stirred the rest of mankind but also from each other. Tribal life was self-contained and savage, the people aware of outsiders only as predators or victims. Tribesmen were motivated purely by tribal traditions or by instinct.

The stasis of Africa was ended only by the coming of the Europeans. The arrival of civilized men provided the stimulus for its emergence from the archaic past. The writing assumes that without this contact Africa would yet be within the changeless cycle of Stone Age life. Cloete illustrates with what reluctance Africa presumably responded to the prod of European entry.

> The African giant . . . was throwing off his chains. He was flexing his muscles. . . . And the rest of African habit and custom had been disturbed, the pattern of 10,000 years shattered in this period of transition. The giant [was] fevered by a dream . . . he wanted to go back into the security of the ancient tribal womb where everything was unchanging and changeless.[27]

So long as the Giant remained inviolate and undisturbed he presented no threat, but the attempt to bring the benefits of civilization to Africa roused it from its centuries-long lethargy. Whatever uneasiness or discomfort the Europeans must endure in this changing Africa are, therefore, to be laid at their own doorstep. Europe alone bears the responsibility for what ensues. Huxley states that ". . . we must answer for our own Frankensteins."[28] And Julian Mockford uses exactly the same idiom.

> Its millions are stirring like a giant—perhaps, from the White man's point of view, like a Frankenstein largely of his own creation; a Frankenstein *ex machina*, from the *Pax Britannica* no less.[29]

Obviously the British mission to bring enlightenment has gone wrong somewhere. If all the effort, the pouring into Africa of wealth and lives, has resulted in a Frankenstein monster then the British have failed signally. The gulf was too deep and wide, the crossing unsuccessful, the bridge too fragile, and the transfer of values and goods incomplete. All they feel they have done was to goad Africa from somnolence and to set a resentful Giant in motion. Van der Post indicates that thus were created the conditions for chaos.

> . . . somewhere in Africa's hidden being is piling up a sinister power of accumulated energy sufficient to shatter the world that is taking away its soul. Africa is being charged like one of the electronic piles used to split the atom. For Africa, from earth and beast, up to the most intelligent of its indigenous children is not letting this loss of

soul take place without a terrible struggle. Even the soil of Africa, this ancient red soil, founded on the original rock of the earth, is rebelling against European methods. . . .[30]

The stirring up of the Giant to threaten the entire world is an elaborate hyperbole that, literally speaking, comes down to African resistance to colonialism. After the end of World War II movements toward African independence accelerated. Nationalism is the new dynamic factor in African politics, and in the literature nationalism is generally equated with antiwhite attitudes. This is a situation scarcely calculated to maintain British equanimity in their relations with their former colonies.

No armed might, no amount of British courage can restore their former position in Africa. The British hark back to past glories, good works, and individual sacrifice as they deplore the course of events. Quite often they blame their own leniency toward the Africans for what has occurred. By allowing the Africans too much freedom, they feel they have undermined their own strength. The response to their present weakness is resentful, frightened, and nostalgic for a past effectiveness.

In the literature from the 1930's on, the British seem profoundly pessimistic about their future in Africa. Their expulsion was inevitable, their accomplishments negated, their works destroyed, and they will be uncompensated by any gratitude or even acknowledgment of the debt they feel Africa owes them.

I thought we came out here to serve these black primitives; we bring them science, the light of progress—and for what? One could write their expressions of gratitude on the head of a pin. . . .

When they throw us out of Africa they won't even lift a hand to wave us goodbye.[31]

The British are even more pessimistic concerning the welfare of independent Africa. Sir Charles Dundas, although more sanguine than most, questions the ability of Africa to succeed on its own: "Whether the African by himself can master both the old and new spi[illegible] of his race remains to be seen."[32] The majority of writers are certain that Africa cannot succeed without European guidance and control. Cary, for example, feels that independent Africa is bound to fail.

> My book was meant to show certain men and their problems in the tragic background of a continent still little advanced from the Stone Age, and therefore exposed, like no other, to the impact of modern turmoil. An overcrowded raft manned by children who had never seen the sea would have a better chance in a typhoon.[33]

This despondent outlook is based upon the familiar premise that the Africans are unable to grasp the essentials of civilization. Only partially acculturated, half-educated and half-Christianized, they are not yet ready to guide their own destiny. The influence of the West prematurely sparked African nationalism and independence. The desire of the Africans for self-government far outran their acceptance or even understanding of the responsibilities of freedom. None of the Africans, say the writers, can adequately replace European colonial officials. Old-style African chiefs are certainly not competent to govern modern states. Leaders must be recruited from the acculturated group whose very Westernization makes them mistrusted. The traditional image of the Westernized African is transferred to the new elite. They are described as ruthless, exploitive, and tyrannical, and they will only restore the older patterns of African despotism, or, perhaps even worse, open the way to complete anarchy.

> I've had enough. Been working over fifteen years with these black bastards and never met a straight one yet and I've been all over the country too. What I say is—hand the bloody place over to them—let them run it . . . and stand back and watch the fireworks. Look at the balls up in Ghana. Bribery and corruption, fighting and murder, the prisons full of the opposition. . . .[34]

Even if the new leaders were to prove politically effective it would be small comfort to the British who see their primary motivation as antiwhite. Effective leadership is thus as much to be feared as ineffective rule. Ineptitude will result in a chaotic eruption of Africa's power, but effectiveness will be equally devastating because of its hostile intent.

The writers, who see the new Africa as a continent where brutish and ignorant masses are ruled by a corrupt and despotic leadership, predict that the new Africa will be in many ways much like the old Africa. There is bound to be a reversion to savagery; all the horrors of a savage condition will sweep away whatever amelioration had been achieved. Lady Joy Packer writes of the colonial period that ". . . this era of African prosperity and education . . . was but a flash between the dark and the dark." [35]

Literary disquietude about African reversion to savagery is all the greater since the reversion is never simply envisioned as the Giant's return to sleep. Africa is awake and moving and will remain a threat to civilization and its values. In *Red Rock Wilderness* Huxley sees the political changes on the continent as

> . . . a battle for the continent, and perhaps even more than that, for the survival of the West. It is a battle between the forces of reason, progress and civilization and the forces of fear, hatred and tyranny—the forces of darkness.[36]

The old conventions and stereotypes have all been resynthesized in the image of the Giant to express the British sense of failure at colonialism and the mission to civilize. The failure is rationalized by the restatement of the impossibility of bridging the Abysmal Gulf which eternally separates Africa from the West. At best, whatever the Africans have adopted of civilization provides them with a thin veneer, false values, and perhaps new motivations and mechanisms for the expression of old savagery. Whatever rationalizations are made, the sense of failure lies just below the surface. The good intentions and the hard work of empire have gone for nought. Enlightenment wakened the Giant, and awake, he exerted his enormous power to reject the givers and their gifts. They earned for their pains not gratitude or acceptance but hate and angry rejection. Even the glib rationales do not quite conceal a hurt bewilderment.

The predominant response to the British sense of failure and to

African rejection is one of reciprocal hostility. Most of the images of the continent presume Africa to be hostile to the British, but heretofore, the British recorded little outright hostility in themselves. At worst, the British response to Africa was ambivalent. At its best it was clearly a case of true love. Africa may have been hostile to the British, but they were entranced with Africa. Reciprocation of the hostility is a newer component; the projection has come full circle.

The entire image is, in fact, a totally hostile one. In the other images hostility is covert, palliated, and perhaps even masked by depictions of devoted servants, loyal subjects, cooperative chiefs, and even noble savages. The British laid claim to love from at least some of the Africans, a love that was sometimes as specious as was perhaps the claim to it. Specious or not, this love of the Africans for their British masters persists in the literature and is a significant expression of British faith in their own goodness and good will. The image of the Sleeping Giant contains no such mitigating good will or expectation of love.

The literature attributes British failure to civilize to the inherent savagery of the Africans, but along with this explanation a certain discomfiture is frequently expressed. The writers fear that African rejection of British values may be justifiable. Their *post hoc* reasoning is that they may have been rejected by Africa because what they were doing in Africa was not worth doing. They, themselves, are no longer certain. In the final analysis, all they have done is to substitute new problems as perplexing and insoluble as the old. In an attempt to assess the final value of British rule in Africa, Dorothy Wellesley questions the worth of Western civilization altogether.

> Personally I have never been able to decide whether or not Western civilization is desirable even in Europe. . . . This is one of the questions which many of us, perhaps, will never be quite sure about. . . . The worst perhaps that can be said of Imperialism is that it gives to the native a new set of troubles in exchange for the old.[37]

The major difference between twentieth- and nineteenth-century writing on Africa is in the self-image of the British. The confidence of the empire-builders is lost in the twentieth century. The literary tradition, however, perpetuates the older stereotypes and, indeed, demonstrates their continued vitality. The liquidation of the empire by no means bankrupted the traditional images. On the contrary, the new situation has been as much a stimulus for proliferation of the tradition as had been the growth of empire.

CHAPTER X

The British Self-Image

THROUGHOUT the literature the image of Africa and the British image of themselves are intimately related; one is the obverse of the other. Africa *is* whatever the British *are not*. The delineation of Africa by means of a set of contrasts is, therefore, dependent upon the British view of themselves. This self-image is not limited to the literature on Africa, but does conform to other evaluations of the British and genuinely seems to express British values and attitudes.

Seen through British eyes, Britain and Africa represent the two poles of a single system of values. These are variously phrased as light opposed to darkness, civilization to savagery, good to evil. Africa is the "continent of dark negation." Contrast with it demonstrates the nature of these values, and confrontation confirms their worth.

The literature on Africa from both the Victorian and the modern periods expresses the same ideals of character, among which discipline and courage are the most important. A man should be so disciplined that he never loses self-control, and his behavior conforms to a rigorous code no matter what the situation. The capacity for heroism, whether in sport or warfare, is the essence of character.

Both Victorian and modern writers share the belief that such character is particularly manifested by members of the upper classes. The literary tradition stresses that the British in Africa are gentlemen. Until well into the nineteenth century the British in Africa were often admittedly from less elevated ranks of society. Class consciousness became a vital aspect of the British self-image only in the mid-nineteenth century and permeated all the subsequent literature.

The modern literature does, however, differ from the Victorian by lessened confidence in England. The exercise of discipline and the display of courage seem underrated and unrewarded. Owing to the changed social structure, England is no longer governed by gentlemen. They have, thus, lost their chief role, and their values are anachronistic. The worth of these values remains an article of faith, but modern England has gone astray. Progress has not fulfilled the promise it held for the Victorians. England is no longer what it was—the nation which created and was created by men of character.

It is an oft-repeated comment in the African literature that only gentlemen should be in positions of authority, since they alone have the requisite character. Whether as army officer, civil servant, or private citizen, an English gentleman, no matter what his feelings, must always be in sufficient command of himself to command others, and to do so justly and effectively. The literature indicates that in the service of the empire discipline demonstrated its worth. In this respect the literature on Africa is no different from the literature on other parts of the British Empire. In Africa, India or anywhere else it is the English gentleman who keeps the imperial sun from setting.

The most effective agency for making gentlemen out of boys is generally thought to be the English public school. There is inculcated the assurance of superior status and the character worthy of its privileges. It is also in the public schools that boys are trained to leadership. Hilaire Belloc terms the public schools "seminaries for the English governing class,"[1] and James Wellard gives ironic consent to this definition.

> The major reward of attending a public school is the firm assurance which never leaves the alumnus afterward, that . . . they are the cream of society and all the rest, the skimmed milk. . . . This simple and useful classification of humanity into two parts is indispensable in later life, in the executive and administrative posts for which public school boys are destined. Hence, in their dealings with subordinates and foreigners and all lesser breeds without the law, these model Englishmen . . . have the unshakeable conviction of intrinsic superiority. Obviously such a conviction together with a complete imperviousness to ideas makes them inviolate and invincible.[2]

The public school builds character, and character is the essential quality of a gentleman. It is precisely because of his character that a gentleman can be entrusted with the welfare of his country. Philip Carr and J. D. Scott, among many other commentators on English life, indicate that in the scale of British values character far outweighs expertise.

> What is certain is that the public schools produce a type of character which has been of great service to the state, as well as being admirable in itself. The system encourages the sense of responsibility; but it tames arrogance and induces modesty. It brings the capacity for practical judgement to early maturity; but it also develops the sense of fairness in general and justice to inferiors in particular.[3]

> . . . the belief that the best kind of man to run anything important, from a merchant banking firm to an African colony or the British embassy in Moscow, is a one-time Captain of the Eton cricket eleven with a good second-class University degree in Classics. . . . It is a source of bitterness to many people that so many important posts are now going to experts, clever men specially trained, who because of their special training cannot take a broad view and because of their cleverness are probably dishonourable and possibly cowardly.[4]

Some writers are approving, others are hostile, and still others are ironic about the character fostered by the public schools. Yet there is consensus that a code of behavior is strongly inculcated and that the code requires a self-abnegating devotion to one's obligations. A gentleman is not governed by emotions or by considerations of his own advantage but by the firmly implanted standards of his class. George Orwell notes the effectiveness of that training.

> After all, they belonged to a class with a certain tradition, they had been to public schools where the duty of dying for your country, if necessary, is laid down as the first and greatest of the commandments. They had to *feel* themselves true patriots. . . .[5]

The mainspring of the gentleman's character is self-control, for only the unrelenting inhibition of impulse permits him to abide by a code that requires conformity in all things, from the style of dress to the manner of death. The goal of public-school education is thus not the full development of the individual, but the conquest of self. Martin Green considers such an education to be appallingly effective.

> . . . a quality . . . lies deep in most modern British figures of authority and intelligence . . . a quality of a revenge taken on one's own spontaneity . . . the source of their energy is a cold joy in the defeat of humanity in themselves and in others.[6]

The literature on the British at home and the African literature both highlight their discussions of the value of discipline by the use of contrast, in one instance with the Africans, and in the other with the lower classes. As Harold Nicolson so coolly phrases it, "internal and external proletariats" are equivalents,[7] and assignment to the category of lesser breed can, obviously, be made either on the basis of race or class. Lower classes, like Africans, lack self-control. For those writers who are critical of the social order, the lack has positive value, and they credit the lower classes with greater warmth, spontaneity, and humanity.[8] This, too, has its parallel in the literature on Africa where writers who question the value system express admiration or envy of the emotional freedom of the Africans.

The writers in both samples, no matter what their point of view, seem to belong to the upper classes. This seems particularly characteristic of the writers on Africa. The generalization is, of course, more nearly valid if one defines upper class quite broadly. Apparently a not-too-rigid definition is permissible. Authorities such as G. D. H. Cole, David C. Marsh, and T. H. Pear suggest that the upper class shades into the upper middle class of intelligentsia, higher civil servants, professional men, and so on.[9] The real break in the English class structure is thus somewhere within the middle class. The significant distinction is between those who have had a public-school education and those who have not. By this token most English writers belong, as Martin Green states, to the upper classes.

> There have never been any working-class writers in England. And during this century, of course, literature has retreated up the social ladder. All our authors are public schoolboys—Waugh, Greene, Auden, Isherwood, Connolly, even Orwell. . . . [Lawrence as the chief exception]. They are "British" gentlemen, ruling class.[10]

Our information on the values of the upper classes, therefore, derives from descriptions given by their members. While these writers have the advantage of intimate knowledge, their observations and judgments are bound to be subjective. Despite their similar social status, the writers differ markedly from one another and have varied political points of view. Nevertheless, the descriptions are all quite consistent, whether the writer is as aloof as Denis W. Brogan, as scornful as Green and Orwell, or as approving as Carr and Nicolson. Consensus among such different writers can hopefully be taken as an indication of reliability, for these literary, impressionistic materials are the only data available. As Pear so justly points out, "there has been little field-work among the English upper class." [11]

Objective studies of the lower classes have, however, been conducted by social scientists. For the most part field work among the English is of the kind Geoffrey Gorer terms " 'slumming sociology,' descriptions of how 'the other half' lives and works." [12] Even in B. M. Spinley's comparative study of upper- and lower-class patterns, the "Deprived" are much more fully described than the "Privileged." [13] Although the studies of the lowest levels of British society are objective and scholarly, they tend to be contrastive in their point of view and so bear a certain resemblance to the literary accounts of the Africans. They, too, "emphasize the differences, not the similarities, between the people studied and the people likely to read the studies." [14] For this reason Gorer's book, *Exploring English Character,* has special value. Although the social extremes are underrepresented, this study includes the large middle segment of English society, which has hitherto been quite neglected. It is worth noticing that despite considerable criticism of the Gorer study, there is as much confirmation of his findings. Since Gorer, furthermore, addresses himself specifically to the nature of English values and attitudes, his work is particularly pertinent.

The most striking conclusion that can be drawn from the studies made by Gorer and others is that the values of the lower middle class and upper working class in English society are similar to those of the upper class. Most writers on English society greatly exaggerate the difference in values between their own class and the rest of English society. The leveling processes of the present century, at least, seem to have created a more homogeneous society than is generally acknowledged. This may, in part, explain the extreme importance attached to speech habits; as other differences become less apparent the public-school or upper-class dialect serves as the most significant, overt symbol of social distinction.

For the English, self-control is both a value in itself and the basis for the entire complex of virtues labeled "character." Implicit in the value of self-control is the underlying puritanical assumption that human beings are naturally evil. Since spontaneous behavior is aggressive and destructive, self-conquest not self-realization is the desired end in the rearing of children. Parents and their surrogates must impose a severe discipline upon children in order to bring all the natural, antisocial tendencies of the self under control.

> The formation of a good English character depends on the parents imposing suitable disciplines as early as possible; the child's character will be spoiled if the discipline is insufficient or not applied soon enough . . . discipline, habit training, is good in itself, and valuable for the formation of a good character, almost without regard to the habits trained or imposed.[15]

Adults who cannot or do not discipline themselves must be controlled by those who do. The demand that authorities take a firm stand, the approbation of what has been till recently a very harsh penal code, seem to derive from this attitude. And without question it is reflected in the African material. The use of force against their African subjects was justified by the English in the name of discipline, and as with children, the Africans were punished for their own good.

To Gorer as well as to other commentators the control of aggression seems the "central problem for the understanding of the English character." [16] Gorer accounts for the repression of other emotions and impulses as by-products, since "the habits of rigid self-control, which we have postulated in the case of aggression, would be likely to generalize to all forms of self-expression." [17] Whether or not control of aggression plays the dynamic, causative role Gorer assigns to it, the fact remains that aggression is firmly controlled. Scott, in his comments on Gorer, writes that he is "quite ready to accept the proposition that every Englishman is his own policeman," [18] and that self-discipline is the chief cause of the orderliness and absence of violence in English society.

Gorer believes that the psychic energy involved in aggression and its control "is not entirely dissipated; it finds outlets in a number of different ways, many of them symbolic." [19] He notes the possibilities in gardening, mastery over pets, and the severe disciplining of children as permitted outlets for aggression. (Perhaps the vicarious excitement to be found in the reading of the literature on Africa is one of them.) And warfare, of course, provides or once did provide an entirely legitimate expression of aggression. In war anger may be fully released because it is in a good cause, and not the indulgence of base instincts.

Sport, particularly the hunting of big game, is an obvious and highly valued outlet for aggression. The delight in hunting and the attraction to Africa because it provides good sport is one of the mainstays of the literature on Africa. But there is more to the satisfaction found in hunting than release of aggression. Sport has its own code: Carr pronounces the judgment that "A true sportsman will refuse to take the opportunity of achieving an easy success." [20] The enormous satisfaction in enduring hardship and discomfort that has always been so much part of the self-image of the British in Africa is related to the rejection of "easy success." Physical discomfort takes on a moral quality, for suffering endured is proof of self-mastery. Neither self-pity nor self-indulgence have deflected the Englishman from his goal. Even more vital is the element of risk; the sportsman faces danger in his pursuit of game and thereby gains assurance that he has overcome fear. Carr defines the best sport as "Difficulty, fatigue, hardship, danger—these are what make the greatest sport; and such magnets are they that men will deliberately seek them. . . ." [21]

The whole lure of Africa is implicitly predicated in Carr's exposition of the sporting spirit: "that a thing may be worth doing for the sake of the adventure—that is, for the sake of the very danger and the discomfort." [22] In Africa, where hardship and danger were embraced with self-congratulatory zeal, these multiple values of release of aggression and the demonstration of control over fear and self-indulgence can be fully realized.

The ethical import of sportsmanship and the code of fair play are extended into all aspects of life. If life can be thought of as a game, then profound emotion is uncalled for, and the English distrust of emotion and its repression are justified. Whether in sport, war, or all of life, there is, therefore, every need for good form and very little need for strong feeling.

> The sporting spirit even means that one must never forget that the whole of life is only a game, which must be played keenly, according to the rules, but without taking the whole thing too seriously, and that its greatest moments should be lived not only with a sense of the game, but with a sense of the sports of the field.[23]

The ethos in which games serve as a model for life has extended the premium on team spirit to a general male solidarity. The segregation of the sexes begins in the schools and tends to persist throughout life. This becomes especially noticeable in leisure pursuits. Carr, for example, attributes the prevalence of men's clubs, mainly an upper-class habit, to a "profound social instinct of the Englishman, the separation of the sexes for relaxation." [24] This "instinct" seems characteristic of all classes, however, including slum dwellers and coal miners as described by Norman Dennis, Fernando Henriques, and Clifford Slaughter.

> Men grow into a status, together with their age-mates, which makes them eligible for participation in these institutions and activities. At

the same time they grow into a set of attitudes and ideas which very consciously exclude women from the activities and permitted liberties of the male group, which can be said to constitute a type of secret society.[25]

These attitudes are also reflected in the African literature where the African experience symbolizes the entrance of the Englishman into an exclusive and esoteric male society. Africa itself provides the ordeal which initiates the youth into the society of men. It is a secret society given no overt formal expression, but the members know one another. They recognize their fellows even over the barriers of race and culture. The Masai and the Zulu are described as such true men, blood brothers to the English—brave, disciplined, and indifferent to women.

The exclusiveness of male society is inevitably accompanied by a sense of masculine superiority to which women give assent. Gorer reports that women would like to join in men's associations and activities if they were permitted.[26] It is interesting to notice how often the African literature tells of British ladies who avail themselves of the unusual opportunities in Africa to behave like gentlemen and sportsmen.

The generally masculine tone of the English ethos tends to devalue women and to set them apart. Some authorities believe that sex, as a social category, leads to greater differences in attitudes and values than any other form of social differentiation.[27] Although legally women have equal status with men, it would appear that women, by and large, are social inferiors who have only limited significance in the lives of men.

From boyhood into manhood the small groups in which males share their actions and thoughts maintain and strengthen the ideas of manliness being opposed to anything to do with girls and women, except in terms of sexual conquest . . . and is invariably reasserted completely after the early years of marriage.[28]

The sociological study of an English coal-mining town from which the above was taken also contains a statement of an attitude toward women that matches the British image of African women.

"In such an ideology women can only be objects of lust, mothers and domestic servants." [29] And the role of an English mother has been described by James H. Wellard as one of "loving drudgery." [30] African and English women are perceived in much the same terms.

Studies which attempt some comparison between English and American sexual behavior concur in their findings that the English, both men and women, are considerably less active sexually than the Americans.[31] The rather general attitude reported by Slater and Woodside in their study of British marriage, that "sex is a duty and women are not trained to expect any particular pleasure," [32] can account for the English woman's indifference. Although sex is deemed a masculine prerogative, men also tend to minimize its importance. Sexual attraction is not considered a reason for marriage or a valuable attribute of one's wife. In fact, a lack of interest in sex on the part of both husband and wife is a matter for complacent, mutual congratulation. Strong sexual feelings suffer the same repression to which all emotion is subject. Scott rather sadly remarks that "British men are not generally *en rapport* with women; it has been questioned whether they are profoundly *en rapport* with pleasure." [33]

There are indications, however, that these attitudes of devaluation of women and of sexuality are presently undergoing some change. The relationship between spouses, it is felt, ought to be more of a partnership than has been customary. In the newer suburbs husband and wife share a common interest in their home, and more of the man's leisure time is spent there with his wife than at a pub with other men. More demands are made on marriage for greater compatibility, emotional responsiveness and sexual satisfaction. If some recent British films and novels are to be taken at face value, the change is a very marked one, especially among the young. It is interesting, however, that the bold depiction of sexuality in the films is not accompanied by any elevation of the status of women, but merely a greater emphasis upon them as sex-objects. These attitudes are echoed in the newer image of Africa, which surrounds the continent with an aura of sexuality and grants African women an intense if passive sexuality.

It is not only in marriage that the English look for greater gratifications. Since World War II, the English standard of living has gone up. Higher wages and the Welfare State have made possible increased consumption. Whatever moral value discomfort may have had for gentlemen, it has not inhibited the working-class Englishman, the chief beneficiary of the postwar situation, from availing himself of the opportunities to enjoy better housing, clothing, and other comforts.

Except for such limited change, the English value system seems intact. Most of Gorer's list of constants—"love of freedom; fortitude; a low interest in sexual activity . . . a strong belief in the value of education for the formation of character; consideration . . . for the feelings of other people" [34]—are values still firmly held by most Englishmen. Yet there is still the feeling that gentlemen and their values have no place in modern England, and it pervades the literature on Africa and on England.

> For the Welfare State is no gentleman's country, and an educated Englishman, whatever he may think about it cannot feel it to be anything but unpalatable, or at best unexciting . . . The facts of life in England in the twentieth century . . . either distress or bore every man of sensibility and discrimination in the country. And yet more people have better health, more money, better education, etc., etc., than ever before. But it is no longer a gentleman's country, and all men of sensibility are gentlemen.[35]

The distress Green attributes to men of "sensibility and discrimination" can hardly be accounted for on the grounds of pure selfishness. Gentlemen surely do not so bitterly begrudge their countrymen access to better health, education, and more comfort. But improvement in the circumstances of the lower classes has been accompanied by a sense of insecurity of tenure in the upper classes. Studies by David Glass and his associates indicate a fairly high rate of downward mobility in recent times.[36] Although G. D. H. Cole partly questions the validity of these findings,[37] they would seem to indicate some realistic basis for the disquietude of the upper classes.

The power position of the upper classes appears weakened. The products of the public schools no longer feel assured of monopoly of leadership in the civil service or the professions. The state-supported schools are modeled on the public schools, and although they cannot give the cachet of superior social status, they do provide an adequate education. They enable their students to qualify for a variety of positions in the modern world where "examination is exalted above personality and trial of personal worth." [38] Even army commissions are no longer prerogatives of the upper classes, for in modern warfare technical skills seem more important than character. Pear suggests that "character" might even be a handicap, since "So far as the Army is concerned, atom- and germ-warfare and the use of hydrogen bombs will never be activities suitable for gentlemen—or sportsmen. . . ." [39]

The sense of alienation reported by upper-class writers is only partly based on the threat, and it is as yet only a threat, to their status. Their values cannot be merely equated with the retention of privilege; a code that places so much more value on discipline than on gratification is probably too austere to permit this. The English do believe that the self-disciplined life is the good life and, therefore, self-rewarding, that " 'righteousness' does in fact exalt a nation." [40] But it is just this sense of exaltation that is now missing. The ideological foundations that gave meaning to self-discipline have been weakened, whether they were found in religion, progress, or imperialism.

Orwell links the decline of the empire with a more profound weakening of British morale.[41] Sir John Strachey, who takes even more pride in the dissolution of the empire than he does in its acquisition, writes of the need for some new great enterprise to reinvigorate English morale.

> It will not do us much good to exhibit all the wisdom and moderation in the world, if we do not find some fresh national purpose, capable of inspiring the spirit and energies of the British people. For to a considerable extent the enlargement or maintenance of the empire has been our national purpose. . . . Yet we shall stagnate unless we can find other purposes to satisfy our hearts.[42]

Responsibility for the empire may well have given purpose and meaning to the austere, self-depriving character of the English.

Imperial England was powerful and wealthy, and as Brogan says, "Virtue was its own reward, and who, looking at the reward, could doubt the virtue?"[43] It is, however, open to question whether imperialism was a truly national ideology. It was more closely allied to the interests of the upper classes, and it was they, rather than the lower classes, who suffered the greater moral loss. David Frost and Anthony Jay do point out that the British of all classes have been deprived by loss of opportunities for validation of manhood.

> Where do you find the challenge, the excitement, the stretching of your capabilities, the test of your courage and nerve that some people need to make them feel that they are living and not just existing. . . . There was a time when you could enlist as a soldier and fight wars; but not any more. There was a time when you could go out to a colony, open up the West, pioneer new frontiers; but not any more.[44]

Protestant Christianity was a system of belief which certainly affected all the social levels of England, and according to the historian K. B. Smellie, ". . . the protestant ethic . . . provided . . . the metaphysical basis for the decencies we still in general observe."[45] Gorer also holds religion to be the strongest sanction for the English moral code.[46] Other accounts, however, stress the weakening of religious faith both in regard to church attendance and to any genuine concern with religion. This loss of faith is regretted because morality is thereby weakened and because human beings have need for faith.[47]

None of the nineteenth-century articles of faith seem secure in the twentieth century. Along with imperialism and religion, the belief in science and progress has been shaken. The cause of progress may once have provided the higher purpose that justified self-denial, but the modern Englishman cannot be confident that social change, increase in scientific knowledge, and expansion of industry will result in the improvement of mankind. Progress has lost its role as a validating purpose, and even more, the direction "progress" has taken seems antithetical to the older values. Orwell is, somewhat unexpectedly, one of the harshest critics of "progress." For his opinion is that "The tendency of mechanical progress is to make your environment safe and soft; and yet you are striving to keep yourself brave and hard." [48] In a world made "safe for little fat men" [49] strength of character and will are superfluous.

Every attitude, major or minor, to be found projected in the literature on Africa has its counterpart expressly stated in the commentaries on England, with one exception—racism. Yet racism is one of the fundamental components of the British literary tradition about Africa; it is equally prevalent in the writing on India, or for that matter, wherever non-white populations come under discussion. Its almost complete omission in the British self-commentary is, therefore, the more striking. Some mention is made of xenophobia, more often phrased as insularity, but even then, it is dismissed as a minor idiosyncrasy, or an attitude held by the ill-educated. Recent events in Great Britain, however, force the recognition that racism is endemic in the whole society. That the British analysts of their own culture do not discuss it indicates a peculiar sort of nescience.

Speculation on this lack of awareness suggests several possible causes. It may be that the liberal and humanitarian values of the British interdict recognition of so antithetical a concept as racism. It is also true that until recently the issue did not have to be faced at home. Racism could be projected out onto the darker-skinned populations of the colonies and there phrased in terms of the master-subject relationship. There had been relatively few non-whites in England, and they were mostly transient students and visitors to whom the British were kind and hospitable, even if patronizing. But the recent immigrants from the former colonies are not transients, nor are they subjects; they are peers to be accorded equal treatment. Great Britain has become a multiracial society in which the new relationship of black and white has evoked the open expression of British racism in acts of discrimination, immigration laws, and race riots.

Contemporary England seems to have undergone a moral revolution evidenced by frivolity in fashions, overt sexuality, youthful rebellion, and aggressive behavior. But one may question whether this self-indulgence is a manifestation of a new hedonism or the froth churned up by the search for new moral purpose. Frost and Jay suggest that the British take up again their mission to civilize, this time donning the mantle of Athens to bring culture and refinement to the new Romans across the Atlantic.[50] Certainly the "angry young men" seem as profoundly motivated by the Protestant passion for righteousness as their Victorian forebears were. They hold the values of the past firmly enough to use them as standards by which to judge and condemn the present.

The values of character have changed less than other aspects of British culture. Victorian values are retained in British writing about themselves and about Africa. And it is the British concept of themselves which has determined their concept of Africa.

Four centuries of writing about Africa have produced a literature which describes not Africa but the British response to it. The literature persistently recounts the fantasy of the Englishman in confrontation with Africa. As in a morality play, the British and the Africans are the exemplars of civilization and savagery, respectively. In the Victorian version civilization equalled the positive good and savagery its abhorrent negation. Modern writers often reverse the equation as an expression of their uncertainties. Whether confident or doubtful, the writers describe Africa in the same conventions. The image of Africa remains the negative reflection, the shadow, of the British self-image.

Notes

Preface

1. Joyce Cary, *The Case for African Freedom* (London, 1944), p. 135.
2. Joyce Cary, *The African Witch* (London, 1951), p. 88.
3. Elspeth Huxley, *Four Guineas* (London, 1954), p. 205.
4. Tom Stacey, *The Brothers M* (New York, 1961), p. 158.

Introduction

1. Katherine George, "The Civilized West Looks at Primitive Africa: 1400–1800," *Isis*, 49 (1958), pp. 62–72.

Chapter I

Commerce in Commodities and Human Beings

1. Richard Hakluyt, *Voyages*, Vol. IV (Glasgow, 1904), p. 194.
2. *Ibid.*, VI, 180.
3. Hakluyt, IV, VI, XI (1904 ed.); Samuel Purchas, *Purchas, His Pilgrimes* (Glasgow, 1905), VI.
4. Richard Jobson, *The Golden Trade, or a Discovery of the River Gambia* (London, 1623).
5. Hakluyt, VI, 167–72.
6. Eden, in J. W. Blake, *Europeans in West Africa*, Vol. II (London, 1942), p. 289.
7. Hakluyt, VI, 184–85.
8. *Ibid.*, p. 151.
9. Towerson, in J. W. Blake, *Europeans in West Africa*, p. 292.
10. Hakluyt, VI, 321.
11. J. Churchill, *Collections of Voyages and Travels* (London, Vols., I–IV, 1704; V–VI, 1752).
12. Archibald Dalzel, *The History of Dahomy, an inland kingdom of Africa* (London, 1793); Robert Norris, *Memories of the Reign of Bosse Whadee, King of Dahomey* (London, 1789); William Snelgrave,

A New Account of Some Parts of Guinea and the Slave Trade (London, 1734); William Smith, *New Voyage to Guinea* (London, 1744).

13. Phillips, in Churchill, *Collection*, VI, 147.
14. Dalzel, *Dahomy*, p. vii.
15. Norris, *Memories*, p. 157.
16. Dalzel, *Dahomy*, pp. xxiv–xxv.
17. Basil Davidson, *Black Mother* (Boston, 1961), p. xvii.
18. Michel Adanson, in Wylie Sypher, *Guinea's Captive Kings: British Anti-Slavery Literature of the XVIII Century* (Chapel Hill, 1941), p. 57.
19. Robert Burns, in E. B. Dykes, *The Negro in English Romantic Thought* (Washington, 1942), p. 20.
20. Mrs. Aphra Behn, *Oroonoko* (London, c. 1677).
21. *Ibid.*, p. 23.
22. Reverend William Dodd, *The Epistle of Zara at the Court of Anamboe, to the African Prince Now in England*, in Dodsley's *Collections* (London, 1783), IV, 222.
23. Roy Harvey Pearce, *The Savages of America* (Baltimore, 1953).

The Early Nineteenth Century: West Africa

1. Plan of the Association from the *Proceedings of the Association for Promoting the Discovery of the Interior Parts of Africa* (London, 1790).
2. Hugh Clapperton, *Journal of a Second Expedition into the Interior of Africa, and the Journal of Richard Lander* (Philadelphia, 1829), p. 3.
3. Captain William Allen and T. R. H. Thompson, *Narrative of the Expedition to the River Niger in 1841*, 2 vols. (London, 1848), I, 218–19.
4. Thomas Thompson, 1758; John Beecham, 1841; T. B. Freeman, 1844; Samuel Crowther, 1855.
5. Reverend R. Montgomery, "Proceedings of the First Public Meeting of the Glasgow Society" in L. J. Saunders, *Scottish Democracy, 1815–1840: The Social and Intellectual Background* (London and Edinburgh, 1950), p. 393.
6. Alexander Laing, *Travels in the Timannee, Kooranko and Soolima Countries* (London, 1825), p. 320.
7. Wallace Notestein, *The Scot in History* (New Haven, 1949), pp. 96, 187.
8. Mungo Park was a physician, Hugh Clapperton an officer in the Navy, and Alexander Laing in the Army; John Duncan had been in the Life Guards. Richard Lander was a literate "Gentleman's gentle-

man." William Baikie was a surgeon and had achieved distinction as a naturalist. At the times of Thomas Bowdich's mission to Ashanti he was a "writer" (clerk) with the African Company of Merchants and later (1820) he lived in Paris, writing and studying mathematics and natural science.

9. Mungo Park, *Travels in the Interior Districts of Africa, 1795, 1796 and 1797* (London, 1799), pp. 62–63.

10. Richard and John Lander, *Journal of an Expedition to Explore the Course and Termination of the Niger,* 2 vols. (New York, 1833), II, 154; see also pp. 62 and 63.

11. Mungo Park, *Journal of a Mission to the Interior of Africa in the year 1805* (Philadelphia, 1815), p. 163.

12. Park, *Travels,* pp. 52, 110, 138–39, 151–52.

13. Thomas Edward Bowdich, *Mission from Cape Coast Castle to Ashantee* (London, 1819), pp. 198–99; John Duncan, *Travels in Western Africa in 1845 and 1846,* 2 vols. (London, 1847), I, 238–39. Park, *Travels,* pp. 26–27, 39–42.

14. Bowdich, *Mission,* pp. 36–44; cf. Duncan, *Travels,* I, 225–40.

15. Duncan, *Travels,* I, 225; see also Bowdich, *Mission,* p. 65.

16. Bowdich, *Mission,* p. 60.

17. Robert A. Lystad, *The Ashanti: A Proud People* (New Brunswick, New Jersey, 1958), pp. 27–28.

18. Duncan, *Travels,* I, 292.

19. Laing, *Travels,* p. 154.

20. Bowdich, *Mission,* pp. 212–25.

21. Duncan, *Travels,* I, 51–54.

22. Samuel Crowther, *Journal of an Expedition up the Niger and Tshadda Rivers* (London, 1855), pp. 128–29.

23. R. Lander in Clapperton, *Journal,* I, 152.

24. Macgregor Laird and R. A. K. Oldfield, *Narrative of an Expedition in the Interior of Africa by the River Niger in 1832–34,* 2 vols. (London, 1837), II, 56.

25. F. Harrison Rankin, *The White Man's Grave: A Visit to Sierra Leone in 1834,* 2 vols. (London, 1836).

The Golden Land: South Africa, 1800–1850

1. John Barrow, *Travels into the Interior of Southern Africa,* 2 vols. (London, 1806), II, 99.

2. *Ibid.,* I, 93–94.

3. *Ibid.,* I, 158–59.

4. Andrew Steedman, *Wanderings and Adventures in the Interior of Southern Africa,* 2 vols. (London, 1910), II, 136–37.

5. *Ibid.*, I, 171.
6. Robert Moffat, *Missionary Labours* (New York, 1842), p. 4.
7. John Campbell, *Travels in South Africa* (Andover, Massachusetts, 1916), p. 262.
8. David Livingstone, *Missionary Travels and Researches in South Africa* (New York, 1859), p. 34.
9. *Ibid.*, p. 47.
10. E.g., Moffat, *Labours;* Campbell, *Travels;* Allen F. Gardiner, *Narrative of a Journey to the Zoolu Country* (London, 1836); Robert Moffat, *Matabele Journals,* 2 vols. (London, 1945; first edition, 1855).
11. Livingstone, *Missionary Travels,* p. 25.
12. *Ibid.*, pp. 21–22.
13. *Ibid.*, pp. 549–50.
14. David Livingstone, *The Last Journals of David Livingstone in Central Africa from 1865 to his Death* (New York, 1875).
15. Douglas Woodruff, "Expansion and Emigration in Early Victorian England" in G. M. Young (ed.), *Early Victorian England* (London, 1934).
16. Thomas Pringle, *African Sketches* (London, 1834), p. 479.
17. Francis Galton, *Narrative of an Explorer in Tropical South Africa* (London, 1853), p. 189.
18. Alfred W. Cole, *The Cape and the Kaffirs* (London, 1852), p. 42; pp. 195ff.
19. Sir William Cornwallis Harris, *The Wild Sports of Southern Africa* (London, 1839), p. 346.
20. Moffat, *Labours,* p. 16.
21. Hugh Murray, Robert Jameson and James Wilson, *Narrative of Discovery and Adventure in Africa* (London, 1849), p. 301.
22. Henry M. Methuen, *Life in the Wilderness, or Wanderings in South Africa* (London, 1856), p. 35.
23. Harris, *Wild Sports of Southern Africa,* p. 65.
24. Livingstone, *Missionary Researches,* p. 69.
25. *Ibid.*, p. 69.
26. Captain Frederick Marryat, *The Mission, or Scenes in Africa* (London, 1845), p. 15.

Chapter II
The Saga of Exploration

1. Ronald Robinson, J. Gallagher and Alice Denny, *Africa and the Victorians, the Climax of Imperialism in the Dark Continent* (New York, 1961), pp. 15–16.

2. *Ibid.*, p. 16.
3. The Church Missionary Society in Uganda in 1877, and the London Missionary Society in Nyasa in 1878.
4. Sir Francis Burton, *The Lake Regions of Central Africa,* 2 vols. (New York, 1961; original edition, 1861), I, 145–57.
5. Alan Moorehead, *The White Nile* (New York, 1960), pp. 61–62.
6. John and Mrs. J. Petherick, *Travels in Central Africa and Explorations of the Western Nile Tributaries,* 2 vols. (London, 1869), II, Appendix A, 78–79.
7. W. E. Houghton, *The Victorian Frame of Mind, 1830–1870* (New Haven, 1957), p. 316.
8. Zoe Marsh, *East African History Through Contemporary Records* (Cambridge, 1961), p. 88.
9. John Hanning Speke, *Journey of the Discovery of the Source of the Nile* (New York, 1864), p. 513.
10. Sir Richard Francis Burton, *A Mission to Gelele, King of Dahomey,* 2 vols. (London, 1877), II, 44.
11. J. B. Thomson, *Joseph Thomson, African Explorer* (London, 1896), pp. 164–65.
12. Sir Samuel Baker, *Albert N'Yanza* (London, 1866), p. 445.
13. Verney Lovett Cameron, *Across Africa (1873–1876)* (New York, 1877), pp. 152–54.
14. Speke, *Journey,* Introduction, p. xxii.
15. David Livingstone, *Narrative of an Expedition to the Zambesi and its Tributaries: and of the discovery of the Lakes Shirwa and Nyassa, 1858–1864* (New York, 1866), p. 725.
16. Baker, *Albert N'Yanza,* "Introduction," p. xxii.
17. Henry M. Stanley, *In Darkest Africa, or the Quest, Rescue and Retreat of Emin, Governor of Equatoria,* 2 vols. (New York, 1890), I, 212 and 244.
18. Livingstone, *Last Journals,* p. 69.
19. J. B. Thomson, *Thomson,* p. 23.
20. Joseph Thomson, *To the Central African Lakes and Back,* 2 vols. (Boston, 1881; 2nd. ed.).
21. Joseph Thomson, *Through Masailand* (London, 1885), p. 574.
22. *Ibid.*, p. 574.
23. James Frederick Elton, *Journals of Travels and Researches among the Lakes and Mountains of Eastern and Central Africa,* edited and compiled by M. B. Cotterill (London, 1879), p. 155.
24. Thomson, *Masailand,* p. 503.
25. Henry M. Stanley, *How I Found Livingtone,* 2 vols. (New York, 1890), I, 311.

26. Baker, *Albert N'Yanza*, p. 297.
27. *Ibid.*, p. 298.
28. Stanley, *How I found Livingstone*, I, 336.
29. Speke, *Journey*, p. 335.
30. *Ibid.*, p. 335.
31. Burton, *Mission to Gelele*, II, 106.
32. Baker, *Albert N'Yanza*, p. 183.

The Setting of the Saga

1. Burton, *Lake Regions*, I, 91–92.
2. Stanley, *Darkest Africa*, I, 282.
3. Thomson, *Masailand*, p. 201.
4. Baker, *Albert N'Yanza*, p. 280.
5. Petherick, *Travels*, II, 6.
6. Baker, *Albert N'Yanza*, p. 130.
7. Burton, *Mission to Gelele*, I, 156.
8. Thomson, *Masailand*, p. 413.
9. *Ibid.*, p. 474.
10. Burton, *Mission to Gelele*, II, 118–19.
11. *Ibid.*, I, 156.
12. Livingstone, *Zambesi*, p. 297; Burton, *Lake Regions*, I, 120.
13. Cameron, *Across Africa*, p. 89; Burton, *Mission to Gelele*, I, 100; Anna Hinderer, *Seventeen Years in the Yoruba Country* (London, 1872), p. 297; Winwood Reade, *African Sketchbooks*, 2 vols. (London, 1873), II, 115.
14. Baker, *Albert N'Yanza*, pp. 152–53.
15. Stanley, *Dark Continent*, pp. 56–63.
16. Burton, *Mission to Gelele*, I, 134–35.
17. Stanley, *Dark Continent*, pp. 17–18, and *passim*.
18. A. M. Mackay, *Mackay of Uganda* (New York, 1890), pp. vi ff.; Speke, *Journey*, chapters XII, XIII, XIV: Robert P. Ashe, *Two Kings of Uganda* (London, 1890).

Mid-Century Fiction and the Work of Winwood Reade

1. Margaret Dalziel, *Popular Fiction 100 Years Ago* (London, 1957); Amy Cruse, *The Victorians and Their Books* (London, 1935).
2. E.g., Charles Reade, *A Simpleton* (Boston and New York, n.d.; original edition, 1873). Reade lists in his introduction at least ten primary sources for his African material.
3. Captain Frederick Marryat, *The Privateersman* (Boston, 1866); Reade, *A Simpleton;* J. A. Skertchly, *Melinda, the Caboceer, or Sport*

in Ashanti (New York, 1876); Henry M. Stanley, *My Kalulu* (New York, 1874); Reade, *African Sketchbooks.*

4. Marryat, *The Privateersman,* pp. 52–53.
5. J. B. Thomson, *Thomson,* p. 191.
6. Reade, *African Sketchbooks,* I, 168.
7. Winwood W. Reade, *Savage Africa,* 2 vols. (New York, 1864), I, 375–82.
8. Reade, *African Sketchbooks,* II, 359.
9. *Ibid.,* I, 55.
10. Reade, *African Sketchbooks,* I, 220–21, 223–25.
11. Reade, *Savage Africa,* I, 440; *African Sketchbooks,* II, 134–35.
12. Reade, *Savage Africa,* I, 454; *African Sketchbooks,* I, 309–19.
13. Reade, *Savage Africa,* I, 159–64, 398; II, 403, 426, 446.
14. Reade, *African Sketchbooks,* I, 223.
15. *Ibid.,* II, 306.
16. Burton, *Lake Regions,* II, 292.
17. Reade, *Savage Africa,* I, 249–50.
18. *Ibid.,* I, 383.
19. *Ibid.,* preface.
20. *Ibid.,* II, 451.

Chapter III
The Bearers of the Burden

1. J. R. Seeley, *The Expansion of England* (London, 1931); Sir Charles Dilke, *The British Empire* (London, 1899); James Bryce, *Impressions of South Africa* (New York, 1897); Rayne Kruger, *Goodbye, Dolly Gray; the Story of the Boer War* (London, 1959).
2. Seeley, *The Expansion of England,* p. 10.
3. Frederick D. Lugard, *The Rise of Our East African Empire,* 2 vols. (Edinburgh and London, 1893), I, 284; see also Alfred J. Swann, *Fighting the Slave Hunters in Central Africa* (London, 1910), pp. 314–15; F. Courtenay Selous, *Travel and Adventure in South East Africa* (London, 1893), p. 325; Thomas Alldridge, *A Transformed Colony, Sierra Leone, As it was and as it is. . . .* (London, 1910), pp. 122, 282.
4. Ewart S. Grogan and Arthur H. Sharp, *From the Cape to Cairo* (London, 1900).
5. Dorothy Wellesley, *Sir George Goldie, Founder of Nigeria* (London, 1934), ix.
6. Winston S. Churchill, *My African Journey* (London, 1908), p. 24.

7. Grogan, *Cape to Cairo,* p. 96.

8. J. B. Thomson, *Thomson,* p. 271.

9. F. Lugard, *Rise of East African Empire,* I, p. 243. See also E. J. Glave, *In Savage Africa; or Six Years of Adventure in Congoland* (New York, 1892), p. 16; and Swann, *Fighting the Slave Hunters,* p. 45.

10. J. Bryce, *Impressions of South Africa,* p. 240; see also Seymour Vandeleur, *Campaigning on the Upper Nile and Niger* (London, 1898), p. 25.

11. Swann, *Fighting the Slave Hunters,* pp. 203–4.

12. Basil Worsfold, *A History of South Africa* (London, 1900), pp. 41–44; Bryce, *Impressions,* pp. 390ff.

13. Grogan, *Cape to Cairo,* p. 324; Lionel Declé, *Three Years in Savage Africa* (London, 1898), p. 203; Sir Harry Johnston, *The River Congo, from its mouth to Bolobo* (London, 1884), pp. 70–71; Worsfold, *History,* p. 41.

14. Lugard, *Rise of East African Empire,* I, 84.

15. Grogan, *Cape to Cairo,* p. 231.

16. H. Rider Haggard, *Cetywayo and His White Neighbours* (London, 1882), p. 35; see also Sir Harry Johnston, *The Story of My Life* (New York, 1923), p. 237.

17. Lugard, *Rise of East African Empire,* I, 301.

18. Sir Harry Johnston, *British Central Africa* (New York, 1897), p. 68; see also W. Churchill, *African Journey,* pp. 43–48; Mrs. M. A. Pringle, *Towards the Mountains of the Moon* (London, 1883), p. 220; Declé, *Three Years,* pp. 125, 185–86; Mary Hall, *A Woman's Trek from the Cape to Cairo* (London, 1907), p. 300.

19. Swann, *Fighting the Slave Hunters,* p. 133; Declé, *Three Years,* pp. 29–31; Sir H. H. Johnston, *The Uganda Protectorate,* 2 vols. (London, 1902), I, 230–31.

20. Johnston, *British Central Africa,* pp. 68–69; Swann, *Fighting the Slave Hunters,* pp. 138–43.

21. Seeley, *Expansion,* p. 225; see also Sir Harry H. Johnston, *The Kilimanjaro Expedition* (London, 1886), p. 508.

22. Churchill, *African Journey,* p. 121.

23. Lugard, *Rise of East African Empire,* I, 204, 462–63.

24. Churchill, *African Journey,* pp. 54–55; Lugard, *Rise of East African Empire,* I, 488; Declé, *Three Years,* p. 369.

25. Ashe, *Two Kings of Uganda,* p. 124.

26. Worsfold, *History,* p. 98.

27. Bryce, *Impressions,* p. 526; Alice Blanche Balfour, *Twelve Hundred Miles in a Waggon* (London, 1895), p. 79; Constance

Larymore, *A Resident's Wife in Nigeria* (London, 1908), Chapter II.

28. Pringle, *Mountains of the Moon,* p. 233.
29. Hall, *Woman's Trek,* p. 231.
30. Mary Kingsley, *Travels in West Africa* (London, 1898), pp. 477–78.
31. Declé, *Three Years,* pp. 136–37.
32. Lady Flora Lugard, *A Tropical Dependency* (London, 1905).
33. Larymore, *Resident's Wife,* pp. 105, 215; see also Lady Florence Dixie, *In the Land of Misfortune* (London, 1882), pp. 109, 130.
34. Declé, *Three Years,* p. 339.
35. Larymore, *Resident's Wife,* p. 14.

The White Man's Burden

1. Johnston, *Uganda,* I, 85–86.
2. Alldridge, *Transformed Colony,* p. 97.
3. W. Churchill, *African Journey,* p. 208.
4. Kingsley, *Travels,* p. 11.
5. Hall, *Woman's Trek,* p. 21.
6. Ashe, *Two Kings of Uganda,* p. 182.
7. Arthur S. White, *The Development of Africa* (London, 1890), pp. 9, 238, 241; Churchill, *African Journey,* pp. 76–79; Johnston, *Uganda,* I, 77–78; Lugard, *Rise of East African Empire,* I, 506–8.
8. Churchill, *African Journey,* pp. 5, 8, 31.
9. Bryce, *Impressions,* pp. 43–44.
10. Johnston, *Uganda,* I, 88.
11. Worsfold, *History,* p. 125.
12. Vandeleur, *Campaigning,* p. 189; see also Johnston, *Kilimanjaro,* pp. 99–100; Selous, *Travel,* p. 346; Swann, *Fighting the Slave Hunters,* pp. 314–15; MacDonald, *Soldiering,* p. 195; Dixie, *Land of Misfortune,* p. 147; Grogan, *Cape to Cairo,* p. 224; Haggard, *Cetywayo,* p. 20; Charles H. Robinson, *Hausaland* (London, 1896), p. 274.
13. Lugard, *Rise of East African Empire,* II, 249–50.
14. *Ibid.,* I, 382.
15. Hall, *Woman's Trek,* pp. 28, 41, 111, 207, 238, 242, 251, 271.
16. Lugard described the Kikuyu (*Rise of East African Empire,* I, 327) as "honest, straightforward, intelligent, good-mannered and friendly." MacDonald (*Soldiering,* pp. 109, 111) asserted that Lugard had been completely misguided in his judgment of the Kikuyu and that they were "really excitable, treacherous, addicted to drink and utter scoundrels."
17. White, *Development of Africa,* pp. 105, 107, 122.
18. Lugard, *Rise of East African Empire,* I, 478–79.

19. Johnston, *Uganda,* II, 647; Churchill, *African Journey,* p. 106.
20. Vandeleur, *Campaigning,* p. 170.
21. Charles H. Robinson, *Nigeria, Our Latest Protectorate* (New York, 1900), pp. 7, 27.
22. Lugard, *Rise of East African Empire,* I, 400.
23. Kingsley, *Travels,* p. 24.
24. Lady Flora Lugard, *A Tropical Dependency,* pp. 21ff.
25. Grogan, *Cape to Cairo,* pp. 149–54.
26. E. E. Evans-Pritchard, "Zande Cannibalism," *Journal of the Royal Anthropological Institute,* 1960; L. and P. Bohannan, *The Tiv* (London, 1953).
27. Johnston, *British Central Africa,* pp. 394–96.
28. Bryce, *Impressions,* p. 359.
29. Johnston, *British Central Africa,* p. 408.
30. All the characteristics are not mentioned by all the writers, but they all mention at least some. Limitations of space do not permit page references for each of the attributions, but, for example, Bryce mentions most of them on pp. 92, 122, 356, 364, 387, 476 (*Impressions*).
31. Bryce, *Impressions,* p. 94; see also Lugard, *Rise,* I, 171.
32. Grogan, *Cape to Cairo,* p. 165; see also Declé, *Three Years,* p. 26; Selous, *Travel,* p. 95; Johnston, *Uganda,* I, 193.
33. Kingsley, *Travels,* p. 488.
34. Bryce, *Impressions,* p. 375; see also Worsfold, *History,* p. 61; Swann, *Fighting the Slave Hunters,* pp. 330–34; Johnston, *British Central Africa,* pp. 202–6; Selous, *Travel,* p. 135.
35. Declé, *Three Years,* p. 5.
36. Vandeleur, *Campaigning,* pp. 161–62.
37. Johnston, *British Central Africa,* pp. 184, 202–3; Bryce, *Impressions,* p. 382; Kingsley, *Travels,* pp. 502–3.
38. Johnston, *Congo,* pp. 8 and 26, and *British Central Africa,* p. 19.

Fiction of Empire

1. Winifred Hall, *The Overseas Empire in Fiction* (London, 1942); Susan Howe, *Novels of Empire* (New York, 1949); William Y. Tindall, *Forces in Modern British Literature, 1885–1946* (New York, 1947).
2. Morton N. Cohen, *Rider Haggard, His Life and Works* (New York, 1960), p. 96.
3. G. A. Henty, *Young Colonists* (New York, n.d.; original edition, 1888).
4. In recent years there has been a small revival of Henty's novels.

His books are being bought up by the toy soldier *aficionados,* to re-enact the battle scenes.

5. Sir Percy Fitzpatrick, *Jock of the Bushveld* (London, 1907).
6. John Buchan, *Prester John* (Boston, 1928; original edition, 1910).
7. Sir Rider Haggard, *Three Novels of Adventure* (New York, 1953).
8. John Chalmers, *Fighting the Matabele* (London, 1898); Sir Bertram Mitford, *The King's Assegai* (London, 1895); Fitzpatrick, *Jock of the Bushveld;* Henty, *Young Colonists.*
9. Mary Gaunt, *The Uncounted Cost* (London, 1904); Sir Bertram Mitford, *John Ames, Native Commissioner* (London, 1900); Ernest Glanville, *The Fossicker* (London, 1891); H. R. Haggard, *Jess* (New York, 1890).
10. Cohen, *Rider Haggard,* p. 113.
11. Mitford, *King's Assegai.*
12. Mitford, *John Ames;* Chalmers, *Matabele;* Glanville, *The Fossickers.*
13. Rudyard Kipling, "The Captive," "A Sahib's War," "Comprehension of Private Cooper," in *Traffics and Discoveries* (New York, 1927; original edition, 1904), also "Egypt of the Magicians", in *Letters of Travel, 1892–1913* (New York, 1927; original edition, 1914).
14. Edgar Wallace, *Sanders of the River* (Garden City, 1930; original edition, 1909).
15. W. Somerset Maugham, *The Explorer* (New York, 1907), p. 180.
16. *Ibid.,* p. 279.
17. *Ibid.,* p. 178.
18. Buchan, *Prester John,* p. 264.
19. Rudyard Kipling, *Something of Myself* (New York, 1937).
20. Olive Schreiner, *The Story of an African Farm* (New York, n.d.; original edition, 1895).
21. *Ibid.,* p. 52.
22. *Ibid.,* p. 170.
23. Joseph Conrad, *Heart of Darkness* (New York, 1961; original edition, 1899) and "An Outpost of Progress," *Tales of Unrest* (New York, 1925; original edition, 1898).
24. Conrad, *Heart of Darkness,* p. 16.
25. *Ibid.,* p. 17.
26. *Ibid.,* p. 18.
27. *Ibid.,* p. 50.
28. Wallace, *Sanders of the River,* p. 277.

29. Conrad, "Outpost of Progress," p. 130.
30. Fitzpatrick, *Jock of the Bushveld,* p. 17.
31. Maugham, *Explorer,* p. 277; see also p. 45.
32. Mitford, *John Ames,* p. 86; see also Chalmers, *Matabele,* pp. 116–17; Buchan, *Prester John,* p. 139; Fitzpatrick, *Jock of the Bushveld,* p. 199; Maugham, *Explorer,* p. 160.
33. Cohen, *Rider Haggard,* p. 21.
34. Conrad, "Outpost of Progress," p. 132.
35. Mitford, *John Ames,* p. 5.
36. Fitzpatrick, *Jock of the Bushveld,* p. 207.
37. Glanville, *Fossicker,* p. 123.
38. Chalmers, *Matabele,* pp. 49–56.
39. William Charles Scully, *Kaffir Stories* (London, 1895).
40. H. Rider Haggard, *Nada the Lily* (London, 1892).
41. Buchan, *Prester John,* p. 201.
42. Fitzpatrick, *Jock of the Bushveld,* p. 197.
43. Haggard, *Allan Quatermain,* p. 430.
44. Buchan, *Prester John,* p. 201.
45. Haggard, *Allan Quatermain,* p. 458.
46. Fitzpatrick, *Jock of the Bushveld,* pp. 167–68.

Chapter IV

The Tradition in the Twentieth Century

1. D. W. Brogan, *The English People—Impressions and Observations* (New York, 1943), pp. 7–8; footnote, p. 8; Rayne Kruger, *Good-bye, Dolly Grey, The Story of the Boer War* (London, 1959), pp. 144ff.; A. Conan Doyle, *The Boer War* (New York, 1900).
2. Calvin Stillman (ed.), *Africa in the Modern World* (Chicago, 1955), pp. 289–90.
3. John Buchan, *Island of Sheep* (London, 1960), pp. 64–65.
4. Buchan, *Prester John,* p. 188.
5. Reginald Coupland, *Kirk of the Zambesi* (Oxford, 1928); Stephen Gwyn, *The Life of Mary Kingsley* (London, 1932); Elspeth Huxley, *White Man's Country,* 2 vols. (London, 1935); Margery Perham, *Lugard,* 2 vols. (London, 1960); Dorothy Wellesley, *Sir George Goldie, Founder of Nigeria* (London, 1934).
6. Ian Henderson, *Man-Hunt in Kenya* (Garden City, 1958).
7. Sir Charles Dundas, *African Crossroads* (London, 1955), p. 143.
8. Peter Viertel, *White Hunter, Black Heart* (London, 1954), p. 18.
9. Winifred Holtby, *Mandoa, Mandoa!* (New York, 1933); Gwyn Griffin, *By the North Gate* (New York, 1959), and *Something of an*

Achievement (New York, 1960); Evelyn Waugh, *Black Mischief* (New York, 1960).

10. Alan Scholefield, *A View of Vultures* (London, 1966), and *Great Elephant* (New York, 1968).

11. Eric Ambler, *Dirty Story* (New York, 1967); June Drummond, *Welcome, Proud Lady* (New York, 1968); Shirley Milne, *Beware the Lurking Scorpion* (New York, 1966).

12. Dr. Grantly Dick Read, *No Time for Fear* (New York, 1955), p. 204.

13. Stuart Cloete, *The African Giant* (Boston, 1955), pp. 290–91.

Chapter V
The Abysmal Gulf

1. Laurens Van der Post, *The Dark Eye in Africa* (New York, 1955), p. 43.

2. Max Catto, *Gold in the Sky* (New York, 1958), pp. 9–10.

3. Richard Wyndham, *The Gentle Savage* (New York, 1936), p. 47.

4. Elspeth Huxley, *The Walled City* (Philadelphia, 1949), p. 176.

5. Joy Packer, *The Glass Barrier* (Philadelphia, 1961), p. 254; see also Harold Bindloss, *The League of the Leopard* (London, 1923), p. 155; Harry Bloom, *Whittaker's Wife* (New York, 1962), p. 36; Gerald Hanley, *The Year of the Lion* (New York, 1954), p. 89; Llewlyn Powys, *Ebony and Ivory* (New York, 1923), p. 40; William Plomer, *Double Lives* (New York, 1956), pp. 107, 156; Laurens Van der Post, *Venture to the Interior* (New York, 1951), p. 102.

6. Cloete, *Giant*, p. 327.

7. Joy Packer, *Apes and Ivory* (London, 1953), p. 204.

8. Elspeth Huxley, *The Flame Trees of Thika* (New York, 1959), p. 67.

9. Robert Lait, *Honey for Tomorrow* (New York, 1961), p. 149.

10. William C. Scully, *Further Reminiscences of a South African Pioneer* (London, 1913), p. 252.

11. John Rowan Wilson, *Double Blind* (Garden City, 1960), p. 283.

12. Augustus C. Collodon, *Congo Jake* (New York, 1933), pp. 212–213.

13. Isak Dinesen, *Out of Africa* (New York, 1938), pp. 134–35.

14. Graham Greene, *Journey Without Maps* (New York, 1961), pp. 36–40.

15. Nicholas Monsarrat, *The Tribe that Lost Its Head* (New York, 1956), pp. 517–18.

16. Raymond Tong, *Figures in Ebony* (London, 1958), p. 86.

17. Greene, *Journey Without Maps,* p. 50.

18. Joyce Cary, *The Case for African Freedom* (London, 1944), pp. 39–40.

Chapter VI

The Dark Labyrinth

1. Elspeth Huxley, *Four Guineas* (London, 1954), p. 292.
2. Greene, *Journey Without Maps,* p. 46.
3. Graham Greene, *In Search of a Character* (New York, 1961), p. 93.
4. Cullen Gouldsbury, *An African Year* (London, 1912), p. 128.
5. Lady Dorothy Mills, *The Golden Land* (London, 1926), p. 13.
6. Tong, *Figures in Ebony,* pp. 28–29; see also, Mills, *Golden Land,* pp. 14, 170.
7. Catto, *Gold in the Sky,* p. 167.
8. Monsarrat, *The Tribe that Lost Its Head,* p. 12.
9. Wyndham, *The Gentle Savage,* p. 125.
10. Cloete, *Giant,* p. 110; see also p. 256.
11. Holtby, *Mandoa, Mandoa!,* p. 163.
12. Cloete, *Giant,* p. 376; see also Joyce Cary, *Aissa Saved* (London, 1952), p. 8; Elspeth Huxley, *On the Edge of the Rift* (New York 1962), p. 269; Bloom, *Whittaker's Wife,* pp. 174–75.
13. Ronald Hardy, *The Men from the Bush* (Garden City, 1959) p. 84.
14. Talbot Mundy, *The Ivory Trail* (Indianapolis, 1919), p. 76.
15. Griffin, *By the North Gate,* p. 116.
16. Huxley, *Four Guineas,* p. 175.
17. Max Catto, *Mr. Moses* (New York, 1961), p. 30; *Gold in the Sky,* p. 100.
18. Collodon, *Congo Jake,* p. viii; Catto, *Gold in the Sky,* p. 34 Gerald Hanley, *Drinkers of Darkness* (New York, 1955), pp. 129, 164
19. Elspeth Huxley, *The Red Rock Wilderness* (New York, 1957) pp. 236–37.
20. Hanley, *Drinkers of Darkness,* pp. 164–65; see also Gerald Hanley, *Gilligan's Last Elephant* (Cleveland, 1962), p. 74; Lady Dorothy Mills, *Road to Timbuktu* (London, 1924), p. 251; Mary Motley, *Devils in Waiting* (London, 1959), pp. 138–41; Robert Shaw *The Sun Doctor* (New York, 1961), p. 90; Marguerite Steen, *Twiligh on the Floods* (Garden City, 1949), pp. 357–58; Tong, *Figures in Ebony,* p. 96.

21. Greene, *Journey Without Maps,* pp. 11 and 33.
22. Laurens Van der Post, *The Heart of the Hunter* (New York, 1961), p. xiv; see also Hanley, *Drinkers of Darkness,* p. 33.
23. Alan Moorehead, *The White Nile* (New York, 1960), pp. 116–117; see also Thomas Sterling, *Stanley's Way* (New York, 1960). This American chronicler of Stanley's journeys gives a parallel interpretation of Stanley. Far from being the indomitable explorer, he views Stanley as the eternal lost boy searching for a father.
24. Powys, *Ebony and Ivory,* pp. 22–23.
25. Greene, *Journey Without Maps,* p. 114; see also Van der Post, *The Dark Eye in Africa,* p. 81.
26. Van der Post, *Venture to the Interior,* p. 198.
27. Van der Post, *Dark Eye in Africa,* p. 250.
28. *Ibid.,* pp. 55–56.

Chapter VII
The Strange Woman

1. Marguerite Steen, *The Sun Is My Undoing* (New York, 1941), p. 319.
2. Margery Perham and Jack Simmons, *African Discovery* (London, 1948), p. 5.
3. Steen, *Twilight on the Floods,* p. 358.
4. Stuart Cloete, *Congo Song* (New York, 1958), p. 97.
5. Cloete, *Giant,* p. 51.
6. Joyce Cary, *Mr. Johnson* (New York, 1961), p. 170.
7. Edwin W. Smith and Andrew Dale, *The Ila-Speaking Peoples of Northern Rhodesia* (London, 1920), pp. 48–49.
8. *Ibid.,* p. 67.
9. John Seymour, *One Man's Africa* (New York, 1956), p. 218.
10. Dinesen, *Out of Africa,* p. 125.
11. Shaw, *The Sun Doctor,* p. 30.
12. Hanley, *Drinkers of Darkness,* p. 57.
13. Cloete, *Giant,* p. 316.
14. Hanley, *Drinkers of Darkness,* p. 55.
15. Hanley, *Gilligan's Last Elephant,* p. 108.
16. Mills, *The Golden Land,* p. 51.
17. Ian Brook, *Jimmy Riddle* (New York, 1961); Richard Llewellyn, *A Man in a Mirror* (New York, 1961).

Chapter VIII
The Land in Amber

1. Hanley, *The Year of the Lion,* p. 176.
2. Huxley, *On the Edge of the Rift,* p. 54.
3. Van der Post, *Venture to the Interior,* p. 294.
4. Huxley, *Walled City,* p. 172.
5. Van der Post, *The Heart of the Hunter,* p. 80.
6. Viertel, *White Hunter,* p. 76.
7. Hanley, *The Year of the Lion,* p. 22.
8. Isak Dinesen, *Shadows on the Grass* (New York, 1961), p. 3.
9. Robert Henriques, *Death by Moonlight* (New York, 1938), p. 220.
10. Elspeth Huxley, *A New Earth* (New York, 1960), p. 66.
11. Griffin, *Something of an Achievement,* pp. 132–33.
12. Lord Vansittart, "Foreword" to H. C. Jackson, *Sudan Days and Ways* (London, 1954).
13. Lord Cranworth, *Kenya Chronicles* (London, 1939), p. 37.
14. A. C. G. Hastings, *Nigerian Days* (London, 1925), p. 77.
15. H. Rider Haggard, *The Days of My Life,* 2 vols. (London, 1926), I, 202.
16. Dinesen, *Shadows on the Grass,* pp. 8–9.
17. Read, *No Time for Fear,* p. 212.
18. Cary, *The Case for African Freedom,* p. 44.
19. Roderick Cameron, *Equator Farm* (New York, 1956), p. 164.
20. *Ibid.,* p. 45.
21. C. W. Hobley, *Kenya from Chartered Company to Crown Colony* (London, 1929).
22. Melville J. Herskovits, *The Human Factor in Changing Africa* (New York, 1962), pp. 82, 477.
23. Cameron, *Equator Farm,* pp. 125–26.
24. Huxley, *Flame Trees of Thika,* p. 116.

Chapter IX
The Antagonist

1. Perham and Simmons, *African Discovery,* p. 15.
2. Huxley, *Red Rock Wilderness,* p. 134.
3. Monsarrat, *The Tribe that Lost Its Head,* p. 120.
4. Van der Post, *Dark Eye in Africa,* pp. 44–45.
5. Greene, *Journey Without Maps,* p. 175.

6. Catto, *Gold in the Sky* and *Mr. Moses;* Stuart Cloete, *Gazella* (New York, 1959), and *Congo Song;* C. S. Forester, *The African Queen* (New York, 1960); Holtby, *Mandoa, Mandoa!;* Huxley, *Red Rock Wilderness;* Monsarrat, *The Tribe that Lost Its Head;* Waugh, *Black Mischief.*
7. Greene, *In Search of a Character,* p. 17.
8. Catto, *Gold in the Sky,* pp. 118–19.
9. Cloete, *Gazella,* pp. 108–9.
10. Dundas, *Crossroads,* pp. 58–59.
11. Alastair Scobie, *Women of Africa* (London, 1960), p. 173.
12. Dundas, *Crossroads,* p. 59.
13. Hanley, *Year of the Lion,* p. 192.
14. Wilson, *Double Blind,* p. 70.
15. Steen, *Twilight on the Floods,* p. 301.
16. Hardy, *Men from the Bush,* p. 108.
17. Beryl Markham, *West with the Night* (Boston, 1942), p. 60.
18. Van der Post, *Venture to the Interior,* p. 93.
19. Elspeth Huxley, *The Sorcerer's Apprentice* (London, 1949), p. 43.
20. Donald L. Wiedner, *A History of Africa* (New York, 1962), p. 11.
21. Cary, *Case for African Freedom,* p. 136.
22. Hanley, *Year of the Lion,* p. 177.
23. Tom Stacey, *The Brothers M* (New York, 1961), p. 11.
24. Hanley, *Drinkers of Darkness,* p. 77.
25. Basil Davidson, *The Lost Cities of Africa* (Boston, 1957), p. 65.
26. *Ibid.,* p. viii.
27. Cloete, *Giant,* p. 368.
28. Huxley, *Walled City,* p. 168.
29. Julian Mockford, *Golden Land* (London, 1949), p. 99.
30. Van der Post, *Dark Eye in Africa,* p. 62.
31. Catto, *Mr. Moses,* p. 8.
32. Dundas, *Crossroads,* p. 242.
33. Joyce Cary, *The African Witch* (London, 1951), p. 12.
34. Lait, *Honey for Tomorrow,* p. 162.
35. Packer, *Apes and Ivory,* p. 298.
36. Huxley, *Red Rock Wilderness,* p. 110.
37. Wellesley, *Sir George Goldie,* pp. 150–51.

Chapter X
The British Self-Image

1. Hilaire Belloc, *An Essay on the Nature of Contemporary England* (New York, 1937), p. 26; see also pp. 28, 29.

2. James Wellard, *Understanding the English* (New York, 1937), p. 90.

3. Philip Carr, *The English Are Like That* (New York, 1941), p. 134.

4. J. D. Scott, *Life in Britain* (New York, 1955), p. 10; see also Harold Nicolson, *Good Behaviour* (Garden City, 1956), p. 250; Roy Lewis and Angus Maude, *Professional People in England* (Cambridge, 1953), p. 263.

5. George Orwell, *A Collection of Essays* (Garden City, 1954), p. 274.

6. Martin Green, *A Mirror for Anglo-Saxons: A discovery of America, a rediscovery of England* (New York, 1960), p. 78.

7. Nicolson, *Good Behaviour*, p. 262.

8. Green, *A Mirror for Anglo-Saxons*, p. 123; Orwell, *Essays*, p. 261; Wellard, *Understanding the English*, pp. 11, 43, 96, 106, 157.

9. G. D. H. Cole, *The Post-War Condition of Britain* (London, 1956), p. 26; T. H. Pear, *English Social Differences* (London, 1955); David C. Marsh, *The Changing Social Structure of England and Wales, 1871–1951* (London, 1958); Nancy Mitford, *Noblesse Oblige* (New York, 1956).

10. Green, *A Mirror for Anglo-Saxons*, p. 51.

11. Pear, *Social Differences*, p. 60.

12. Geoffrey Gorer, *Exploring English Character* (New York, 1955), p. 2.

13. B. M. Spinley, *The Deprived and the Privileged: Personality Development in English Society* (London, 1953).

14. Gorer, *Exploring English Character*, p. 2.

15. *Ibid.*, p. 163.

16. *Ibid.*, p. 13; see also Margaret Mead, *The Application of Anthropological Techniques to Cross-National Communication* (New York, 1947), p. 136; Scott, *Life in Britain*, pp. 19–20; Spinley, *The Deprived and the Privileged*, p. 104; Martha Wolfenstein and Nathan Leites, *Movies* (Glencoe, 1950), p. 295.

17. Gorer, *Exploring English Character*, p. 288.

18. Scott, *Life in Britain*, p. 20.

19. Gorer, *Exploring English Character*, pp. 289–91.

20. Carr, *The English Are Like That*, p. 265.
21. *Ibid.*, p. 265.
22. *Ibid.*, p. 19.
23. *Ibid.*, p. 19; see also Denis W. Brogan, *The English People—Impressions and Observations* (New York, 1943), pp. 144, 285; Pear, *Social Differences*, p. 176; Wellard, *Understanding the English*, p. 76.
24. Carr, *The English Are Like That*, p. 74; see also p. 81; Norman Dennis, Fernando Henriques and Clifford Slaughter, *Coal Is Our Life* (London, 1956), p. 218; Gorer, *Exploring English Character*, pp. 75, 76; Scott, *Life in Britain*, pp. 16–17.
25. Dennis, Henriques and Slaughter, *Coal Is Our Life*, p. 211.
26. Gorer, *Exploring English Character*, p. 75.
27. *Ibid.*, p. 303; Spinley, *The Deprived and the Privileged*, p. 136; Wellard, *Understanding the English*, p. 53.
28. Dennis, Henriques and Slaughter, *Coal Is Our Life*, p. 226.
29. *Ibid.*, p. 231.
30. Wellard, *Understanding the English*, p. 54.
31. R. F. L. Logan and E. M. Goldberg, "Rising Eighteen in a London Suburb," *British Journal of Sociology*, IV, 333; Eliot Slater and Moya Woodside, *Patterns of Marriage* (London, 1951), p. 167.
32. Slater and Woodside, *Patterns of Marriage*, p. 167.
33. Scott, *Life in Britain*, p. 15.
34. Gorer, *Exploring English Character*, p. 287.
35. Green, *Mirror for Anglo-Saxons*, pp. 31–32.
36. David Victor Glass (ed.), *Social Mobility in Britain* (Glencoe, 1954), pp. 177–217.
37. Cole, *Post-War Condition of Britain*, p. 38.
38. Lewis and Maude, *Professional People*, p. 220.
39. Pear, *Social Differences*, p. 152.
40. Brogan, *The English People*, p. 254.
41. Orwell, *Essays*, p. 278.
42. John Strachey, *The End of Empire* (New York, 1960), p. 204.
43. Brogan, *The English People*, p. 5.
44. David Frost and Anthony Jay, *The English* (New York, 1968), p. 57.
45. K. B. Smellie, *The British Way of Life* (London, 1955), p. 148.
46. Gorer, *Exploring English Character*, p. 117.
47. Brogan, *The English People*, pp. 82, 83, 101, 103, 106; Dennis, Henriques and Slaughter, *Coal Is Our Life*, p. 169; Lewis and Maude, *Professional People*, pp. 138, 141, 264; Marsh, *Social Structure*, pp. 188, 189; Orwell, *Essays*, p. 241; Slater and Woodside, *Patterns of Marriage*, pp. 124, 193, 256, 260; Smellie, *British Way of Life*, p. 48;

B. S. Rowntree and G. R. Lavers, *English Life and Leisure* (London, 1951), Chapter XIII.

48. George Orwell, *The Road to Wigan Pier* (New York, 1961), p. 162.

49. *Ibid.*, p. 175.

50. Frost and Jay, *The English*, pp. 254–55.

Bibliography

BACKGROUND

'he background materials include critical biographies, African history nd anthropology, and other studies of the Western view of alien eople. The works listed are selective; those which were directly per-inent and to which we had immediate reference. Ideally, such a ibliography should be limitless, since there is almost no end to the terature which helped to formulate the ideas basic to this study. Many of the ideas are the ineluctable consequence of two lifetimes pent as anthropologists, and to document them would require listing ost of the significant works in anthropology.

nnals of the American Academy of Political and Social Science. Sept. 1954.

aines, Jocelyn. *Joseph Conrad—A Critical Biography*. New York: McGraw-Hill, 1960.

ohannan, Laura and Paul. *The Tiv of Central Nigeria. Ethnographic Survey of Africa*, Part VIII. London: International African Institute, 1953.

ovill, W. E. *The Golden Trade of the Moors*. London: Oxford University Press, 1958.

rodie, Fawn M. *The Devil Drives: A Life of Sir Richard Burton*. New York: W. W. Norton, 1967.

urns, Sir Alan. *History of Nigeria*. London: Allen and Unwin, 1929.

arrington, John F. *Talking Drums of Africa*. London: Kingsgate Press, 1949.

ohen, Morton N. *Rider Haggard: His Life and Works*. New York: Walker and Co., 1961.

oupland, Reginald. *Kirk on the Zambesi*. Oxford: Clarendon Press, 1928.

———. *The Exploitation of East Africa, 1856–1890: The Slave Trade and the Scramble*. London: Faber and Faber, 1939.

CURTIN, PHILIP D. *The Image of Africa*. Madison: The University of Wisconsin Press, 1964.

DAICHES, DAVID. *White Man in the Tropics: Two Moral Tales*. New York: Harcourt, Brace and World, Inc., 1962.

DAVIDSON, BASIL. *The Lost Cities of Africa*. Boston: Little, Brown and Co., 1957.

———. *Black Mother*. Boston: Little, Brown and Co., 1961.

DIKE, K. ONWUKA. *Trade and Politics on the Niger Delta, 1830–1885*. Oxford: Clarendon Press, 1956.

DRIVER, DAVID MILLER. *The Indian in Brazilian Literature*. New York: Hispanic Institute in the United States, 1942.

DYKES, E. B. *The Negro in English Romantic Thought*. Washington 1942.

EVANS-PRITCHARD, E. E. "Zande Cannibalism," *Journal of the Royal Anthropological Institute*, 90, Pt. 2. 1960, 238–58.

FAGE, J. D. *An Introduction to the History of West Africa*. Cambridge: Cambridge University Press, 1961.

———. *Ghana—A Historical Interpretation*. Madison: University of Wisconsin Press, 1959.

FAIRCHILD, HOXIE N. *The Noble Savage: A Study in Romantic Naturalism*. New York: Columbia University Press, 1928.

GEORGE, KATHERINE. "The Civilized West Looks at Primitive Africa 1400–1800." *Isis*, 49 (1958), 62–72.

GLUCKMAN, MAX. "The Kingdom of the Zulu of South Africa," in FORTES, M., and E. E. EVANS-PRITCHARD (eds.), *African Political Systems*. London: Oxford University Press for the International African Institute, 1940, 25–55.

GWYNN, STEPHEN. *Mungo Park*. New York: G. P. Putnam Sons, 193[illegible]

———. *The Life of Mary Kingsley*. London: Macmillan, 1932.

HAINES, C. GROVE (ed.). *Africa Today*. Baltimore: Johns Hopkins University Press, 1955.

HAMMOND, DOROTHY. "The Image of Africa in the British Literature of the Twentieth Century," Ph.D. dissertation. University of Michigan Microfilm, 1963.

——— and ALTA JABLOW. "The African in Western Literature" *Africa Today*, Dec. 1960 and Jan. 1961.

HANKE, LEWIS. "Aristotle and the Indian," *Texas Quarterly*, Spring 1958.

HENNESSEY, MAURICE. *The Congo—A Brief History and Appraisal*. New York: Frederick A. Praeger, 1961.

HERSKOVITS, MELVILLE J. *The Human Factor in Changing Africa.* New York: Alfred A. Knopf, 1962.

———. *Man and His Works.* New York: Alfred A. Knopf, 1949.

———. *Dahomey.* Vol. II. New York: J. J. Augustin, 1938.

HOBLEY, G. W. *Kenya from Chartered Company to Crown Colony.* London: H. F. and G. Witherby, 1929.

HODGKIN, THOMAS. *Nigerian Perspectives.* London: Oxford University Press, 1960.

HUXLEY, ELSPETH. *White Man's Country.* 2 vols. London: Macmillan Co., 1935.

ISAACS, HAROLD. *Scratches on Our Minds: American Images of China and India.* New York: John Day Co., 1958.

JABLOW, ALTA. "The Development of a Literary Tradition: The British in Africa, 1530–1910." Ph.D. dissertation. University of Michigan Microfilms, 1963.

KLINEBERG, OTTO. "Pictures in Our Heads," *UNESCO Courier,* 8, No. 4 (Sept. 1955), 5–9.

KRUGER, RAYNE. *Goodbye, Dolly Grey: The Story of the Boer War.* London: Cassell and Co., 1959.

LYSTAD, ROBERT A. *The Ashanti, A Proud People.* New Brunswick: Rutgers University Press, 1958.

MAHOOD, MOLLY M. *Joyce Cary's Africa.* London: Methuen, 1964.

MARSH, ZOE (ed.). *East African History Through Contemporary Records.* Cambridge: Cambridge University Press, 1961.

MERKER, M. *Die Masai.* Berlin: D. Reimer, 1904.

MERRIAM, ALAN P. "A Prologue to the Study of African Arts," *Antioch College Founder's Day Lectures.* No. 7. Yellow Springs: Antioch Press, 1961.

MOOREHEAD, ALAN. *The White Nile.* New York: Harper and Brothers, 1960.

———. *The Blue Nile.* New York: Harper and Row, 1962.

MPHAHLELE, EZEKIEL. *The African Image.* New York: Frederick A. Praeger, 1962.

PEARCE, ROY H. *The Savages of America.* Baltimore: Johns Hopkins University Press, 1953.

PEDRAZA, HOWARD J. *Borrioboola Gha: The Story of Lokoja, the First British Settlement in Nigeria.* London: Oxford University Press, 1960.

PERHAM, MARGERY. *Lugard.* 2 vols. London: Collins, 1960.

——— and JACK SIMMONS. *African Discovery.* London: Penguin Books, 1948.

Pope-Hennessy, James. *Sins of the Fathers: A Study of the Atlantic Slave Traders, 1441–1807*. New York: Knopf, 1968.

Rattray, Robert S. *Ashanti Law and Constitution*. London: Oxford University Press, 1929.

———. *Religion and Art in Ashanti*. London: Oxford University Press, 1927.

Schneider, Harold K. "Pakot Resistance to Change," in William Bascom and Melville J. Herskovits (eds.), *Continuity and Change in African Culture*. Chicago: University of Chicago Press, 1954.

Simmons, Jack. *Livingstone and Africa*. New York: Crowell, 1962.

Smith, Bernard. *European Vision and the South Pacific, 1768–1850*. London: Oxford University Press, 1960.

Smith, Edwin W. and Andrew M. Dale. *The Ila-Speaking Peoples of Northern Rhodesia*. 2 vols. London: Macmillan, 1920.

Sterling, Thomas. *Stanley's Way*. New York: Atheneum, 1960.

Stillman, Calvin W. *Africa in the Modern World*. Chicago: University of Chicago Press, 1955.

Sypher, Wylie. *Guinea's Captive Kings: British Anti-Slavery Literature of the XVIII Century*. Chapel Hill: University of North Carolina Press, 1942.

Weischoff, H. A. *Colonial Policies in Africa*. Philadelphia: University of Pennsylvania Press, 1944.

Wellesley, Dorothy. *Sir George Goldie, Founder of Nigeria*. London: Macmillan, 1934.

Wiedner, Donald L. *A History of Africa South of the Sahara*. New York: Random House, 1962.

Wolfson, Freda. *Pageant of Ghana*. London: Oxford University Press, 1958.

Wright, Andrew. *Joyce Cary, A Preface to His Novels*. New York: Harper and Brothers, 1958.

THE BRITISH IN AFRICA: 1530–1910

The works listed below comprise the sources for the first half of this study. They contain the historical data and include primarily the journals of explorers, traders, settlers, officials, missionaries, and visitors; there are also some early compendia of travelers' accounts in the collections of Hakluyt, Purchas, Churchill, and Blake, and a few later books on the whole of Africa compiled by armchair commentators. We have, undoubtedly, omitted many items to which particular readers may be committed, but the sample is sufficient to indicate that even the exceptional work would scarcely change the over-all picture. Omissions were not intentional, save in a very few instances. For example, we deliberately did not include the great pioneer work of James Bruce, *Travels to Discover the Source of the Nile,* first published in 1790. He was, for us, an explorer in the wrong place at the wrong time, since his explorations in Ethiopia, and his concern with the Nile sources were well in advance of the mainstream of such activity on the part of the British. Ethiopia was, in any event, outside the major areas of British concern in Africa, and its culture differed greatly from the African cultures south of the Sahara. The British literature on Ethiopia merits separate study.

The bibliographic listings will follow the main chapter headings as far as possible. Some of the authors may be assigned to more than one chapter, since their lifetimes and interests range over several time periods and areas. In such cases we have separated their works for listing in the appropriate chapters. The fiction of this entire period is listed separately, and only those novels to which we have made direct reference are included in the bibliography.

Chapter I. First Light on the Dark Continent

ALLEN, CAPTAIN WILLIAM and T. R. H. THOMPSON. *Narrative of the Expedition to the River Niger in 1841.* 2 vols. London: Richard Bentley, 1848.

BAIKIE, WILLIAM BALFOUR. *Narrative of an Exploring Voyage up the Rivers Kwora and Binue in 1854.* London: John Murray, 1856.

BARNARD, LADY ANNE. *South Africa a Century Ago* ("Letters from the Cape of Good Hope: 1798–1801"). W. H. WILKINS (ed.). London: 1901.

BARROW, JOHN. *Travels into the Interior of Southern Africa.* 2 vols. 2nd ed. London: T. Cadell and W. Davies, 1806.

BEECHAM, JOHN. *Ashantee.* London: John Mason, 1841.

BLAKE, J. W. *Europeans in West Africa, 1450–1560.* Vol. II. London: Hakluyt Society, 1942.

BOWDICH, THOMAS EDWARD. *Mission from Cape Coast Castle to Ashantee, with a statistical account of that Kingdom, and geographical notices of other parts of the interior of Africa.* London: John Murray, 1819.

BURCHELL, W. J. *Travels in the Interior of Southern Africa.* 2 vols. London: Batchworth Press, 1949 (reprinted from the original edition of 1822).

CAMPBELL, JOHN. *Travels in South Africa.* Andover, Mass.: Flag and Gould, 1916.

CHURCHILL, J. *Collections of Travels and Voyages.* London: Vols. I–IV, 1704; V–VI, 1732.

CLAPPERTON, HUGH. *Journal of a Second Expedition into the Interior of Africa, and the Journal of Richard Lander*. Philadelphia: Lea and Corey, 1829.

COLE, ALFRED W. *The Cape and the Kafirs*. London: Richard Bentley, 1852.

COOLEY, WILLIAM D. *Inner Africa Laid Open*. London: Longman, Brown, Green and Longmans, 1852.

CROWTHER, SAMUEL. *Journal of an Expedition up the Niger and Tshadda Rivers*. London: Church Missionary House, 1855.

CRUICKSHANK, BRODIE. *Eighteen Years on the Gold Coast of Africa*. 2 vols. London: Hurst and Blackett, 1853.

DALZEL, ARCHIBALD. *The History of Dahomy, an inland kingdom of Africa, compiled from authentic memoirs*. London: T. Spilsbury, 1793.

DUNCAN, JOHN. *Travels in Western Africa in 1845 and 1846*. 2 vols. London: Richard Bentley, 1847.

FREEMAN, T. B. *Journals of Various Visits to the Kingdom of Ashanti*. London, 1844.

GALTON, FRANCIS. *Narrative of an Explorer in Tropical South Africa*. London: John Murray, 1853.

GARDINER, CAPTAIN ALLEN F. *Narrative of a Journey to the Zoolu Country*. London: William Crofts, 1836.

HAKLUYT, RICHARD. *Voyages*. Vols. IV, VI, VII, and XI. Glasgow: Maclehose and Sons, 1904.

HARRIS, SIR WILLIAM CORNWALLIS. *The Wild Sports of Southern Africa*. London: John Murray, 1839.

HUTCHINSON, T. J. *Narrative of the Niger, Tshadda, and Binue Exploration*. London: Longman, Brown, Green and Longmans, 1855.

JOBSON, RICHARD. *The Golden Trade, or a Discovery of the River Gambia*. London: Nicholas Okes, 1623.

LAING, ALEXANDER GORDON. *Travels in the Timannee, Kooranko and Soolima Countries*. London: John Murray, 1825.

LAIRD, MACGREGOR and R. A. K. OLDFIELD. *Narrative of an Expedition in the Interior of Africa by the River Niger in 1832–34*. London: John Murray, 1837.

LANDER, RICHARD and JOHN. *Journal of an Expedition to Explore the Course and Termination of the Niger*. 2 vols. New York: J. and J. Harper, 1833.

LIVINGSTONE, DAVID. *Missionary Travels and Researches in South Africa*. New York: Harper and Brothers, 1859.

MASON, JOHN. *Life with the Zulus of Natal*. London: Longman, Brown, Green and Longmans, 1855.

METHUEN, HENRY E. *Life in the Wilderness, or Wanderings in South Africa.* London: Richard Bentley, 1846.

MOFFAT, ROBERT. *Matabele Journals.* 2 vols. London: Chatto and Windus, 1945 (first published in 1855).

———. *Missionary Labours and Scenes in Southern Africa.* New York: Robert Carter, 1842.

MURRAY, HUGH, ROBERT JAMESON and JAMES WILSON. *Narrative of Discovery and Adventure in Africa.* London: Thomas Nelson, 1849 (first published in 1830).

NORRIS, ROBERT. *Memoirs of the Reign of Bossa Ahadee, King of Dahomey.* London, 1789.

PARK, MUNGO. *Journal of a Mission to the Interior of Africa in the year 1805, to which is prefixed an Account of the Life of Mr. Park by J. Whishaw.* Philadelphia: Edward Earle, 1815.

———. *Travels in the Interior Districts of Africa, 1795, 1796, and 1797.* London: J. M. Dent and Co. n.d. (first published in 1799).

PRINGLE, THOMAS. *African Sketches.* London, 1834.

PURCHAS, SAMUEL. *Purchas His Pilgrimes.* Vol. VI. Glasgow: James Maclehose and Sons, 1905.

RANKIN, F. HARRISON. *The White Man's Grave: A Visit to Sierra Leone in 1834.* 2 vols. London: John Murray, 1836.

SMITH, WILLIAM. *A New Voyage to Guinea.* London, 1744.

SNELGRAVE, WILLIAM. *A New Account of Some Parts of Guinea and the Slave Trade.* London, 1734.

STEEDMAN, ANDREW. *Wanderings and Adventures in the Interior of Southern Africa.* 2 vols. London: Longmans and Co., 1835.

THOMPSON, THOMAS. "An Account of Two Missionary Voyages," in F. Wolfson, *Pageant of Ghana.* London: Oxford University Press, 1958.

Chapter II. The Dawn of Empire

ASHE, ROBERT P. *Two Kings of Uganda.* London: Sampson Low and Co., 1890.

BAKER, SIR SAMUEL W. *Ismailia, a Narrative of the Expedition to Central Africa for the Suppression of the Slave Trade.* 2 vols. London: Macmillan, 1874.

———. *Albert N'Yanza.* 2 vols. London: Macmillan, 1866.

BURTON, SIR RICHARD FRANCIS. *A Mission to Gelele, King of Dahomey.* 2 vols. London: Tinsley Brothers, 1877.

———. *The Lake Regions of Central Africa.* 2 vols. New York: Horizon Press, 1961; reprinted from the original edition of 1861.

———. *First Footsteps in East Africa.* London and New York: Everyman's Edition, 1910 (first published in 1856).

CAMERON, VERNEY LOVETT. *Across Africa (1873–1876).* New York: Harper and Brothers, 1877.

ELTON, JAMES FREDERICK. *Journals of Travels and Researches among the Lakes and Mountains of Eastern and Central Africa.* Edited and compiled by M. B. COTTERILL. London: John Murray, 1879.

HINDERER, ANNA. *Seventeen Years in the Yoruba Country. Memorials gathered from her journals and letters.* London: Seeley, Jackson and Halliday, 1872.

JOHNSTON, SIR HARRY H. *The Kilimanjaro Expedition.* London: Kegan Paul, Trench and Co., 1886.

———. *The River Congo, from its mouth to Bolobo.* London: Sampson Low, Marston, Searle and Rivington, 1884.

LIVINGSTONE, DAVID. *The Last Journals of David Livingstone in Central Africa from 1865 to his death.* New York: Harper and Brothers, 1875.

———. *Narrative of an Expedition to the Zambesi and its Tributaries; and of the discovery of the Lakes Shirwa and Nyassa, 1858–1864.* New York: Harper and Brothers, 1866.

PETHERICK, JOHN. *Egypt, the Soudan and Central Africa.* Edinburgh and London: W. Blackwood and Sons, 1861.

——— with MRS. PETHERICK. *Travels in Central Africa and Explorations of the Western Nile Tributaries.* 2 vols. London: Tinsley Brothers, 1869.

READE, WINWOOD W. *Savage Africa.* New York: Harper and Brothers, 1864.

SPEKE, JOHN HANNING. *Journey of the Discovery of the Source of the Nile.* New York: J. and J. Harper, 1864.

STANLEY, HENRY M. *Coomassie and Magdala: The story of two British campaigns in Africa.* New York: Harper and Brothers, 1874.

———. *How I Found Livingstone: travels, adventures, and discoveries in Central Africa, including an account of four months' residence with Dr. Livingstone.* 2 vols. New York: Charles Scribner, 1890.

———. *In Darkest Africa, or the Quest, Rescue and Retreat of Emin, Governor of Equatoria.* 2 vols. New York, Charles Scribner, 1890.

———. *Through the Dark Continent, or, The Sources of the Nile Around the Great Lakes of Equatorial Africa.* 2 vols. London, 1899 (first published in 1878).

THOMSON, J. B. *Joseph Thomson, African Explorer.* London: Sampson Low, Marston and Co., 1896.

THOMSON, JOSEPH. *Through Masailand.* London: Sampson Low, Marston, Searle and Rivington, 1885.

———. *To the Central African Lakes and Back.* 2 vols. 2nd. ed. Boston: Houghton Mifflin and Co., 1881.

Chapter III. The Height of Empire

ALLDRIDGE, THOMAS J. *A Transformed Colony, Sierra Leone, As it was and as it is. . . .* London: Seeley and Co., 1910.

ARKELL-HARDWICK, A. *An Ivory Trader in North Kenia.* London: Longmans, Green and Co., 1903.

BALFOUR, ALICE BLANCHE. *Twelve Hundred Miles in a Waggon.* London: Edward Arnold, 1895.

BATEMAN, LATROBE C. S. *The Ascent of the Kasai.* New York: Dodd, Mead and Co., 1889.

BOISRAGON, CAPTAIN ALAN. *The Benin Massacre.* London: Methuen and Co., 1897.

BRYCE, JAMES. *Impressions of South Africa.* New York: The Century Co., 1897.

CHURCHILL, WINSTON S. *My African Journey.* London: Hodder and Stoughton, 1908.

COOPER-CHADWICK, J. *Three Years with Lobengula and Experiences in South Africa.* London: Cassell and Co., 1894.

DECLÉ, LIONEL. *Three Years in Savage Africa.* Introduction by H. M. Stanley, London: Methuen and Co., 1898.

DIXIE, LADY FLORENCE. *In the Land of Misfortune.* London: Richard Bentley and Son, 1882.

DOYLE, ARTHUR CONAN. *The Great Boer War.* New York: McClure, Phillips, 1900.

FREEMAN, RICHARD AUSTIN. *Travels and Life in Ashanti and Jaman.* London: Archibald Constable and Co., 1898.

GLAVE, E. J. *In Savage Africa; or Six Years of Adventure in Congo-land.* New York: R. H. Russell and Son, 1892.

GROGAN, EWART S. and ARTHUR H. SHARP. *From the Cape to Cairo.* London: Hurst and Blackett, 1900.

HAGGARD, H. RIDER. *Cetywayo and His White Neighbours.* London: Trubner and Co., 1882.

HALL, MARY. *A Woman's Trek from the Cape to Cairo.* London: Methuen and Co., 1907.

HORE, ANNIE B. *To Lake Tanganyika in a Bath Chair.* London, 1886.

JOHNSTON, SIR HARRY H. *The Story of My Life*. New York: Bobbs, Merrill and Co., 1923.

———. *The Uganda Protectorate*. 2 vols. London: Hutchinson and Co., 1902.

———. *British Central Africa*. New York: Edward Arnold, 1897.

KINGSLEY, MARY. *West African Studies*. London: Macmillan and Co., 1899.

———. *Travels in West Africa*. London: Macmillan and Co., 1898.

KIPLING, RUDYARD. *Something of Myself*. New York: Doubleday, Doran and Co., 1937.

———. *Letters of Travel 1892–1913*. New York: 1927 (first published in 1914).

LARYMORE, CONSTANCE. *A Resident's Wife in Nigeria*. London: George Rutledge and Sons, 1908.

LEONARD, MAJOR ARTHUR GLYN. *How We Made Rhodesia*. London: Kegan Paul, Trench, Trubner and Co., 1896.

LUGARD, FREDERICK D. *The Dual Mandate in British Tropical Africa*. Edinburgh and London: W. Blackwood and Sons, 1929.

———. *The Rise of Our East African Empire*. 2 vols. Edinburgh and London: W. Blackwood and Sons, 1893.

LUGARD, LADY FLORA. *A Tropical Dependency: An Outline of the Ancient History of the Western Soudan, with an account of the modern settlement of Northern Nigeria*. London: J. Nisbet and Co., 1905.

MACDONALD, MAJOR J. R. L. *Soldiering and Surveying in British East Africa, 1891–1894*. London: Edward Arnold, 1897.

MACKAY, A. M. *Mackay of Uganda*. New York: A. C. Armstrong and Son, 1890.

MACKENZIE, JOHN. *Day-Dawn in Dark Places*. London: Cassell and Company, 1883.

PRINGLE, MRS. M. A. *Towards the Mountains of the Moon*. Edinburgh and London: W. Blackwood and Sons, 1883.

ROBINSON, CHARLES H. *Nigeria, Our Latest Protectorate*. New York: Oakside Press, 1900.

———. *Hausaland*. London: Sampson Low, Marston and Co., 1896.

SELOUS, F. COURTENAY. *Travel and Adventure in South East Africa*. London: Rowland Ward and Co., 1893.

SWANN, ALFRED J. *Fighting the Slave Hunters in Central Africa*. London: Seeley and Co., 1910.

TUCKER, BISHOP ALFRED R. *Eighteen Years in Uganda and East Africa*. 2 vols. London: Edward Arnold, 1908.

VANDELEUR, SEYMOUR. *Campaigning on the Upper Nile and Niger.* Introduction by G. T. Goldie. London: Methuen and Co., 1898.

WHITE, ARTHUR SILVA. *The Development of Africa.* London: George Philip and Son, 1890.

WORSFOLD, BASIL W. *A History of South Africa.* London: J. M. Dent and Co., 1900.

THE FICTION TO 1910

BEHN, APHRA. "Oroonoko," in *The Shorter Novels of Aphra Behn.* Vol. II. London: Everyman's Edition, 1929 (first published around 1677).

BUCHAN, JOHN. *Prester John.* Boston and New York: Houghton Mifflin Co., 1928 (first published in 1910).

CHALMERS, JOHN. *Fighting the Matabele.* London: 1898.

CONRAD, JOSEPH. *Heart of Darkness.* New York: Signet, 1961 (first published in 1899).

———. "An Outpost of Progress," in *Tales Of Unrest.* New York: Doubleday, Page and Co., 1925 (first published in 1898).

DODD, REVEREND WILLIAM. "The Epistle of Zara at the Court of Anamaboe, to the African Prince now in England," in *Dodsley's Collections.* Vol. IV. London, 1780.

FITZPATRICK, SIR PERCY. *Jock of the Bushveld.* London: Longmans, Green and Co., n.d. (first published in 1907).

GAUNT, MARY. *The Uncounted Cost.* London, 1904.

GLANVILLE, ERNEST. *The Fossicker, A Romance of Mashonaland.* London: Chatto and Windus, 1891.

HAGGARD, H. RIDER. *Nada The Lily.* London, 1892.

———. *Allan Quatermain.* New York: Dover, 1951 (first published in 1888).

———. *She.* New York: Dover, 1951 (first published in 1887).

———. *Jess.* New York: Longmans, Green and Co., 1918 (first published in 1887).

———. *King Solomon's Mines.* New York: Dover, 1951 (first published in 1886).

HENTY, G. A. *Young Colonists.* New York: F. M. Lupton Co., n.d. (first published in 1888).

KIPLING, RUDYARD. *Traffics and Discoveries.* New York: Doubleday and Co., 1927 (first published in 1904).

MARRYAT, CAPTAIN FREDERICK. *The Privateersman.* Boston: Roberts Brothers, 1866.

———. *The Mission, or Scenes in Africa.* London: J. M. Dent and Co., 1845.

MAUGHAM, SOMERSET. *The Explorer.* New York: George H. Doran Company, 1907.

MITFORD, SIR BERTRAM. *The King's Assegai.* London, 1895.

———. *John Ames, Native Commissioner, or a Romance of the Matabele Uprising.* London: F. V. White and Company, 1900.

READE, CHARLES. *A Simpleton.* Boston and New York: Colonia Press, n.d. (first published in 1873).

READE, WINWOOD W. *African Sketchbooks.* 2 vols. London: Smith, Elder and Co., 1873.

SCHREINER, OLIVE. *Story of an African Farm.* New York: A. L. Burt, n.d. (first published in 1883).

SCULLY, WILLIAM CHARLES. *Kaffir Stories.* London: 1895.

SKERTCHLY, J. A. *Melinda the Caboceer, or Sport in Ashanti.* New York: D. Appleton and Co., 1876.

STANLEY, HENRY M. *My Kalulu.* New York: Scribner, Armstrong and Co., 1874.

WALLACE, EDGAR. *Sanders of the River.* Garden City: Doubleday, Doran and Co., 1930 (first published in 1909).

THE BRITISH EMPIRE AND VICTORIANISM

This bibliography makes no attempt to list all the books about the Victorian era, only those to which there is direct reference, or those of sufficient significance to warrant inclusion in such a brief listing. The interested reader can easily find himself inundated with Victoriana merely for the looking. Our concern was directed primarily to those works about the literature of the Victorian period and about the British Empire.

BAKER, JOSEPH E. *The Reinterpretation of Victorian Literature.* Princeton: Princeton University Press, 1950.

BRIGGS, ASA. *Victorian People.* Chicago: University of Chicago Press, 1955.

British Broadcasting Corporation. *Ideas and Beliefs of the Victorians.* London: 1949.

BUCKLEY, JEROME H. *The Victorian Temper: A Study in Literary Culture.* Cambridge: Harvard University Press, 1951.

Cambridge History of English Literature. Vols. XII and XIV. Cambridge University Press, 1953.

COLE, G. D. H. and RAYMOND POSTGATE. *The British Common People, 1746–1938.* New York: Alfred A. Knopf, 1939.

CRUSE, AMY. *The Victorians and Their Books.* London: Allen and Unwin, 1935.

DALZIEL, MARGARET. *Popular Fiction 100 Years Ago.* London: Cohen and West, 1957.

DILKE, SIR CHARLES. *The British Empire.* London: Chatto and Windus, 1899.

———. *Great Britain: A Record of Travel in English Speaking Countries in 1866 and 1867.* London: Macmillan and Co., 1872.

HALÉVY, ELIE. *A History of the English People in the Nineteenth Century,* translated from French by E. I. Watkin and D. A. Baker. 6 vols. New York: Barnes and Noble, 1961.

HALL, WINIFRED. *The Overseas Empire in Fiction.* London: Oxford University Press, 1942.

HOBSON, J. A. *Imperialism, A Study.* London: Archibald Constable and Co., 1905.

HOUGHTON, W. E. *The Victorian Frame of Mind, 1830–1870.* New Haven: Yale University Press, 1957.

HOWE, SUSAN. *Novels of Empire.* New York: Columbia University Press, 1949.

LUCAS, SIR CHARLES. *The British Empire.* London: Macmillan, 1924.

NOTESTEIN, WALLACE. *The Scot in History.* New Haven: Yale University Press, 1949.

PETRIE, SIR CHARLES. *The Victorians.* London: Eyre and Spottiswoode, 1960.

ROBINSON, RONALD and J. GALLAGHER, with ALICE DENNY. *Africa and the Victorians: The Climax of Imperialism in the Dark Continent.* New York: St. Martin's Press, 1961.

SAUNDERS, LAURANCE JAMES. *Scottish Democracy, 1815–1840, The Social and Intellectual Background.* London and Edinburgh: Oliver and Boyd, 1950.

SEELEY, J. R. *The Expansion of England.* London: Macmillan, 1931 (first published in 1883).

THORNTON, A. P. *The Imperial Idea and Its Enemies.* London: Macmillan, 1959.

TINDALL, WILLIAM Y. *Forces in Modern British Literature, 1885–1946.* New York: Alfred A. Knopf, 1947.

WINGFIELD-STRATTON, ESME. *The Victorian Aftermath.* New York: William Morrow and Co., 1934.

———. *The Victorian Sunset.* New York: William Morrow and Co., 1932.

———. *Those Ernest Victorians.* New York: William Morrow and Co., 1930.

Young, G. M. *Victorian England: Portrait of an Age.* London: Oxford University Press, 1936.

——— (ed.). *Early Victorian England.* 2 vols. London: Oxford University Press, 1934.

Zimmern, Alfred. *The Third British Empire.* London: Oxford University Press, 1934.

THE TRADITION IN THE TWENTIETH CENTURY

The listing of books that follows is a selective, working bibliography. The British have written so much on Africa since 1910, and especially since 1930, that we could not include everything we had read, let alone particular books that anyone else had read. Nor were we concerned to list all of any author's output. Our wish was rather to be sufficiently inclusive and wide-ranging to provide an adequate sample.

The bibliographic organization differs from that of the first part of the book; it was not feasible to follow the chapter headings. Though some of the writers adhere strongly to one or the other of the predominant images, too many of them use conventions that are appropriate to several of the images. It is possible to isolate some of the books that deal primarily with the hunting ethos, such as D. R. Sherman's *Into the Noonday Sun,* or Colin Willock's *The Animal Catchers,* but more frequently even the mystique of the hunt is only part of a more eclectic view of Africa in which other themes and images are incorporated. We have, therefore, been content merely to separate out the fiction from the nonfiction.

We have included also a separate list of a selected bibliography of South African novels of social protest. Though not dealt with in the text, they are the most important and probably the best-known novels about Africa in the United States. They are pertinent here in that they carry on the traditional humanitarian line of Olive Schreiner. Some of these novelists move into the area of African imagery in certain of their books or in parts of others. Harry Bloom's *Whittaker's Wife* clearly belongs in the realm of British imagery about Africa, while his *Episode in the Transvaal* is a classic novel of social protest. William Plomer's *Turbott Wolfe* has been called by Laurens Van der Post (Introduction to Turbott Wolfe) one of the pivotal works of South African fiction, combining the traditions of Haggard and Schreiner. It does, indeed, properly belong to the data of the African image as well as to the fiction of social protest.

The work of Pauline Smith has been listed along with the South African material, but hers are novels and tales of social realism rather than social protest, and primarily concern the Afrikaners rather than the British or Africans. Her view of the barren, open veldt and the stolid Boers is in the Schreiner tradition, though she evokes them as few other novelists have done.

Nonfiction

BAKER, RICHARD ST. BARBE. *African Drums.* Revised edition. Oxford: George Ronald, Wheatley Co., 1951.

BIGLAND, EILEEN. *The Lake of the Royall Crocodiles.* New York: Macmillan, 1939.

BINKS, H. K. *African Rainbow.* London: Sidgwick and Jackson, 1959.

BIRKBY, CAROL. *Limpopo Journey.* London: Frederick Miller, 1939.

BLAKE, W. T. *Rhodesia and Nyasaland Journey.* London: Alvin Redman, Ltd., 1960.

BUCHAN, JOHN. *Pilgrim's Way.* Boston: Houghton Mifflin Co., 1940.

CAMPBELL, ROY. *Light on a Dark Horse.* Chicago: Henry Regnery, 1952.

CARY, JOYCE. *The Case for African Freedom.* London: Secker and Warburg, 1944.

CLOETE, STUART. *The African Giant.* Boston: Houghton Mifflin Company, 1955.

COLLINS, DOUGLAS. *A Tear for Somalia.* London: Jarrolds, 1960.

COLLIS, ROBERT. *African Encounter.* New York: Charles Scribner's Sons, 1961.

COLLODON, AUGUSTUS C. *Congo Jake.* New York: Claude Kendall, 1933.

———. *Congo Jake Returns.* London: John Long, 1934.

CRANWORTH, LORD. *Kenya Chronicles.* London: Macmillan, 1939.

DICKSON, MORA. *New Nigerians.* London: Dennis Dobson, 1960.

DINESEN, ISAK. *Out of Africa.* New York: Random House, 1938.

———. *Shadows on the Grass.* New York: Random House, 1961.

DUNDAS, SIR CHARLES. *African Crossroads.* London: Macmillan, 1955.

DURRELL, GERALD M. *The Overloaded Ark.* New York: The Viking Press, 1953.

GIBBS, PETER. *A Flag for the Matabele.* New York: Vanguard, 1956.

GORER, GEOFFREY. *Africa Dances.* London: John Lehmann, 1949.

GOULDSBURY, CULLEN. *An African Year.* London: Edward Arnold, 1912.

GREEN, LAWRENCE G. *Lands of the Last Frontier: The Story of South West Africa and Its People of All Races.* London: Stanley Paul and Co., 1953.

GREENE, GRAHAM. *In Search of a Character: Two African Journals.* New York: Viking Press, 1961.

———. *Journey Without Maps.* New York: Compass, 1961 (first published in 1936).

HAGGARD, H. RIDER. *The Days of My Life.* 2 vols. London: Longmans, Green and Co., 1926.

HASTINGS, A. C. G. *Nigerian Days.* London: John Lane, 1925.

HENDERSON, IAN. *Manhunt in Kenya.* Garden City: Doubleday, 1958.

HENNINGS, R. D. *African Morning.* London: Chatto and Windus, 1951.

HIVES, FRANK and LUMLEY GASCOINE. *Ju-Ju and Justice in Nigeria.* New York: Ballantine Books, 1961.

HOARE, RAWDON. *Rhodesian Mosaic.* London: John Murray, 1934.

HORN, ALOYSIUS and E. LEWIS. *Trader Horn.* New York: Grosset and Dunlap, 1927.

HUNTER, J. A. *Hunter.* New York: Harper and Bros., 1952.

——— and DANIEL P. MANNIX. *Tales of the African Frontier.* New York: Harper and Bros., 1954.

HUXLEY, ELSPETH. *On the Edge of the Rift.* New York: William Morrow and Co., 1962.

———. *A New Earth.* New York: William Morrow and Co., 1960.

———. *The Flame Trees of Thika.* New York: William Morrow and Co., 1959.

———. *Four Guineas.* London: Chatto and Windus, 1954.

———. *The Sorcerer's Apprentice.* London: Chatto and Windus, 1949.

JACKSON, SIR FREDERICK. *Early Days in East Africa.* London: Edward Arnold and Co., 1930.

JACKSON, H. C. *Sudan Days and Ways.* London: Macmillan, 1954.

JARRETT-KERR, MARTIN. *African Pulse.* London: Faith Press, 1960.

MARKHAM, BERYL. *West with the Night.* Boston: Houghton Mifflin and Co., 1942.

MARSH, JOHN and LYMAN ANSON. *Skeleton Coast.* New York: Dodd, Mead and Co., 1958.

MATURIN, EDITH. *Adventures Beyond the Zambesi.* London: Eveleigh Nash, 1913.

MAUGHAM, ROBIN. *The Slaves of Timbuktu.* New York: Harper and Brothers, 1961.

MICHAEL, MARJORIE. *I Married a Hunter.* New York: G. P. Putnam's Sons, 1957.

MILLS, LADY DOROTHY. *Road to Timbuktu.* London: Duckworth and Co., 1924.

———. *The Golden Land.* London: Duckworth and Co., 1926.

MOCKFORD, JULIAN. *Golden Land.* London: Adam and Charles Black, 1949.

MORTON, H. V. *In Search of South Africa.* London: Methuen and Co., 1948.

MOTLEY, MARY. *Devils in Waiting.* London: Longmans, Green and Co., 1959.

NEAL, JAMES H. *Jungle Magic.* New York: David McKay, 1966.

NEVINSON, HENRY W. *More Changes More Chances.* New York: Harcourt, Brace and Co., 1925.

PACKER, JOY. *Apes and Ivory.* London: Eyre and Spottiswoode, 1953.

PATTERSON, JOHN HENRY. *The Man-Eaters of Tsavo and Other African Adventures.* New York: Macmillan, 1927.

PLOMER, WILLIAM. *Double Lives.* New York: Noonday Press, 1956.

POWYS, LLEWELLYN. *Ebony and Ivory.* New York: Harcourt, Brace and Co., 1923.

PRETORIUS, MAJOR P. J. *Jungle Man.* New York: E. P. Dutton and Co., 1948.

RANIER, PETER. *My Vanished Africa.* New Haven: Yale University Press, 1940.

RAYNE, MAJOR H. *Sun, Sand and Somals.* London: H. F. and G. Witherby, 1921.

READ, GRANTLY DICK. *No Time for Fear.* New York: Harper and Bros., 1955.

REDMAYNE, SIR RICHARD. *Men, Mines and Memories.* London: Eyre and Spottiswoode, 1942.

REEVE, ALAN. *Africa, I Presume.* New York: Macmillan, 1948.

RYAN, MARGARET G. *African Hayride.* New York: Rand McNally, 1956.

SCOBIE, ALASTAIR. *Women of Africa.* London: Cassell and Co., 1960.

SCULLY, WILLIAM CHARLES. *Further Reminiscences of a South African Pioneer.* London: Fischer Unwin, 1913.

———. *Reminiscences of a South African Pioneer.* London: Fischer Unwin, 1911.

SEYMOUR, JOHN. *One Man's Africa.* New York: John Day, 1956.

SIMPSON, ALYSE. *The Red Dust of Kenya.* New York: Thomas Y. Crowell Co., 1952.

SMITH, ANTHONY. *High Street Africa.* London: Allen and Unwin, 1961.

STATHAM, COL. J. C. B. *With My Wife Across Africa By Canoe and Caravan.* London: Simpkin, Marshall, Hamilton, Kent and Co., 1924.

SWEENEY, R. C. H. *The Scurrying Bush.* New York: Random House, 1965.

TAYLOR, JOHN. *Maneaters and Marauders.* New York: A. S. Barnes and Co., 1960.

TONG, RAYMOND. *Figures in Ebony*. London: Cassell and Co., 1958.

VAN DER POST, LAURENS. *The Heart of the Hunter*. New York: William Morrow and Co., 1961.

———. "Portrait of a Continent," *Holiday*, April 1959.

———. *The Dark Eye in Africa*. New York: William Morrow and Co., 1955.

———. *Venture to the Interior*. New York: William Morrow and Co., 1951.

WYKES, ALAN. *Snake-Man*. New York: Simon and Schuster, 1961.

WYNDHAM, RICHARD. *The Gentle Savage*. New York: William Morrow and Co., 1936.

Fiction

ALLAN, RALPH. *Ask the Name of the Lion*. New York: Doubleday and Co., 1962.

AMBLER, ERIC. *Dirty Story*. New York: Atheneum, 1967.

BAKER, RICHARD ST. BARBE. *Kabongo*. Oxford: George Ronald Co., 1955.

BEAVON, ERIC A. *Sindiga the Savage*. London: Harpers, 1930.

BINDLOSS, HAROLD. *The League of the Leopard*. London, 1923.

Blackwood Magazine, collections from. "Tales from the Outposts." Vol. V. *Jobs of Work*. Edinburgh and London: William Blackwood and Sons, 1932.

BLOOM, HARRY. *Whittaker's Wife*. New York: Simon and Schuster, 1962.

BROOK, IAN. *The Black List*. New York: G. P. Putnam's Sons, 1962.

———. *Jimmy Riddle*. New York: G. P. Putnam's Sons, 1961.

BUCHAN, JOHN. *The Island of Sheep*. London, 1936.

———. *The Runagates Club*. London, 1928.

BURGESS, ANTHONY. *Devil of a State*. New York: W. W. Norton and Co., 1961.

CAMERON, RODERICK. *Equator Farm*. New York: Roy, 1956.

CANAWAY, W. H. *Find the Boy*. New York: Viking Press, 1961.

CANNING, VICTOR. *The Burning Eye*. New York: William Sloane Associates, 1960.

CARY, JOYCE. *Aissa Saved*. Carfax Edition. London, 1952.

———. *An American Visitor*. Carfax Edition, 1952.

———. *Mr. Johnson*. New York: Berkley Medallion Books, 1961.

———. *Spring Song*. New York: Harper and Bros., 1960.

———. *The African Witch*. Carfax Edition. London, 1951.

———. *Castle Corner*. London: Michael Joseph, 1938.

Catto, Max. *Mr. Moses.* New York: William Morrow and Co., 1961.
———. *Gold in the Sky.* New York: William Morrow and Co., 1958.
Caute, David. *Decline of the West.* New York: Macmillan, 1966.
———. *At Fever Pitch.* New York: Pantheon, 1961.
Cloete, Stuart. *Gazella.* New York: Pocket Books, 1959.
———. *Congo Song.* New York: Monarch, 1958.
Drummond, June. *Welcome, Proud Lady.* New York: Holt, Rinehart and Winston, 1968.
Forester, C. S. *The Sky and the Forest.* Boston: Little, Brown and Co., 1948.
———. *The African Queen.* New York: Bantam Books, 1960.
Glanville, Ernest. *The Hunter, A Story of Bushmen.* New York: Harcourt, Brace and Co., 1926.
Greene, Graham. *The Heart of the Matter.* New York: The Viking Press, 1948.
———. *A Burnt-Out Case.* New York: The Viking Press, 1961.
Griffin, Gwyn. *Something of an Achievement.* New York: Henry Holt and Co., 1960.
———. *By the North Gate.* New York: Henry Holt and Co., 1959.
Hanley, Gerald. *Gilligan's Last Elephant.* Cleveland: World, 1962.
———. *Drinkers of Darkness.* New York: Macmillan, 1955.
———. *The Year of the Lion.* New York: Macmillan, 1954.
Hardy, Ronald. *The Savages.* New York: G. P. Putnam's Sons, 1967.
———. *The Men from the Bush.* Garden City: Doubleday and Co., 1959.
Henriques, Robert D. Q. *Death by Moonlight.* New York: William Morrow and Co., 1938.
Holtby, Winifred. *Mandoa, Mandoa!* New York: Macmillan, 1933.
Horne, Geoffrey. *The Man Who Was Chief.* London: Chapman and Hall, 1960.
Huxley, Elspeth. *The Red Rock Wilderness.* New York: William Morrow and Co., 1957.
———. *The Walled City.* Philadelphia and New York: J. B. Lippincott Co., 1949.
Jenkins, Geoffrey. *A Twist of Sand.* New York: Viking Press, 1960.
Lait, Robert. *Massacre at Tangini.* New York: Random House, 1963.
———. *Honey for Tomorrow.* New York: Random House, 1961.
Lane, Margaret. *A Calabash of Diamonds.* New York: Duell, Sloan and Pearce, 1961.
Llewellyn, Richard. *A Man in a Mirror.* New York: Doubleday and Co., 1961.
Lodwick, John. *Equator.* London: Heinemann, 1957.

MATHEW, DAVID. *The Mango on the Mango Tree.* New York: Alfred A. Knopf, 1951.

MILLIN, SARAH GERTRUDE. *The Herr Witchdoctor.* London: William Heinemann, 1941.

———. *God's Stepchildren.* New York: Boni and Liveright, 1924.

———. *Adam's Rest.* London, 1922.

MILNE, SHIRLEY. *Beware the Lurking Scorpion.* London: House and Maxwell, 1966.

MONSARRAT, NICHOLAS. *The Tribe that Lost Its Head.* New York: William Sloane Associates, 1956.

MUNDY, TALBOT. *The Ivory Trail.* Indianapolis: Bobbs, Merrill Co., 1919.

NEAME, ALAN. *The Adventures of Maud Noakes.* New York: New Directions, 1960.

PACKER, JOY. *The Glass Barrier.* Philadelphia: J. B. Lippincott, 1961.

PLOMER, WILLIAM. *Turbott Wolfe.* New York: William Morrow, 1965 (first published in 1926).

RAND, JAMES. *Run for the Trees.* New York: Putnam, 1967.

REID, VICTOR STAFFORD. *The Leopard.* New York: Viking Press, 1958.

ROOKE, DAPHNE. *A Lover for Estelle.* Boston: Houghton Mifflin Co., 1961.

———. *Wizard's Country.* Cambridge, Mass.: Riverside Press, 1957.

SCHOLEFIELD, ALAN. *Great Elephant.* New York: William Morrow and Co., 1968.

———. *A View of Vultures.* London: Heinemann, 1966.

SCHOLEY, JEAN. *The Dead Past.* New York: Macmillan, 1962.

SHAW, ROBERT. *The Sun Doctor.* New York: Harcourt, Brace and World, 1961.

SHERMAN, D. R. *Into the Noonday Sun.* Boston: Little, Brown and Co., 1966.

SMITH, WILBUR. *The Train from Katanga.* New York: Viking, 1965.

STACEY, TOM. *The Brothers M.* New York: Pantheon Books, 1961.

STEEN, MARGUERITE. *Twilight on the Floods.* Garden City: Doubleday and Co., 1949.

———. *The Sun Is My Undoing.* New York: Viking Press, 1941.

TREVOR, ELLESTON. *The Freebooters.* Garden City: Doubleday and Co., 1967.

VAN DER POST, LAURENS. *The Hunter and the Whale.* New York: William Morrow and Co., 1967.

———. *Flamingo Feather.* New York: William Morrow and Co., 1955.

VIERTEL, PETER. *White Hunter, Black Heart.* London: W. H. Allen, 1954.

WALLACE, EDGAR. *Mr. Commissioner Sanders*. New York: Doubleday, Doran and Co., 1930.

WAUGH, EVELYN. *Black Mischief*. New York: Dell Publishing Co., 1960.

WILLOCK, COLIN. *The Animal Catchers*. New York: Doubleday and Co., 1964.

WILSON, JOHN ROWAN. *The Double Blind*. New York: Doubleday and Co., 1960.

YOUNG, FRANCIS BRETT. *The City of Gold*. London: William Heinemann, 1939.

———. *They Seek a Country*. Baltimore: Waverly Press, 1937.

South African Fiction of Social Protest

ABRAHAMS, PETER. *A Wreath for Udomo*. New York: Alfred A. Knopf, 1956.

———. *Mine Boy*. New York: Alfred A. Knopf, 1955.

———. *Tell Freedom*. New York: Alfred A. Knopf, 1954.

BLOOM, HARRY. *Episode in the Transvaal*. London: Collins, 1956.

COPE, JACK. *The Tame Ox*. London: William Heinemann, 1960.

———. *The Golden Oriole*. London: William Heinemann, 1958.

GORDIMER, NADINE. *Friday's Footprints*. New York: Simon and Schuster, 1960.

———. *A World of Strangers*. New York: Simon and Schuster, 1958.

———. *Six Feet of the Country*. New York: Simon and Schuster, 1956.

———. *The Lying Days*. New York: Simon and Schuster, 1953.

———. *Soft Voice of the Serpent*. New York: Simon and Schuster, 1952.

JACOBSON, DAN. *The Zulu and the Zeide*. Boston: Little, Brown and Co., 1959.

———. *The Evidence of Love*. Boston: Little, Brown and Co., 1959.

———. *The Price of Diamonds*. London: Weidenfeld and Nicolson, 1957.

———. *A Dance in the Sun*. London: Weidenfeld and Nicolson, 1956.

KRIGE, UYS. *The Dream and the Desert*. London: Collins, 1953.

LESSING, DORIS. *Martha Quest and a Proper Marriage* (volumes 1 and 2 of *Children of Violence*). New York, 1965.

———. *A Ripple from the Storm and Landlocked* (volumes 3 and 4 of *Children of Violence*). New York, 1966.

———. *African Stories*. London: Michael Joseph, 1964.

———. *Five Short Novels*. London: Michael Joseph, 1953.

———. *This Was the Old Chief's Country*. London: Michael Joseph, 1952.

———. *The Grass Is Singing*. London: Michael Joseph, 1950.

PATON, ALAN. *Tales from a Troubled Land*. New York: Charles Scribner's Sons, 1964.

———. *Too Late the Phalarope*. New York: Charles Scribner's Sons, 1953.

———. *Cry, the Beloved Country*. New York: Charles Scribner's Sons, 1948.

SMITH, PAULINE. *The Beadle*. New York: Vanguard, 1954 (first published in 1927).

———. *The Little Karoo*. New York: Vanguard, 1952 (first published in 1926).

The British on Themselves

BELLOC, HILAIRE. *An Essay on the Nature of Contemporary England*. New York: Sheed and Ward, 1937.

BRADBURY, MALCOLM. "The Taste for Anarchy," *Saturday Review*, June 30, 1962.

BROGAN, DENIS W. *The English People—Impressions and Observations*. New York: Alfred A. Knopf, 1943.

CARR, PHILIP. *The English Are Like That*. New York: Charles Scribner's Sons, 1941.

CHAUDHURI, MRAD C. *A Passage to England*. New York: St. Martin's Press, 1959.

CHESSER, EUSTACE. *The Sexual, Marital and Family Relationships of the English Woman*. New York: Roy Publishers, 1957.

COLE, G. D. H. "The Idea of Progress," *British Journal of Sociology*, IV (1953), 266–85.

———. *The Post-War Condition of Britain*. London: Routledge and Kegan Paul, 1956.

DENNIS, NORMAN, FERNANDO HENRIQUES and CLIFFORD SLAUGHTER. *Coal Is Our Life*. London: Eyre and Spottiswoode, 1956.

FARBER, MAURICE L. "English and Americans: A Study of National Character," *Journal of Psychology*, XXXII (1951).

———. "English and Americans: Values in the Socialization Process," *Journal of Psychology*, XXXVI (1953).

FROST, DAVID and ANTONY JAY. *The English*. New York: Stein and Day, 1968.

GLASS, DAVID VICTOR (ed.). *Social Mobility in Britain*. Glencoe: The Free Press, 1954.

GORER, GEOFFREY. *Exploring English Character.* New York: Criterion Books, 1955.

GREEN, MARTIN. *A Mirror for Anglo-Saxons: A Discovery of America, a rediscovery of England.* New York: Harper and Brothers, 1960.

GUTTSMAN, W. L. "Aristocracy and the Middle Class in the British Political Elite 1886–1916," *British Journal of Sociology,* V (1954).

KERR, MADELINE. *The People of Ship Street.* London: Routledge and Kegan Paul, 1958.

LEWIS, ROY and ANGUS MAUDE. *Professional People in England.* Cambridge: Harvard University Press, 1953.

LOGAN, R. F. L. and E. M. GOLDBERG. "Rising Eighteen in a London Suburb," *British Journal of Sociology,* IV (1953), 323–45.

MACK, JOHN. "Review of Gorer—*Exploring English Character,*" *British Journal of Sociology,* VI (1955).

DE MADARIAGA, SALVADOR. *Englishmen, Frenchmen and Spaniards.* London: Oxford University Press, 1929.

MARSH, DAVID C. *The Changing Social Structure of England and Wales, 1871–1951.* London: Routledge and Kegan Paul, 1958.

MEAD, MARGARET. *The Application of Anthropological Techniques to Cross-Cultural Communication. Transactions of the New York Academy of Science.* Series 2, no. 9 (1947).

MILLER, S. M. "Comparative Social Mobility," *Current Sociology,* IX, no. 1 (1960).

MITFORD, NANCY. *Noblesse Oblige.* New York: Harper and Bros., 1956.

MOGEY, JOHN. *Family and Neighbourhood.* London: Oxford University Press, 1956.

NICOLSON, HAROLD. *Good Behaviour.* Garden City: Doubleday and Co., 1956.

ORWELL, GEORGE. *The Road to Wigan Pier.* New York: Berkeley Publishing Co., 1961.

———. *A Collection of Essays.* Garden City: Doubleday Anchor Books, 1954.

PEAR, T. H. *English Social Differences.* London: George Allen and Unwin, 1955.

ROWNTREE, B. SEEBOHM and G. R. LAVERS. *English Life and Leisure.* London: Longmans, Green and Co., 1951.

SCOTT, J. D. *Life In Britain.* New York: William Morrow and Co., 1955.

SLATER, ELIOT and MOYA WOODSIDE. *Patterns of Marriage.* London: Cassell and Co., 1951.

SMELLIE, K. B. *The British Way of Life.* London: William Heinemann, 1955.

SPINLEY, B. M. *The Deprived and the Privileged: Personality Development in English Society.* London: Routledge and Kegan Paul, 1953.

STERLING, PAUL. "Review: *Exploring English Character,* Geoffrey Gorer," *American Anthropologist,* LVIII, no. 6 (1956).

STRACHEY, JOHN. *The End of Empire.* New York: Random House, 1960.

TITMUSS, RICHARD M. *Essays on "The Welfare State."* London: George Allen and Unwin, 1958.

WELLARD, JAMES HOWARD. *Understanding the English.* New York: McGraw-Hill, 1937.

WILLMOTT, PETER and MICHAEL YOUNG. *Family and Class in a London Suburb.* Routledge and Kegan Paul, 1960.

WOLFENSTEIN, MARTHA and NATHAN A. LEITES. *Movies.* Glencoe: The Free Press, 1950.

Index